Visions of Desirable Societies

SYSTEMS SCIENCE AND WORLD ORDER LIBRARY

General Editor: Ervin Laszlo

Explorations of World Order

DE ROUGEMONT, D.
The Future is Within Us

GIARINI, O. & LOUBERGE, H.
The Diminishing Returns of Technology: an Essay on the Crisis in Economic Growth

LASZLO, E. & BIERMAN, J.
Goals in a Global Community
Vol. 1: Studies on the Conceptual Foundations
Vol. 2: The International Values and Goals Studies

LASZLO, E.
The Inner Limits of Mankind: Heretical Reflections on Today's Values, Cultures and Politics

MARKLEY, O. & HARMAN, W.
Changing Images of Man

SAUVANT, K.
Changing Priorities on the International Agenda: The New International Economic Order

TÉVOÉDJRÈ, A.
Poverty: Wealth of Mankind

Innovations in Systems Science

AULIN, A.
The Cybernetic Laws of Social Progress

COOK, N.
Stability and Flexibility: An Analysis of Natural Systems

CURTIS, R. K.
Evolution or Extinction: The Choice Before Us

GEYER, R. F.
Alienation Theories: A General Systems Approach

GEYER, R. F. & VAN DER ZOUWEN, J.
Dependence & Inequality: A Systems Approach to the Problems of Mexico & Other Developing Countries

JANTSCH, E.
The Self Organizing Universe: Scientific and Human Implications of the Emerging Paradigm of Evolution

LAVIOLETTE, P. (ed.)
Systems Anthropology: Selected Papers by Ludwig von Bertalanffy

NOTICE TO READERS

If your library is not already a standing order customer to this series, may we recommend that you place a standing or continuation order to receive immediately upon publication all new volumes published in this valuable series. Should you find these volumes no longer serve your needs your order can be cancelled at any time without notice.

Visions of Desirable Societies

Edited by

Eleonora Masini

for the World Futures Studies Federation
in cooperation with
El Centro de Estudios Economicos y Sociales del Tercer Mundo and the
United Nations University Goals, Processes and Indicators for Development Project

PERGAMON PRESS

OXFORD · NEW YORK · TORONTO · SYDNEY · PARIS · FRANKFURT

U.K.	Pergamon Press Ltd., Headington Hill Hall, Oxford OX3 0BW, England
U.S.A.	Pergamon Press Inc., Maxwell House, Fairview Park, Elmsford, New York 10523, U.S.A.
CANADA	Pergamon Press Canada Ltd., Suite 104, 150 Consumers Road, Willowdale, Ontario M2J 1P9, Canada
AUSTRALIA	Pergamon Press (Aust.) Pty. Ltd., P.O. Box 544, Potts Point, N.S.W. 2011, Australia
FRANCE	Pergamon Press SARL, 24 rue des Ecoles, 75240 Paris, Cedex 05, France
FEDERAL REPUBLIC OF GERMANY	Pergamon Press GmbH, Hammerweg 6, D-6242 Kronberg-Taunus, Federal Republic of Germany

First English edition 1983

Library of Congress Cataloging in Publication Data

Visiones de sociedades deseables. Spanish
Visions of desirable societies.
(Systems science and world order library.
Innovations in systems science)
Proceedings of a meeting held at CEESTM,
Mexico City, Apr. 1978.
Translation of: Visiones de sociedades deseables.
Includes bibliographies.
1. Twentieth century—Forecasts—Congresses.
2. Twenty-first century—Forecasts—Congresses.
3. Utopias—Congresses. 4. Social problems—
Congresses. I. Masini, Eleonora. II. World
Futures Studies Federation. III. Centro de
Estudios Económicos y Sociales del Tercer Mundo.
IV. United Nations University. V. Series.
CB161.V5713   1983   303.4'9   82-18069

British Library Cataloguing in Publication Data

Visions of desirable societies.—(Systems science
and world order library)
1. Social change—Congresses
2. Twentieth century—Forecasts—Congresses
3. Twenty-first century—Forecasts—Congresses
I. Masini, Eleonor II. Series
300   HM101
ISBN 0-08-026089-6

Printed in Great Britain by A. Wheaton & Co. Ltd., Exeter

Dedication

THIS book is dedicated to John McHale, a great pioneer in the field of future studies who was both a participant at and a contributor to one of the meetings on which this book was based.

John was born in Scotland, was trained as a sociologist, and was also an artist and a designer with expositions in Europe and in the United States. *The Future of the Future* (1969), *The Ecological Context* (1970), *World Facts and Trends* (1972), *The Changing Information Environment* (1976) and all his work on basic needs, for the Aspen Institute and for the United Nations Environment Programme, bear testimony to his broad range of interests, his deep knowledge, his sense of urgency and dedication, his humane attitudes and his brilliant intellect. All of us who had the good fortune to meet him and be with him remember his mild, yet incisive discourse; his ability to cut through nonsense whether in the field of research or in the organization of research. It can be said of him that he did not suffer fools gladly; and that he was an enemy of pretentiousness, of fake studies. He was in his work and manners a beautiful model for others to try to live up to. And he will continue to live in us, with his pipe, his wonderful Scottish r's, his deep sense of humour.

For all of us who admired his work it gives great comfort to know it will be carried on by his wife and colleague, and indeed co-author, Magda Cordell McHale. On behalf of the World Future Studies Federation and of everybody engaged in future studies we thank you, John. We shall do our best to continue the work in your spirit.

ELEONORA MASINI

Note

THE essays in this book are selected, edited and, in one or two cases, revised from papers presented at two meetings held in Mexico City in 1978 and 1979, and organized by the World Futures Studies Federation in cooperation with El Centro de Estudios Economicos y sociales del Tercer Mundo and the United Nations University under the general title of Visions of Desirable Societies.

The views of the authors of individual papers do not necessarily reflect those of the co-sponsoring organizations.

Contents

viii   *Contents*

Preface

In 1978 a project of the United Nations University, within the Human and Social Development Programme, was conceived on the topic "Goals, Processes and Indicators of Development". The aim was to investigate new ways and new ideas on a form of development which would involve the whole human being. It was thought of as a reaction against the failure of considering development problems solely in terms of "economic growth" which in turn leads to solutions mainly in the shape of material necessities.

Within such a framework, what would be the goals of societies of the future which could bring about an alternative form of development? Which cultures and societies currently in the making would lead to such development alternatives?

On the basis of these questions and within the goal of looking into the future, not only as a consequence and continuation of the present, but as an alternative to the present, a different future "vision of desirable societies" emerged as a subproject of GPID.

The search started among and between people involved in futures studies and future thinking — people who are used to probing the historical processes for change and for continuity.

One section of the discussion was on the obstacles in the present world to thinking about and finding alternatives. The pressure of the requests for food, health, work and basic needs is growing, hence visions which take into account not only these requirements, but also other requirements, such as solidarity among people, human relationships, friendship and love, are vital. Do the obstacles to visions thinking, to alternative thinking, emerge from a society which is built on Western principles, mainly using science and technology to solve problems and meet needs, forgetting such ingredients as imagination, fantasy and beliefs?

Such was the debate of the first year and first meeting, which is described in the introduction written by Bart van Steenbergen and myself to the papers presented in Mexico City at CEESTEM (Centro de Estudios Economicos y Sociales del Tercer Mundo) in 1978.

Some alternative visions did emerge in the framework of Western societies as the "frugal society", based on austerity, on the capacity of autodetermination of people in small groups joining into forms of political aggregations such as federalism, in the search for diverse visions which may become compatible.

VDS-A*

On the whole, though, it was necessary to search more for alternatives or the seeds of change. The search proceeded to see if such visions could be found in cultures which are not Western.

The deeper researchers went into the search for cultures which have not been affected by the West, the more they realized the fact that such societies are difficult to find, and as a consequence, four hypotheses emerged.

Do we have to search deeper in the roots of cultures to find the alternatives, where societies seem to emerge which are not based on "science as a product of the West", but on "other sciences" which have not been able to develop except in their own small environment?

Do we search for alternatives in dialogues between cultures? In such contact cultures should not radically transform themselves but as a result of it the deeper states of human aspiration may be brought to the surface onto a social level. We are, in fact, speaking of societies and not of individuals in the search for social change.

A third hypothesis was the fact that women, outside the main stream of thinking, may have visions which are more holistic and alternative to the present.

Finally, a fourth hypothesis was developed: alternatives based on imagination and fantasy can emerge from the thinking of artists. These four hypotheses were examined in the second year of the project.

In the present volume the whole process of thinking, which is the result of two years work on the project "Visions of Desirable Societies", is presented.

A special thanks goes to Kinhide Mushakoji, for the support he gave to the project and to all the participants in the three meetings of Visions of Desirable Societies, who all, in different ways, contributed to developing a new concept of Futures Studies, taking into account the changes already taking place at present as well as desirable future changes, in the search for projects as builders of an alternative future.

ELEONORA BARBIERI MASINI

PART I

1

Introduction

BY ELEONORA MASINI
World Futures Studies Federation, Italy
and BART VAN STEENBERGEN
University of Utrecht, The Netherlands

Theoretical Issues, Insights and Understandings at the Mexico Meeting

In this introduction we shall try to clarify some of the theoretical insights which seemed to emerge from the discussions among the twenty-five participants at the Mexico meeting on "Visions of Alternative Societies". This stimulating and difficult topic brought out many issues and topics for further analysis based on an awareness that much is being done in the present world to create more and more instruments or means to organize and steer society, while a consideration of the goals towards which these means should be directed is very weak.

Visions of desirable societies can be a great help in this context and this brief introduction is intended simply to indicate a few points for further analysis and development in the awareness that the main stream of future thinking devoted to extrapolation trends now needs to be balanced by an equivalent development of visions.

Visions are no longer to be considered a luxury, but a need springing from the feeling of many people that we have come to the end of a particular period in history.

Visions, the present and the future

Visions of the future are the stimulus to change the present. Fred Polak[1] says that from the antithesis of the present and the imagined, the future is born and that from this dualism in temporal terms the movement of events emerges.

I will also say that the present and the future are linked by the vision. The vision, we think, lies in a perception of the elements of change in the present, and hence is in itself the possibility of change, of building a future which is different from the present.

---

[1]Fred Polak, *The Image of the Future*, Elsevier, 1973.

3

Vision captures change in the present and makes it the future, diverse, other. Hence I believe that the future is born from the antitheses of the present and the vision, as discontinuous transformation or else it is born from the continuous flow, from the seeds in the present into a continuous building of visions which are the future reflecting the changing present.

Both forms of vision exist, the one dialectic and the other emerging from the flow of time, both have their value and may even coexist and strengthen each other. A revolt among the people of a country emerges from the vision as antithesis to the present, but could not emerge concretely if it was not also germinating in the awareness of the people themselves.

Again Fred Polak speaks for completed and non-completed time, the present and the vision, and I also speak of the different rhythm of time: the present is brief even if completed, the past is long term, the future is long term, non-completed time. The present is but a moment although springing from the cumulation of the past, the past stretches through the centuries, the future stretches into the infinite. The vision catches the different time dimension of the past and the future around the seeds of the present but transcends them beyond the present. The decentralized society's vision, the β society in its multiplicity as described at the Mexico conference, grows into the future from the seeds which are alive in the present while its origins lie back in the Communes of medieval Italy or in the Taoist communities described by Lao-tse.

Difficulty of visions

Is it true that we are living at a time when visions are not really visions, a time when we are living according to worn-out visions of the present or worse, of the past? As was said at the Mexico conference "our current alternatives have a feeling of statis". The vision of a feminist world is no longer a vision, for the present can potentially create a world in which man and women are both searching for their identity and are at the same time persons. The vision of a communist society realized in a structure which shows the possibilities of oppression, depersonalization and exploitation, is in the past, while a socialist vision that takes different shapes springing from present thinking but which will realize itself as a decentralized socialism, a humanistic socialism, a communitarian socialism, as described at the Mexico conference, remains a vision.

Does the fact that visions are weakening indicate a decaying society? Is it true that the strength of a culture shows in the energy, in the intensity of its visions? If this is true, is our culture, the Western culture which is weakly capable of creating visions of the future, only capable of visions which search for the seeds of change in other cultures? Or is it maybe capable of visions which reflect the differences between itself and that which has been called the "changing paradigm?" Are maybe those the "faith" visions in Taoistic terms where the concept of time is that of continuous flow and the antithesis is between the completion and innovation? The visions based on a faith that emerge from being oneself as part of the flow of human history? In this sense the "faith visions" search for the seeds of human history in every movement of human existence.

Is this the meaning of the visions discussed in Mexico as being those of women, which are again seen in Taoistic terms as being part of a flow and of a whole in a commensalistic spirit, beyond any dychotomy of man-woman, black-white, etc? Maybe it is the moment to realize that on this basis mankind's objective's are now being met by non-Westerners, or is this another step towards "the other" understood as the "non-self" in Western terms? Or is it rather the refusal of the "other" and, in this case, is Fred Polak right when he says that it is the crippling awareness of "the other" that makes us incapable of visions hence of change and of even understanding the present where the seeds of the future capable of creating visions lie? Or is it that we Westerners understand our limits in history, future history while we do not deny our creative past? Are the Third World cultures capable of visions which are not the reflection of Western visions? These are the questions that were raised at the Mexico meeting and which we hope will stimulate further debate from which we hope will also emerge another meeting and another set of papers.

There is another aspect to visions: I said previously that the present is perceived as a moment, even if rich of the past, the vision is perceived as a long-term happening, it does not have limits, and as Westerners we wish to see the result, the limit. Perhaps this is one of the reasons for our present inability to create visions of the future.

Having encountered difficulties in finding visions in our present adult world, we have searched for visions of the future in children, through surveys, through simply reading the way Italian children describe their future, their home, their country in drawings or in writings and what did we find? We found rebellion, anguish, despair in their description of a future where nuclear holocaust, world hunger and destructive violence as well as the loneliness of big towns with no open spaces or parks or friendships, are central and overpowering.

On first analysis, these descriptions seem to reproduce the present but a closer inspection reveals the rejection of the present, the wish to change it, maybe a desire for revolution, and the descriptions acquire the character of a vision of a different reality in the future which contrasts with the present like the negative of a photograph. Would children of other countries, continents, cultures have the same or different visions? We should find out more about this.

Multiplicity of visions

This brings us to another concept: visions are multiple, they are not exclusive, the failure of visions to which we have referred has probably partly been caused by the fact that they usually aim at being exclusive. The Christian vision of society, and the communist vision, as normally seen, are exclusive and therefore limited, being structure-based and structure-oriented, and therefore not flexible but static.

Visions are diverse, continuously changing and interrelating because they are part of the process of human history. Visions in this sense aim to understand the processes from which the emerging structures will be more dynamic, more flexible, more democratic. At the same time they are not being born from structures but from processes. Visions born from structures are themselves crystallized, fixed, exclusive visions while visions born of ever-changing reality are dynamic and multiple and by generating energy tend towards flexible dynamic structures.

The visions of the various feminist movements are different, being born from processes with seeds in other processes, they are multiple, hence progress towards flexible structures. The vision of the Catholic Church is one and static, the vision of a structure born from a structure. The visions of the different movements within the Christian church are different parts of a sane process, hence dynamic and multiple, reflecting the growth of the people as well as their needs and wishes, a process of visions which have in themselves flexible, dynamic structures.

Perhaps I am trying to indicate that the very strength of a vision lies in its diversity.

The flexibility of structures, the search for the seeds of change in the present, and the multiplicity of visions are tightly linked to a democratic and participatory society where the general public should be involved in the processes of decision-making. In this sense the emergence of visions, of desirable societies can help the emergence of a democratic participatory society.

The fact that the people asked to prepare papers for Mexico were also willing to revise them afterwards demonstrates yet again that visions are multiple and interact when men and women really interact and are capable of generating change. The danger is that once a vision is completely and beautifully defined it is presented, felt and thought of as being "The Vision" and is not that anymore. In this sense it both makes for a good society and sets a trap, a device to limit freedom, hence it can and will betray.

Whose visions?

We wish to stress at this point the fact that visions are not the domain of the futurists, who have in fact not contributed much in this field, certainly not as much as many social groups and institutions.

The visions builder is one who understands the processes whereby the seeds of the vision, hence of the future are latent in the present. He is also one who sees the future vision as the antithesis to the present. He looks beyond his own culture for visions in other cultures, is open-minded and therefore gets close to the multiple essence of life.

We hope that this volume will encourage the creation of multiple visions in the sense of linking the present and the future, as well as perceiving the future as emerging from the dychotomy of the present and the vision. It is a process, as we have said, where seeds of change are present and have to be perceived to by all, not just by experts and futurists.

Visions and desirables

When we asked people to present and describe their visions, we knew very well that they were all identifying themselves with their visions because we all, in our visions, describe what we wish will happen, we search in fact for the seeds in the process which we believe will be the seeds of "good" things. There is no need to be afraid of this, visions are in fact value loaded and consciously or not are constructed according to value choices and value priorities.

Fred Polak says that "awareness of ideal values is the first step in the conscious creation of images of the future". Are we able, however, to interpret among the seeds which are in the present and which may develop in the future the ones which will be chosen by groups, societies, cultures, or are the vision builders choosing for themselves?

Visions interact, they express the desires of many people and groups and have a variety of derivations. We are not discussing visions, but those which reflect and in turn are a reflection of the changes which are in the historical process, that is to say social visions. In this sense the illustrations of fear which were found in the Italian children's drawings, the suggestion of the loneliness of life in big towns indicate certain desirable features of the future which people like the participants at the Mexico meeting are describing in their visions: The visions of the β society in its multiplicity, the "instant visions" do not just represent the vision and the wishes of one man but one felt by the many. Here emerges the value of visions as policy indicators or maybe, as discussed at length in Mexico, as indicators for strategies. To what extent do strategies kill visions or to what extent do they influence them into becoming other visions, into a further multiplication of visions?

Some people, we said, are capable of perceiving the seeds in processes and create "visions" based on their value choices, but these visions must be easily communicative, understood and in a certain sense capable of being verified or changed; only at this point are strategies found.

The visions of self-determined communities as described in Mexico must interact with society, with the people that have the need for that vision and also the need for the implementation of the vision, while at the same time the vision is part of the participatory democratic process and springs from it and is not forced onto it. It is a social vision.

In these terms the vision has an anticipatory function which verified, transforms itself in a policy-orientated function, maybe into a strategy function. But again, if it is a characteristic of a vision to be multiple, its verification by the people will feed back into the vision which will, in a certain sense, be at the same time vision generating as long as it responds to the seeds in the process; beyond that it becomes a trap again, a crystallization, no longer a vision. This brings me to make the point that a vision is not such *ad eternum*, which is why at the present time we are referring to visions at a stasis and are searching for the "new" visions which will always have to be "new".

We hope that the present activity of the World Future Studies Federation will stimulate the ever-creating, ever-generating process of visions for a few years to come. Such activity we hope "lives" the basic concept of visions, perceiving the seeds in the process of change towards the creation of the future. This was the reason for holding the Mexico conference on "Visions of Desirable Societies" as well as the stimulus to prepare this volume with contributions from people who are capable of perceiving the seeds of change. The World Future Studies Federation hopes in this way to contribute to the building of the future.

The project on "Visions of Desirable Societies" became a reality in the meeting at CEESTM (Centro Estudios Economicos y Sociales del Tercer Mundo), Mexico City, in April 1978 and the following papers are the proceedings of that meeting. The project is an ongoing one as subproject of the larger project "Goals, Processes and Indicators of Development" of The United Nations University. It is part of the Goals aspect of the same project.

The entire endeavour is the result of the combined efforts of The World Future Studies Federation, Centro de Estudios Economicos y Sociales del Tercer Mundo and the United Nations University, although the "vision" was the WFSF's.

Its aim is towards "Understanding contradictions within and between diverse visions and to find ways in which they become more compatible in a diverse world".[2]

---

[2]Sam Cole and Ian Miles, "Summary of proceedings of the meeting Visions of Desirable Societies", held in Mexico City at CEESTM published in *Futures*.

2

Women's Visions of the Future

Elise Boulding

University of Colorado at Boulder, USA

THERE is a profound ambiguity in the concept of women visioning the future. Their historic role has been that of stewards and conservers of resources for their families, as nurturers, fending off the effects of change as much as possible to preserve a space of tranquillity for those in their care. They are therefore seen as conservative, cautious, unwilling to take risks, and as needing to be protected from the vicissitudes of larger social processes. Yet at the same time women are the womb of the future in every society. They dream for each babe they carry through 9 months of pregnancy, and they dream for each child that plays at the family hearth — dream what the future will bring. They dream for their husbands, they dream for themselves. They are continually preparing in their minds for future possibilities, anticipated needs. The dreaming interacts with the constantly changing reality of each family member growing older, taking on new characteristics, assimilating new life experiences, making new demands. The dreaming is also grounded in the practical necessity of providing for the family — a task shared with men from time immemorial.

The experience worlds of women have been somewhat different from those of men in that they have travelled less far in their daily round, and stayed closer to the hearth because of childbearing. The differences are not so great as commonly supposed, nor are they likely to continue to be so in the future. But women have in general dreamed from the more private spaces of society, and known less of the public, civic spaces where grand designs for the future have been planned by men. To the extent that this is true, the thoughts women have about the future have a special quality that sets them apart from the manipulative futurism of planners, who develop a model of the social processes they are concerned with project trends, and then try to alter the values of the variables of their model to assure outcomes approaching the desired end state. Women's futurism is the futurism of the Tao, the way, rather than the futurism of projected end states. In its idealized form it involves an attunement to cosmic processes which makes action seemingly effortless because it is based on the intersecting realities

9

and potentials of the individual and the social order. It is not a heroic futurism, overcoming all obstacles, but a gentle, listening futurism, moving with the sun, the moon, the tides and the seasons of the human heart. Although it appears effortless, however, the imaging process is a highly developed one, based on lifelong discipline in the skills of listening, watching, attunement to realities of the physical and social environment and in the skills of representation of the path. Women have often not realized they were futurists because they only know of manipulative futurism. They will be shown here as identifiers of the way. This process approach is by no means the exclusive province of women, of course. Because men and women are perhaps more alike than they are different, many men have dreamed as women have dreamed. This is true of all the great religious teachers. Because my assignment in this paper is to identify the special characteristics of women's thinking about alternative futures, I will be emphasizing certain aspects of that thinking which stem from their special life experiences but which are in no way exclusive to women. I will also be emphasizing a certain tradition of visioning that has it roots in an acknowledgement of the spiritual dimensions of humanity. In doing so I will perhaps not do full justice to the more secular feminist socialist vision, though the socialist vision lies at the very core of the future society as presented here. In looking at women's visions of all kinds it must be remembered that many women accept the conquest visions of the men around them and behave in ways that support systems of domination and the consumption ethic.

Women's visions have a strongly commensalist character. That is, the metaphor of the human family comes easily and naturally to them, and they draw on it frequently in visioning a future society more peaceful, just and humane than the present one. Also, because women are used to operating from the private spaces of society although their responsibilities are public in the fullest meaning of that word, they are very ingenious in visualizing changes that can be made "from inside", in the cracks of the microstructures of the existing society. Finally, women are perhaps more aware than men of the goodness factor in creating futures — the limitations set by the behavioural potentials of human beings. Because human capability for goodness is the least fashionable talking-point in discussions about the future, a further exploration of this concept may be useful before going on to discuss women's contributions to future visioning under the three headings just proposed of (1) commensalism, (2) "working in the cracks", and (3) the production of human goodness.

Human beings: the raw materials of the future

The question of the kinds of future societies which the human race will have to choose from cannot be separated from the question of our potentials as a human species. So far, we have had extensive experience of the capacities of the species to fight, to settle into dominance–submission relationships and to be incredibly inventive in harnessing the physical environment to the needs of the species. We also have experience with the nurturant capacities of the species as expressed by females in family-type settings, and as expressed by some peaceable small-scale folk societies in their tribal life styles. We have further witnessed the deliberate attempt to create such peaceful mini-societies in utopian experiments within aggressive conquest societies. Deeds of nurturance, it must be confessed, rate only a minor footnote to the pages of history.

The social structures of all complex societies from the times of ancient empires to the present are reflections and embodiments of the dominance capacities of the species. The nurturant roles exist in the interstices of social systems, and the nurturers, largely but not exclusively women, have no power over the shaping of those structures. There is no evidence whatsoever from history that the present twin crises of excess of military capability and rapidly dwindling natural resources in the face of expanding populations will be handled any differently than past crises have been handled. War is still the favoured instrument for settling problems. New Third World centres of power may reorganize social structures to correspond to the desires of the new haves, but injustice, war and human misery are very likely to continue.

This is because large-scale structural rearrangements, whether socialist or reformist capitalist, even when extremely beneficent and designed to meet the needs of the poor, are planned on the assumption that human beings will behave reasonably, responsibly and with good will when their basic needs, including their needs to be recognized as citizens, are met. In fact, it is extraordinarily difficult for humans to "be good", even in the most intimate setting of the family. Human goodness I will define here as a quality of inner security and well-being involving the possession of vast reservoirs of surplus emotional energy for listening to, loving and caring for others, linked to a discerning intellect that will utilize that reservoir wisely. We identify people having this quality of goodness as saints, and separate them conceptually from "ordinary persons", i.e. the rest of us. It is a fact that every religious tradition maintains (with some provisos) that humans generally are capable of this goodness if they follow the teachings of the tradition, and it is also a fact that every society disbelieves its own traditions. Every society also, in self-contradictory self-righteousness, expects its women, its children, its minorities and its poor to "be good". There is great indignation when they are not. The training minorities get for goodness is training to be nurturant and compliant without discernment. When they develop discernment, with the help of consciousness-raising social movements, they reject what is clearly a false goodness,[1] and are all too

---

[1]False goodness would involve going through the external motions of goodness behaviour because the individual perceives no other option, without any inner dynamic to correspond to the outward behaviour. It is coerced, not voluntary behaviour.

often left with nothing in its place but the aggressive behaviour model of those who have dominated them. Yet human life even at its best is so full of contradictions, paradoxes and conflicting needs that surplus energy for loving is absolutely necessary to keep human relationships from deteriorating to mutual distrust, regardless of the economic system in which people live.

Consciousness-raising for all kinds of oppressed groups has been occurring very rapidly in recent decades, and goodness has got short shrift because it is associated with the false nurturance behaviour forced on the oppressed. The tragedy is that without a careful tending of our goodness capacity as a species, we cannot break the cycles of dominance and misuse of power. To say that no utopia, no social arrangement, can be better than the people in it would seem to be a counsel of despair. But while we cannot guarantee through social structure, we can provide for processes that promote inner growth and goodness within structures. This, if I understand him correctly, is one of the points Galtung is making in his paper on utopias. However, inner growth, goodness and nurturance skills are not high public priorities. The leaders who are to lead us into the new social order were not trained for nurturance, but for commanding. Newly liberated minorities who want to share in shaping the new social order do not find their old compliant behaviour helpful in their new roles (if they do they are accused of Uncle Tomism) and are pushed to emulate their former "masters" whether they want to or not.

Many counter-culture religions, whether they are Eastern imports to the West or Western imports to the East (including Third World "modernization religions" and cargo cults), are based on concepts of the instant transformation of persons and societies, ignoring hard-won knowledge accumulated over the centuries by each religious tradition on its own home ground about how to realize human potentials most fully. They therefore make little contribution to the production of social goodness. The established religions, to which counter-culture religions are a reaction, have long since settled for a Sunday morality which is a far cry from the vision of human potential which is still kept alive by a small creative minority within each religious establishment.

Today we are caught in one of those difficult, exciting periods in history known as an axial age, in which many new insights, technologies and social capabilities have come together (the last was in the thirteenth century). Many people think we could step over a threshold into a new phase of social evolution. What holds us back is undeveloped spiritual and moral potential. There is much talk about human transformation, transcendance, and so on, just as there was in the thirteenth century. The evidence today, however, is that our existing societies are not capable of producing the new kinds of persons required for the new era, any more than they were in the thirteenth century. Neither the old or the new international economic order enable this to be done, nor will the liberation movements, or the established churches or the counter-culture religions. Yet we do have nurturance resources at work in the cracks of existing social structures including, imperfect as they are, in families. We also have a high probability of the breakdown of many centrally administered bureaucratic systems in the most industrialized societies, because organizational technology cannot keep pace with bureaucratic complexity. The Stanford Research Institute study on bureaucratic complexity and breakdown only describes at a theoretical level what we read daily in our newspapers about the serious local malfunctioning of the economic and social welfare infrastructures of the modern state. When energy shortages generate massive shortfalls in the provision of electrical power from centralized sources, we may be forced to go local and develop a whole set of innovations in energy production, economic processes and political organization that will enable people to organize their lives at the local community level. Since the fostering of growth in human goodness is basically a local, labour-intensive enterprise, a localist scenario is the most promising vision of the future from that perspective.

All of the most highly developed skills of women as initiators of futurist visioning and futurist processes can be brought to play when the emphasis is local. Nurturance resources can be released from private into public spaces. While some of that nurturance has been rejected as false, when the coercive aspect is removed genuine nurturance can flourish. The specialization of women in such nurturance roles should be regarded as a strictly transitional phenomenon, preparing the way for equal opportunities in nurturance training for men and women in the future. This nurturance training will be essential in rounding out the assertive character already overdeveloped in many men, making persons of both sexes more flexible and empathic in their social behaviour so that structural design can accomplish its human welfare goals.

Women's commensalist visions of planetary sharing

Women were leaders in two major world movements for planetary sharing in the last century, and much of today's visioning owes its strength to the experience of the women who worked 100 years ago. One movement was the Christian missionary movement, which brought women from Europe and the Americas together with women of Africa and Asia in countless local community development projects including the development of schools and medical services. The other was the world women's movement, expressed through the formation of fifteen different international non-governmental women's organizations between 1880 and 1915, and embodied today in about fifty transnational women's organizations. The forty-seven organizations for which I have information can be classified into: religious (9), international relations (10), professional (18), educational (7) and sports (3).

All the organizations have certain characteristics in common. They all promote international cooperation and understanding, as well as some concept of justice and social welfare, both for people in general and for women in particular. They all have a high ethical and altruistic tone. To some degree, therefore, they are all addressing themselves to some of the major problems of the twentieth century. They are all to an extent concerned with the gathering of data that will enable them to act more effectively in solving the problems they address, and for each of them the very existence of the organization itself provides a new set of social roles for acting on the world scene (Boulding, 1977).

World sisterhood is strong within and to some extent between these organizations, and while they fall short of their goals, each organization contributes to some modest extent to a redistribution of information, training and resources toward Third World women and away from Europe and North America. If one were to distill a common utopia from their various organizational visions, it would be of a pluralistic world society with equal life chances for each woman, man and child, equal participation opportunities for all, and innumerable interlacing networks of local people sharing common interests as private individuals concerned for public welfare. It would be a world conscious of its grass roots, and adept at individual-to-individual communication from anywhere to anywhere. It would be a world of diverse lifestyles freely chosen, ranging from rural voluntary simplicity to urban high technology. The most important feature of this vision is that *no community would exist in isolation.* Through the use of two-way television, radio and telephone, people would be immediately present to one another across great distances. Because of this two-way immediacy, human needs would be seen, shared and acted upon directly and non-bureaucratically, from community to community regardless of national borders.

The great commensalist vision of the Jubilee Year, which long ago mandated the Jews to "return every man unto his possession" (Leviticus 25:1-28) every fiftieth year, so that no one should oppress another, has received a striking reformulation by a Catholic women sociologist and futurist, Sister Marie Augusta Neal. She has developed a theology of relinquishment, an approach to teaching the haves to let go so they will be able to obey the mandate to share with have-nots. With one sweep of the hand she dismisses all arguments about triage and lifeboat ethics. We are four billion people in the world and our primary responsibility is to the poor among us. No other priority may override that of sharing the fruits of the planet (Neal, 1977). Her work provides the type of underpinning without which the New International Economic Order would be meaningless, since it must be based on commitment to action.

Other women visionaries have tried to spell out the details of how a commensalist world could work. Barbara Ward first gave us the imagery of the spaceship earth. Hazel Henderson has spelled out the "end to economics" as we have known it, the end of a system that mines the planet and its people (Henderson, 1977). She visualizes a counter-economy based on a realistic awareness of the entropy–syntropy cycle, with sustainable modes of production and consumption involving simple lifestyles and more labour-intensive production. While old industrial structures crumble, the following post-industrial phenomena will flourish: alternative technologies and alternative marketing structures for alternative technology products, developed with the aid of alternative publishing ventures; increase in labour-intensive household production; the rebirth of the cooperative movement, neighbourhood and block development; the rise of worker-participation and self-management movements; the world-wide linkage of the networks of the global ecology movement, the indigenous peoples' movement, and the feminist movement, to provide the technical and psychological skills required for the more labour-intensive society. The theme is local self-sufficiency embedded in a system of global networks that provide continuous feedback on how the human family is doing. The political science of commensalism was developed as far back as 1920 by Mary Follett, a little-known futurist who described how non-governmental networks might work to debureaucratize and make more human large-scale political systems (Follett, 1920).

Militarism, the great enemy of commensalism, has been tackled by women with visions of alternative, demilitarized societies for over a century, Bertha Suttner, who persuaded Alfred Nobel to institute the Nobel Peace Prize, wrote *Down With Arms,* a "how-to" on disarmament, in 1894. Jane Addams, half a century ahead of her time, linked problems of urban neighbourhood reform to global peace and disarmament, and saw women as "housekeepers for the world", in *Peace and Bread.* One of the major women futurists of this century is Alva Myrdal, whose utopian efforts were first bent to a restatement of the role of minorities and women in society, and in recent decades has focused on how to create a disarmed world (Myrdal, 1970). By keeping their eye on the main vision of a peaceful, sharing world, each of these women has avoided being dragged into the pseudo-rational deterrence theorizing of their male colleagues, and instead stayed with the task of delineating the functioning of social systems leading to injustice and war. More than that, they have gone on as far as they were able to a systems analysis of the alternative future societies they envisage.

Women's visions of rebirth: the production of human goodness

While we tend to think of the most powerful images of the future as images of future societies, we find over and over again that at critical times in history people have been transported by images of what human beings as individuals could become. While there is a social dimension implicit — and often explicit — in these images, the significance and power derive from ideas of what the Creator had in mind when humans were first formed. Such visions tend to arise in axial ages, as suggested earlier. During one such axial age, the visions of the human potential developed in Jainism and Buddhism in India in the sixth century B.C. led thousands of women to leave their homes and become wandering nuns, travelling from place to place teaching other women about the great spiritual developments that lay ahead for them if they would open themselves to enlightenment. The teachings of Jesus about human potential also brought thousands of women out of their homes to help shape a new society, in travelling missionary bands. By the fourth century when the Christian church was already becoming institutionalized and the urban corruption of Mediterranean society was clearly continuing unchecked by the new vision, many women fled these cities to live in the desert and work more seriously at the problem of human transformation. Some of them were wealthy Roman matrons, like St. Jerome's friend and collaborator Paula, who settled into a severely ascetic way of life in Jerusalem. Others were fun-loving city play-girls, like St. Mary of Egypt, who according to legend subsisted on the meagre fruits of the desert in solitary sanctity for 47 years before she died. Thousands of their sisters crowded into convents in the Syrian and Egyptian deserts in that same fourth century. That which tore them loose from old settings and nourished them in arid new ones was an overpowering vision of human beings under divine guidance. They felt instinctively that the currupt environments of cities could not let this new dimension of spirituality flower in their own lives or in the lives of others. Yet their departure from the cities was not a denial but an affirmation. They were affirming the reality of the new possibility, and stayed where they could prepare body, mind and spirit for a new order in which everyone would love God and each other.

What characterized the rebirth experiences of these desert ascetics was an overwhelming experience of the love of God which endowed them in turn with a great capacity for love and joy, and with a great energy for the work of reconstructing, through prayer, the society they had known. These drastic methods may have had little effect on the cities, but they became embodied in a great classic literature of reconstruction through prayer, an approach which has yet to be adequately tested in any society. The thirteenth and fourteenth centuries were another axial age when European women in large numbers left homes and families to enter convents, or create lay urban communes like the *béguinages,* or to live in solitude in huts by forests and streams and on the outskirts of villages. It was generally thought that the Age of the Holy Spirit was about to begin, but humans were still bogged down in their old beastliness, so it took fervent searching to discover the path to goodness for a corrupt society. Lady Julian of Norwich was one of the great solitary visionaries of this period who also wrote about her visions (Colledge and Walsh, 1978). She is particularly important in an account of women futurists, because she wrote of the motherhood of God in a way that is still beyond the understandings of church officialdom, and laid the groundwork for contemporary feminist theology.

In our era, filled with so many diverse opportunities to work, play and explore the planet, it is hard to imagine an experience of insight into the divine-human enterprise so powerful that the rest of one's lifetime would be spent in working out that insight. While many of the women infected with "New Ageism" were recluses or nuns, they had a powerful impact on their own time and are reappearing in our own, like a delayed time-bomb, this after an apparent break of some centuries in the tradition of seeking to understand and develop the human potential with divine guidance. Today, many women's religious orders are rediscovering the hermit tradition, and there is more demand for hermitages and places of solitary retreat in every country than there are facilities. Again we are in an axial age, standing at a threshold, and business as usual will not take care of the insistent inner demands for a return to the old unfinished business of the reconstruction of human beings. While that work has often called women out of families to a life of celibacy, countless women embark on this task in the midst of an apparently ordinary working and home life. Others, like Simone Weil, plunge passionately into the hardest kind of work among the poor, but live a life of deepest prayer even while struggling with utter physical exhaustion (Weil, 1959).

The process being described here is not a once-for-all pentecostal experience, but a life-long disciplined attention to inward leadings that produces what might be called an accelerated growth in the capacity for discerning, loving and acting. It produces the quality of love described by Paul in I Corinthians 13, including the capacity in an obstinate world to "bear all things, believe all things, hope all things, endure all things". It involves a high degree of development of the intellecting and imaginative capacities, including a development of what St. Augustine calls the five inward senses, corresponding to the five outward senses. It produces people of great serenity, lovers of simplicity and frugality, with highly active social imaginations and often with great capacity for local community work. In short, it produces the kind of people who can make a new social order a viable ongoing reality.

Women as practical utopists: building the new society in the cracks of the old

Alternative societies are continuously in process of creation. Every family is in a sense an alternative society. It creates its own culture, its own values. Usually the variations in family culture in relation to mainstream culture are of such a nature that family culture as such has little effect on the larger society. In times of change like the present, however, families belonging to minority subcultures become vital experimental ventures in the creation of a new society. Children of "movement families" are usually trained in movement skills. To the extent that women are involved as change agents outside the home, they will also be contributing to social change through what they teach in the family. The family is the proving ground for the localist utopia. It is here that habits of analysis of the social scene, habits of egalitarian relationship, skills of give and take in joint decision-making, ways of handling conflicts, habits of personal simplicity and frugality, and useful life maintenance skills and recycling skills are first developed. The family can also be the graveyard of undeveloped personalities and undeveloped futures. In every industrialized country where home television is prevalent, and most of all in the USA where television is most widely distributed in homes, this danger of undevelopment exists. Passive TV-mesmerized families will produce no utopias, because there is not enough family interaction to produce anything but passivity. In general, however, utopia-building community processes should be thought of as flowing back and forth across the boundaries between family and community and not just as occurring at the community level.

The rejection of the family as a historically oppressive institution and all the roles associated with it, and the insistence that society as a whole should take over the nurturance tasks associated with the family, is an important alternative feminist vision. This rejection, however, is of one particular form of the family mistakenly thought of as the family. In fact the communist cell and the lesbian commune are also families in the most appropriately inclusive sense of the term — caring groups committed to each other over a period of time. Lesbian communes also rear children — though communist cells probably do not. It is important to affirm the desirability of diversity in types of family groupings. The lesbian commune in particular seeks a new quality of human relationship and can be thought of as a model for all families in that respect. So can the convent, which is indeed a family as the Benedictine Rules emphasizes, even though no children are raised there. The old patriarchal image of the family which makes women exclusively responsible for the domestic sphere has no place in the future, when all nurturance activities will be shared between women and men. That all human beings should in some way share in the care of very young children, whether in families, communes, neighbourhood centres or in other ways that the childless and the celibate can enter into, is a basic tenet of the localist image of the future.[2] Another basic tenet of localist futurism is that ageism must disappear. Children must be treated as persons with participatory capacities from a young age. They should be brought in as co-shapers of community life from at least the age of 5 (when they enter the family labour force in all preindustrial societies). Elder persons must

---

[2]The image of all children cared for by the state in child-care centres, all people fed in state restaurants, and a total provision of individual needs by the state, belongs to an older socialist vision of the state which has questionable viability given what we know of the weaknesses of bureaucratic centralism, including the socialist variety. A decentralist image of neighbourhood care and neighbourhood communal eating is completely compatible with the existence of a diversity of *family style* groupings in neighbourhoods and is not an "anti-familistic" image.

likewise be treated as persons with full participatory capabilities, and not be artificially retired from productive and civic status (Boulding, 1978).

Historically much of women's practical utopia-building experience has come, ironically, in their role as rebuilders of society after wars. At that time their labour is needed everywhere, both in reconstructing physical environments — buildings, roads, etc., and in reconstructing the social environment — schools, hospitals, recreational areas, welfare facilities. In the twentieth century women of Europe, Africa and Asia have had many such reconstruction opportunities in the aftermath of World War II and wars of liberation. In the war-torn socialist countries of Europe new types of neighbourhood centres and activities, particularly for children, were developed by women to orient the next generation towards a new society. As I write this I think particularly of the Society of the Friends of Children in Poland, which I visited in 1962. This was an old pre-war women's organization galvanized into new life in the rubble of post-holocaust Warsaw. Combing the ruined city block by block, members of the society found Warsaw's children, and began by clearing safe spaces in each block for them to play in. Moving step by step with their perceptions of the children's needs, they have created a whole "alternative society" for children "in the cracks" of the official society, and have even been acknowledged and honoured by an overburdened government in the process.

In Japan, China and India, each of which traditionally had few public roles for women, women themselves created the public organizations they needed, in which they could develop their own civic consciousness and pursue their own ideas for the future of their respective countries. The famous "Frying Pan March" down the main streets of Tokyo of Japanese women as the 1950s turned into the 1960s, when they announced to an astonished male public that there were serious problems in terms of goods and services to households was one of the more dramatic examples. The women followed up in March with the creation of a whole new set of monitoring institutions to ensure safe food and safe production processes. Bit by bit Japanese women tackled the problems that men left unsolved: sewage and garbage disposal and the safety of children walking to school on narrow streets crowded with speeding cars were among the items they took into their own hands. Because they were creating institutions that had not existed before, and were needed in the new society growing inside the shell of old Japan, this is properly speaking utopia creations "in the cracks". In Vietnam, women are playing a shaping role in the new socialist republic such as few women have played in any country. In other countries where women fought side by side with men in wars of liberation, they have not always "been allowed" to stay in public roles to shape the new society. In every country where they have been pushed aside, that country has suffered in its development.

At the global level, the most dramatic "in the cracks" futurism has been seen in the International Women's Year Conference. Although officially sponsored by the UN and its member governments, the resources set aside for this consideration of the situation of women and their role in furthering development and peace were so meagre that the conference was only able to produce meaningful work because of the in-the-cracks participation of countless women volunteers, inside and outside the transnational non-governmental women's organizations. The International Women's Year Tribunal, which is the voice of these women from the cracks, is the only active follow-up body still functioning 3 years after the Conference.

The vision presented at the International Women's Year Conference of the future society is simple but revolutionary: it involves the participation of women as co-creators in the civic sphere, nationally and internationally; as co-producers of development plans as well as co-implementers of them; as co-designers of disarmament and peace plans; it calls for the removal of all impediments due to custom and law which hinder women from full participation with men as equals in their respective societies and in the UN.

Neither co-creation nor the removal of impediments have had much attention since International Women's Year. The international women's movement is divided now as it was then over the issue of whether to press for admittance to a man's world, which is what the International Women's Year Plan of Action calls for, or whether to ignore the man's world and set about creating the alternative society on a whole new pattern right now. Ironically, women are equally marginal whether they choose to press for admittance into the man's world or whether they choose for creating alternatives themselves. Yet both approaches continue to have validity. The more women enter the "man's world" the more they alter it by their very presence, if they have not already completely modelled themselves on the men with whom they seek colleagueship. The more they work on alternatives, the more visible and compelling these alternatives become, as other solutions break down. Since the New International Economic Order seems to have little place for women, more and more women of the non-industrial, as well as of the industrial world, are opting for pilot experiments to see what works in local communities. The visioning process cannot be assigned to a few well-known women. It is literally a community process among communities of women. This is in itself a testimony against the "great person" theory of history and social change, and a commitment to the *process* of futures building as compared to static statements of goals.

In Africa this commitment to process has brought new life to traditional women's village councils and work groups. They plan development projects that will ease their work load (the heaviest in the world, perhaps), enhance the life of the community, and increase their own sense of worth and creativity. It may be building a road for transport to improve their trading activities, or a mill to grind their grain, or a school for lifelong learning programmes, or food storage bins that are rat-proof. Whatever it is, they have decided it, they will make it, and from that point on personal and social growth cannot be stopped. They already have the localist society industrial women sometimes dream of, but they have it in an impoverished, artificially dependent form because of the structures of the old economic order. They will not wait for those structures to go. Life is where life is, and these women, once they have decided to act communally, have life.

Socialist revolutionaries have always worked in the cracks. Clara Zetkin and Rosa Luxemburg's vision was of a peaceful localist/transnational socialist world, as was that of many women socialists at the turn of the century. The localist/transnational vision lost to a militant centralist nationalism in the socialist movement. Terrorist Sofia Parovskaya and anarchist Emma Goldman were also revolutionaries with a tender-hearted vision of a localist world, but social circumstances in old Russia led Perovskaya to abandon her native gentleness for terrorism, and led Goldman to a lifetime of heartaches amidst labour violence in the U.S.A. The rejection of family life and childbearing by so many revolutionaries was often at great personal cost. Some of them wrote longingly of that other life they might have lived. Secular saints, they responded to the needs of society with the same intensity as those who went to the desert, the hermitage or to the convent. Neither the revolutionary nor the nun, however, negate the family as an institution. Rather they reaffirm the family metaphor at a deeper level.

Tania, the Argentinian-born revolutionary who died a violent death with Che Guevara in the jungles of Bolivia, was another gentle idealist who sought the peaceful localist society but was trapped in violence. A poem she wrote in April 1966 while waiting for an underground contact somewhere in Latin America, testified to the poignancy of knowing that one is working in the cracks, that one's vision may never be known:

> So I must leave, like flowers that wilt?
> Will my name one day be forgotten
> And nothing of me remain on the earth?
> At least, flowers and song.
> How then, must my heart behave?
> Is it in vain that we live, that we appear on the earth?
> (in Rojas and Calderon, 1971:178)

At the other extreme are the women trained as global modellers who have a localist vision of equally shared wealth around the world and use their skills to try to translate their visions into forms understandable by international decision-makers. This is an exercise in frustration. Donella Meadows, senior author of the Club of Rome study, *Limits to Growth* (1972), points out that few people have ever noticed what she was really trying to say in the last chapter of *Limits to Growth* about the alternative society. Graciela Chichilniski, who has worked with the Bariloche Foundation in Argentina as economics–mathematician world modeller, also finds that people do not really *hear* what she has to say. (Herrera, Skolnik and Chichilniski, 1976 provides an example of her type of work.) In each case, a woman trained like men is trying to speak to men, yet each is coming from a different place, has different dreams and cannot make herself understood.

The Ecology Movement is perhaps one of the few places today where women's visions take equal place with the visions of men. The world as a precióus, rather fragile ecosystem which must be tended with loving care, and continually replenished when something is taken from it by humans, is a woman's metaphor but one that more and more men are coming to adopt. The model of women and men working together for the new society will then come largely from this movement. Women are running for political office on ecology platforms in Europe and the US, and being elected. The ecology movement has so many forms that no generalizations can be made about it, but some of the most innovative local community organizing seen in the past decade in the industrialized societies comes from various national and local offshoots of the ecology movement. Much of women's civic zeal that was formerly isolated in the women's world is now linking up with the zeal of men in this common vision of a planet to be preserved for itself and for all life, including humanity. The humility of the ecology movement, the placing of human wants and needs in the perspective of the planetary ecosystem and the well-being of life itself, not just human life, represents the triumph of the women's conserving vision as a viable vision of the future in a hypertechnologized society.

The urban neighbourhood renewal movement in the world's cities represents another such triumph of women's visions. Now men work side by side with women to encourage the capacity to plan an action initiated in the residents of the city block, a social unit long despised by all but city ward heelers. The most improbable things happen. Not only is crime and violence brought under control, but vegetables start growing where no food has grown for half a century; solar heaters and greenhouse energy systems appear in tenements scheduled for demolition. People dance in the streets. Humanness and joy sprout inside the dead husks of urban decay. The antecedents of the new neighbourhood renewal movement lie at least in part in institutions like Dorothy Day's Hospitality Houses, developed by the Catholic Workers movement she founded in the 1930s. Dorothy Day began opening community houses in the most abandoned areas of New York, and later of other big cities, when no one else wanted to think about the poorest of the unemployed. She has specialized in loving and caring for the bums, the outcasts, those no one else wants to help. A brilliant woman who could have entered many fields, she chose to work in the cracks, creating gardens of human caring in city deserts. Like so much work in the cracks, it has had ramifications far beyond the city blocks in which she has worked. Her face and figure, her words and her work are known around the world. She is one of those new humans, living a life of inward contemplation in the midst of extreme outward activity, and the inwardness shines through every act. Dorothy's vision is a world vision, for she has travelled and worked for peace and justice world-wide, but it consists of neighbourhoods at peace and caring for one another: neighbourhoods in the city, and neighbourhoods in the country. It includes farms such as the Catholic Worker farm she has established outside New York City, which sends food into the city and takes human derelicts out to the farm, nursing them back to health (Day, 1952, 1963, 1972).

The rural renewal movement represents another triumph of women's visions. In the US, the country where decay of rural life and the obsolescence of the family farm had gone the furthest, women have started a national movement to affirm the values of rural life and the family farm. Farm women wear T shirts inscribed "I'm proud to be a farmer's wife" and their daughters wear T shirts inscribed "I'm proud to be a farmer's daughter". If the gender role differentiation seems to belong to an earlier era, this is only so to the outsider. Watch farm women in the US work side by side with their husbands in the field, and listen to them express pride in the fact that they know how to do everything that is done on the farm, and are their husband's partners.[3] Here is where labour-intensive activity can be seen at its most intense, and in a context of pride and contentment. Here are the role models for the localist communities of the future in the industrial world, for these women, and their children as well as their husbands, know how to work with their hands for whatever hours are necessary at harvest and other peak-load times. They also know how to rest, and how to play.

Women do not work side by side with their husbands in the fields in all parts of the world. Many women work alone in the fields, or work at more menial tasks than their men. A fair distribution of the work load, and companionship with men in work as well as in the home is an ideal for women everywhere. Labour-intensivity is a bad concept or westerners because they associate it with exploitation. Partnership in labour-intensive work is one part of women's vision of the future, including partnership in labour-intensive child care. Technology is to be used where appropriate, but never for its own sake. Time to enjoy the rhythm of the seasons and to observe the festivals, and a reasonable return on labour, completes the rural woman's vision of the future in whatever country.

The various components of women's visions of the future which I have described here — the concept of the planetary household at peace with itself, of the localist self-sufficient community connected with the world society through the technology of communication, of joy in work and in

---

[3]These statements are based on a current study of women farmers in the southwest of the United States, and come from personal observation.

relationships, and a high view of the human potential for goodness and love — all these are shared by a growing number of men. They represent a new direction, away from old patterns of expanding control over ever-larger social units, and increasing social stratification with attendant release from labour for some at the expense of others who must work longer hours; away from consumerism and away from a denigration of simplicity and rural lifestyles. To the extent that men are increasingly sharing women's values, we may say that the alternative future is already at least a possibility. How probable it is depends in part on the skills of human beings in forming coalitions across their usual social boundaries, and in identifying common interests where these may not appear to exist on the surface. Finally, it also depends on there being enough surplus energy for love, trust and action.

References

BOULDING, ELISE (1977) *Women in the Twentieth Century World.* New York: Halsted Press, John Wiley & Sons.

BOULDING, ELISE (1978) *Children's Rights and the Wheel of Life.* New Brunswick: Transaction Press.

CHICHILNISKI, GRACIELA with AMILCAR HERRERA, HUGO SKOLNIK *et al.* (1976) *Catastrophe or New Society? A Latin American World Model.* Buenos Aires: Fundacion Bariloche.

COLLEDGE, EDMUND and WALSH, JAMES (1978) *Julian of Norwich: Showings.* New York: Paulist Press.

DAY, DOROTHY (1952) *The Long Loneliness.* New York: Harper & Row.

DAY, DOROTHY (1963) *Loaves and Fishes.* New York: Harper & Row.

DAY, DOROTHY (1972) *On Pilgrimage: The Sixties.* New York: Curtis Books.

FOLLETT, MARY (1920) *The New State.* New York: Longmans Green.

HENDERSON, HAZEL (1978) *Creating Alternative Futures: The End of Economics.* New York: Berkeley Publishing Corporation, a Berkeley Windhonor Book.

MEADOWS, DONELLA and DENNIS (1972) *Limits to Growth.* New York: Universal Books.

MYRDAL, ALVA (1976) *The Game of Disarmament.* New York: Pantheon Books.

NEAL, MARIE AUGUSTA, S.N.D. deN. (1977) *A Socio-Theology of Letting Go.* New York: Paulist Press.

ROJAS, MARTA and CALDERON, MERTA RODRIGUEZ (eds.) (1971) *Tania: The Unforgettable Guerrilla.* New York: Random House.

WEIL, SIMONE (1959) *Waiting on God.* Fontana Books. London: Collins Clear-Type Press.

3

Loose Connections: A Vision of a Transformational Society

JIM DATOR

Department of Political Science, University of Hawaii at Manoa, USA

OVER the past 15 years, during which time I have devoted myself profes-
sionally to the study of the future, I have almost evenly divided my efforts
between either discovering and analysing what other people think the future
will or should be, or determining and clarifying what I would prefer the
future to be. I state these two activities as being separate because I have
learned that what I prefer is not what many other people seem to want or
consider possible. You can get a good estimate of the differences involved
by comparing my preferred future, briefly indicated below, with other contributions to this volume. There are substantial differences.

Moreover, while I am by no means predicting that my preferred future
will actually happen, I am describing what I believe to be a possible future. I
am presenting a *eutopia* (a preferred real future, i.e. a good place), not a
utopia (preferred but impossible future, i.e. no place). That is to say, I
believe that there are trends and possible events which could lead to the
future I prefer, and I am merely highlighting what I believe to be one possible set of consequences deriving from those trends and events.

There is no doubt that my preferred future is both highly personal and
highly ethnocentric. It is a future which one might expect from a white,
middle-aged, reasonably successful American university professor, though
it is equally clear that most white, middle-aged, successful American university professors do not by any means adhere to it. Nonetheless, one would
not expect my preferred future to come from the typewriter of a well-
socialized Indian farmer, Nigerian bureaucrat, Sicilian peasant, Polynesian
chief, or what have you — although it is possible that some one thus
described might in fact like my preferred future even better than I do.

To call my future, "personal and ethnocentric", however, is not to condemn it, in my opinion. As you will see, the essence of my future is the
assumption that we are more or less rapidly moving into a situation where
more and more people in the world will find themselves in the company of

others who have genetic, linguistic, experiential, and expectational differences from themselves. That is to say, in contrast to the assumption I find underlying most of the papers in this volume, I believe that we are rapidly moving away from "community" and precedence-oriented living situations, and towards "individualized" and consequence-oriented circumstances.

Moreover, I believe this is happening globally, though obviously each section of the world will feel the impact of this trend differently. And just as some will feel it sooner (or are, as I believe, already experiencing it now — the US and some of Western Europe) so others (e.g. the People's Republic of China) might be able to avoid it entirely.

Theoretical Assumptions

One of the reasons futures studies is often considered to be an emerging art (not to say a pseudo-science) by persons uninvolved in it is because most writings about the future are so devoid of theoretical underpinnings. Presumably, one should not speak about the future unless one has first developed and specified a clear theory of a social structure and social change. Yet, most writings on the future either ignore the subject entirely, or offer only veiled hints as to what causes what to change and what does not change in human societies.

With such a statement, I should immediately launch into my own clear theory of social morphology, but, alas, I can do little better than the worse who have gone before me. I do wish to make a comment about my theoretical *assumptions,* however, because I believe that unless you understand them, you cannot begin to understand why I make the statements I do about my preferred future. Also, it should make it much easier for you to pinpoint and refute my errors if I can show you at the outset where I will subsequently be going wrong.

Figure 1 depicts an attempt I have made to analyse all of the various theories of social change that I am familiar with. It is unlikely that any one theory is correct, or wholly wrong. Rather, our understanding of social structure and dynamics is so primitive (and neglected) that it is likely not only that a complex combination of several of these theories is nearer the truth, but also that important factors have not been picked up by any theorist so far. It is also possible that we are humanly incapable of developing an adequate theory in this area, but I assume such is not the case.

Probably the most popular "theory" used by futures researchers is that which is operationalized by various forms of trend analysis: one's theory of social change (whether that theory is rigorously defined or only a hunch) specifies the factors in society which are most important (e.g. population growth, energy utilization, the proportion of the population in various kinds of occupations, etc.); indicates how to determine the growth (or decline) of that factor or factors from historical data; and then extrapolates

CHARACTERISTIC DISTINCTIONS BETWEEN THEORIES OF SOCIAL CHANGE

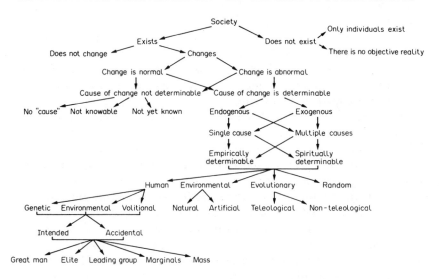

PATTERNS OF CHANGE: 1. Linear 2. Curvilinear (e.g. hyperbolic, exponential, logistic, etc.) 3. Cyclical 4. Envelope 5. Step 6. Dialectic 7. Stochastic 8. Random
SCALE OF CHANGE: 1. Individual 2. Communal 3. Societal 4. Cultural 5. Global 6. Extraterrestrial
HIERARCHY OF CHANGE: Movement → Change → Development
LOCUS OF CHANGE: 1. Endogenous change: Dynamic equilibrium; biological growth; "the social DNA"
2. Exogenously-imposed change: Disease; evolution; revolution; invasion; operant conditioning; education
3. Exogenously-sought change: Feedback, information, learning
ILLUSTRATION OF CHANGE *IN* THE SYSTEM VS. CHANGE *OF* THE SYSTEM: a. Stagnant pond; b. Flowing stream with standing-wave pattern; c. I step in the stream and change the wave-pattern temporarily; d. I dam the stream and permanently alter the flow and wave-pattern; e. I heat the stream and change water into steam and sand into glass. SO, WHAT IS CHANGE? I SAY BETWEEN "B" AND "C". Thus, even a waterfall doesn't "change" according to this understanding because the speed of change is not the most important factor; the stability of the system — the alteration of patterns of or within the system — is the point.
    Also, there is the question of SCALE: The "stagnant pond" actually changes microscopically, and with the seasons. Similarly, the changes of the heated stream may be irrelevant, or small parts of another system when seen from the moon.

FIG. 1

the historical curve into the future, utilizing either simple linear regression or complex systems dynamics — or merely intuitive — techniques. Though they did not say so, I gather that many of the contributors to this book used such a method, explicitly or implicitly.

So have I, but with a certain twist to it. Out of the many factors that might be thought to shape the future, I have utilized only two — and then not rigorously operationalized them. First of all, I believe that Marshall McLuhan's statement, "We shape our tools and thereafter our tools shape us", captures a very important cause of social change. Hence, I believe that technology helps shape the future.

Secondly, I am persuaded that what sociologists call "age cohort analysis" — the studies of differences in attitudes and behaviours between human generations caused by differences in diet, child-rearing practices, significant commonly-shared social events, and the like — is also helpful for understanding what is not yet.

Now, in choosing these two to utilize in developing my eutopia, I am focusing on factors which tend to work against or break currently-dominant trends. This may be one reason why my future looks so different from that of others. Yet is seems to me that usual trend analysis, while valuable in many respects (for predicting the short-range future of a well-defined closed system), is not as helpful for my purposes (designing the long-range future of a poorly-understood open system). Thus, I am not interested in the future that normal trend analysis proports to reveal so much as in exploring what Theodore Gordon calls "the nature of unforeseen developments".

But let me be a bit more specific about how I intend to use technological/societal interactive analysis and age-cohort analysis to illuminate my preferred future.

On technology

Currently, there seem to be three competing notions of the relationship between technology and society. The first, and most widely held, I call "mere technology" — the belief that "technology" designates simply the tools which humans use to enable them to do things. Technology refers merely to various types of hardware, nothing more. These tools have no special effect upon human nature, nor on what it means to be human, nor even upon the environment of humans. Of course, certain tools might be used in ways that humans feel are harmful. But this is only of trifling significance: once the evil has been identified, the problem can be corrected, either by changing the way the tool is used, by developing a new tool, or by reverting to some earlier mode of pre-tool usage. Technology is basically helpful to humans, and societies can be classified according to the primitiveness or complexity of their technologies. Generally speaking, the more complex, the better.

A second view, which has always existed but is currently gaining intellectual popularity, I call "dehumanizing technology" — the belief that technology is basically anti-human. Each culture has a collection of great myths which essentially says the same thing: technology is bad. It easily gets out of control. Technology is to be avoided. It is unnatural. Prometheus' fire; Pegasus' attempts to fly; Pandora's box. Shelley's Frankenstein, and the Sorcerer's Apprentice are merely a sampling of the cautionary tales in Western culture alone. Even the Adam and Eve story in Genesis One of the Bible has been interpreted as a warning against the original sin of linking human purpose with technological know-how in order to modify the perfectly-adapted Garden of Eden.

Thus, every increase in technological complexity is a step away from essential humanity. Small is beautiful. We are mere humans, always trying to play god through our technological mastery of nature, but only able to make things worse and worse until finally we develop a doomsday machine that will destroy us all. We must rid ourselves of technology, and live as simply as possible.

The view I hold is different still. For good or ill (and it may be ill), humans become humans and change the meaning of what it is to be human (i.e. change "human nature") in large measure by interacting with themselves and their environment through their technologies. The technological–human relationship is thus symbiotic and not parasitical. We may think that interrelationship is trivial, but in fact humans have been, are, and will be further changed by the interaction. We may think the interaction is demonic (probably because many of the changes which occur are unanticipated), but who we are now is largely a consequence of changes which occurred through past interactions, and it is dubious whether we should attempt to make the present immutable when its own characteristics are in part only the result of past interactions with technology which altered earlier human conditions.

In addition, it is doubtful whether certain types of technology are superior to others, *per se.* Small (or large) may or may not be beautiful. Scale is not the only criterion. It certainly does not seem likely that agricultural technologies — which wrought such incredible changes in human life thousands of years ago — are naturally superior to industrial ones. Is it more "human" to get up with the chickens than to get up with an alarm clock or a factory whistle? What is the inherent nobility in milking a cow twice a day every day of one's life, rather than tightening a screw on an assembly line forty hours a week? Why is a sabretooth tiger less dehumanizing than an automobile? And those questions are not made in defence of the moral superiority of factory whistle assembly lines or automobiles, necessarily. Rather, *all* technologies both restrain and liberate us, and we should evaluate them solely in terms of whether they help us live the way we wish to live or not, and whether we are so reactionary that we prefer the certainties of past technological arrangements to the uncertainties and possibilities of new ones.

I wish to make several more comments about technology. First of all, I am drawn to the definition which says simply that "technology" is how humans "get things done". This makes it easier to understand that technology is a good deal more than physical tools alone. Indeed, I find it helpful to distinguish between three types of technologies: biological, social and physical. The distinction I find important because often the question of whether a technology is "good" or "bad" revolves around whether one prefers a new physical technology to an established biological or social one. Figure 2 lists a variety of functions which have been, are, or perhaps will be performed by two or three of the modes of technology.

TYPE OF TECHNOLOGY	BIOLOGICAL	SOCIAL	PHYSICAL
FUNCTION			
Communication	Extra-sensory perception	Spoken language	Television
Acquiring children	Sexual intercourse	Adoption Kidnapping	Test-tube babies
Food production	Mother's milk/ Wetnurse	Slave-based agriculture	Synthetic pills
Information transfer	DNA	School system	Learning pills
Killing	Strangulation	Voodoo	ICMB
Moving mountains	Manual labour	Faith	Bulldozer

FIG. 2

Generally speaking, humans have only recently developed powerful physical technologies which are capable of rivalling and replacing the older biological or social ones. A great deal of conflict over technological development comes in part, then, from not recognizing that technology consists of more than physical tools. But another important part of the conflict also comes from people who gain advantage from present technological arrangements, and who are loath to see the presently powerless made more powerful by newer technologies. Admittedly, a significant portion of the argument is also that modern technologies take power away from the already relatively powerless and give more power to the already relatively powerful. There are certainly instances where this is the case. But it is my belief that, overall and in the long run, more individuals gain more freedom in more areas of their lives through modern technologies (especially physical ones, but also social, and perhaps even biological technologies, if for example, "paranormal" abilities become more prevalent). Indeed, that individual freedom (as a fact of human experience and not merely as an intellectual concept) is in large part a (generally unintended) consequence of technological development is one of the most important contentions underlying my preferred future. While I am impressed by the arguments of such people as Ivan Illich and Jacques Ellul to the contrary, I am not convinced by them.

To put it extremely briefly, technological development shapes the future of society by (1) making possible human behaviour that was previously impossible, or making easier that which was previously difficult. Contrarily, (2) it makes unnecessary the previously necessary or highly likely. Thus (3) technological developments usually create choice where there was previously virtual inevitability. Hence, it changes, or at least threatens, established behaviours and values. (4) Since it creates choice where there was inevitability before, and since (while we may be able to do anything, we can't do everything) choices made frequently foreclose other opportunities, technological development also operates in a fashion contrary to that I have indicated so far. Thus, it may make impossible the previously possible; it may make necessary the previously unnecessary: and it may foreclose choice by creating inevitability. The critics of modern technology seem to feel that this latter is more nearly the true character of technology than that which I discern.

Let me make some final remarks about this point.

1. The way a specific technological development is introduced into a society; the local "software" (rules for use) surrounding the hardware; and the specific existential structure and values of the society into which it is introduced (or out of which it develops) all affect the way in which the generalized rules, outlined above, operate. Thus, assuming the general rules to be correct, we can at best only indicate the general tendencies of the technological development, not predict the specific resulting behaviour and values — not now, and perhaps not at all.

2. There are important differences between the social impact of specific pieces of hardware (e.g. a particular automobile); generalized types of hardware (the automobile *per se,* vs. other modes of transport, for example); and "levels" of technology (such as industrial technologies *per se* vs. agricultural technologies, vs. hunting and gathering societies). It is much easier to indicate the general impact of a change from one level to another than it is to predict the impact of a specific piece of hardware — yet the impact of specific pieces of hardware is all that really happens. Indicating the probable impact of generalized types is in between the two in difficulty.

Inasmuch as I believe we are moving rapidly from an industrial to a "post-industrial" technological system, I am discussing the implications of that shift in what follows, not the impact (say) of holographic television on Egyptian society (still less the consequence of whether that television is produced and distributed by Phillips or by Sony before or after an Arab–Israeli war!).

3. There is a difference between the social impact of the *invention* of a tool (whether invented by individual chance or by social research and development); the *development* of it (whether by entrepreneurship or by political decision); and its *diffusion* so that it has a mass impact through market and/or other modes of distribution. I am interested mainly in the impact of technology at the stage of mass diffusion.

4. Finally, methods of technology assessment attempt to distinguish between "orders" of technological impact: primary, or first-order effects; secondary, or second-order effects, and so on. Primary effects are much easier to identify than are later-order effects, yet it is probably the later-order effects that are most socially significant, as Lynn White, Jr., pointed out in his interesting article on technology assessment from the point of view of a medieval historian.

Cross-impacts (the impact of one effect upon another) are also important, as is the sequence in which the technology is introduced and the impacts felt (again, always in a specific historical situation, with specific—and unpredictably motivated—actors).

5. There is much, much more to "the causes of social change" than technological development alone. The statement, "we shape our tools and thereafter our tools shape us", starts out with the primacy of human action: *we* shape our tools. Why we shape which tools, and who controls that action, is also highly significant. And so are decisions, actions and values totally unrelated to "technology". I by no means minimize the role of politics in all of this. Indeed, I consider that to be central.

Finally, let me make it clear that I do not own stock in any manufacturing company, nor am I in the pay of any modern industry (save that of the industry of publicly-supported higher education). My interest in technology may come from misguided intellectual curiosity, but it is not from ideological privilege: while some of my best friends may be technocrats, most of them are not!

On age-cohort analysis

Let me offer some extended examples of age-cohort analysis from the writings of Leonard Cain, a sociologist at Portland State University in Oregon, specializing in the future of old age.

> "My wife and I had from time to time discussed the differences between her parents and mine. Their rural and regional and social class backgrounds were somewhat similar, but their life styles were quite different. One day we discussed the possibility that their differences in age may be crucial. My father was born in 1896, my mother in 1900, my inlaws in 1903 and 1905. My father was well into

his thirties when the Depression hit, and managed to keep a job. My father-in-law had not achieved job security by 1929; he spent a decade and more searching, working temporarily, moving, and searching, moving. I set about the task of determining if there were what may be called a generational watershed which routed those born just before the new century began down one set of life-style paths, and those born early in the century down another set. Out of such observations hypotheses are born.

The data I managed to collect suggested that the age cohort born in the decade before 1900 had attributes and experiences which set its members distinctly apart from members of the cohort born during the 1901-1910 span. The younger cohort had a much better educational opportunity than the older: the shift from typical grammar school termination of education to high school experiences for most youths took place about the time of World War I. The younger may be classified as our first 'native born' cohort, with hardly one in twelve an immigrant; the older cohort reflected the heavy immigration of early years of this century much more fully, with one in six an immigrant.

The women in the younger cohort produced the smallest rate of births of any cohort before or since; their older sisters still reflected childbearing practices of an agricultural economy, though trends in birthrate had already become downward.

The 1901-1910 cohort was too young for World War I, too old for World War II, service. The men of the 1890's cohort supplied most of the manpower for World War I. Prohibition; women's suffrage; the 1920 Census, which reported America had finally become more than 50% urban; the new style of the Roaring Twenties; the widespread use of the automobile, the radio, and the movies; mass production; labour union expansion; came about after the older cohort was already of age, and provided new conditions for growing up and stepping into adulthood for the younger cohort.

I even tried to imagine the differential impact on health-related discoveries and new health programs on the physical bodies of the two cohorts. I have not yet found a way to deal systematically with the generational watershed which may have been produced by the discovery of vitamins beginning in 1913, of the movement to chlorinate water and pasteurize milk and vaccinate children against smallpox and to develop and expand public health services early in this century. But I suspect that the ravages of childhood diseases, of poor nutrition, of physically demanding labor, are manifest now in the bodies of those already being served by Medicare. The currently middle aged, with the health advantages from developments mentioned above, may produce a whole new challenge for Medicare, and for geritricians. And dare we speculate on the health care needs of the recent cohorts who have had vitamins and innoculations and intensive pediatric care, when they become old, after 2001? . . .

I tried in this first formal venture into cohort analysis to add a practical note to gerontologists. It had been my observation that most of the studies by gerontologists were of samples of the already old. I reasoned that, by the time a systematic study of the characteristics and needs of the already old were made, the data processed and analysed, the results interpreted and published, then introduced to policy makers and legislators, and translated into law and finally into programs for the aged, many in the cohort studied would be deceased. Rather, I suggested, gerontologists need very much to become anticipatory, to study the not yet old in order to plan for effective programs as successive cohorts step into new old age roles. And, I hardly need add, an anticipatory gerontology would surely benefit social planners." (From Leonard D. Cain, "Planning for the Elderly of the Future", read before the Conference on "Planning and the Urban Elderly", 1971, pp. 3-5.)

I draw several conclusions from the method Cain suggests here (and uses more rigorously in several papers):

1. We are likely to err if we predict the salient values and behaviour of people in the future from those of "the average person" today.

2. There are significant value and behavioural differences between cohorts at present. If we wish to predict the values and behaviours of future decision-makers (for example), we cannot simply ascertain the values and behaviours of present decision-makers and project them into the future. Rather, we should determine those of the presently young who will (presumably) assume positions of power in the future, discounting appropriately for the effects of maturation, and also for the possibility that all "power holders" by definition may be significantly alike on the one hand and significantly different from non-power holders at all times by virtue of their power-seeking and/or holding propensities.

3. The differences between cohorts is due in part to diet (especially infant feeding practices), child-rearing practices (in the US, pre-Spock, Spock, and now post-Spock differences seem important), and significant, commonly-shared social events (such as wars, depressions, "Woodstock", fads, films, educational curricula and the like). These, and other events, mark the cohorts who experience them and distinguish them from other cohorts who, in essence, live in a different world, and interpret the same objective events quite differently.

4. Thus, as a cohort exercising social power more or less abruptly relinquishes that power to a succeeding cohort on death or retirement, there may be "sudden" changes in perception and thus in policy, and hence the smoothly extrapolated future suddenly shifts and a new trend line comes in-

to place. For example, in the 1950s, American students seemed to be well-socialized achievement-oriented youngsters with slight interests in politics. It was thought this would always be the case of good American youth, living in the best of all possible (Eisenhower) worlds. By the mid-1960s, American campuses were "aflame", and forecasters saw student activism ever-increasing. Today's students, however, seem to be even more apathetic than were those of the Fifties. And tomorrows?

5. Cain warns against expecting too much of even the best age-cohort analysis, however, He discusses the distinctiveness of the 1916-1925 cohort who "should" have exercised political power in the United States during the late 1960s and early 1970s, according to "normal" expectations of succession:

"The thirty year political history of the cohort is considerably less rosy than its economic history. The cold war, McCarthyism, the slow pace of the Eisenhower years, faced the members as young adults. Then came 1960; a man of the 19th Century was to be replaced in the presidency by one of their very own. 'The torch passes . . .' The so-called 'fifteen years after' phenomenon was operable again. The thesis is that approximately fifteen years after a major crisis (such as war), those who were entering adulthood at the time of the crisis are able to move into positions of power. In 1960, the youth of the 1940s, that is, the 1916-1925 cohort, was ready to take over and in many ways, did. With the assassination of 1963, the torch was passed back to an older cohort, and has remained there since. If there is impeachment and conviction, there will be Gerald Ford, also older than JFK.

Apart from the killing of younger minority members such as George Jackson and Fred Hampton, the victims of recent assassinations have been members of the cohort under review: John Kennedy, Robert Kennedy, Malcolm X, Medgar Evers, Martin Luther King may be considered an 'honorary' member of the cohort. George Wallace had a nearly successful attempt made on his life. And with the exposure of the dirty tricks by the Republicans in 1972. George McGovern experienced a type of political assassination.

The point is that the 1916-1925 cohort assumed responsible political leadership at the appointed time, but has been thwarted since 1963 in the sustaining of that responsibility. Will this denial of power continue?" (Leonard D. Cain, "The Futuristics of Aging", mimeograph, 1974.)

Cain was writing in 1974, and we know the answer to that question: Jimmy Carter, a Southerner who wears Levis and was born in 1924, is president. Does it make a policy difference? Could it have been predicted?

An approach to social design

Every semester for the past 12 years I have been asking students in my introductory futuristics classes to undertake something like the following assignment:

"In 15 to 25 typewritten pages, indicate your design of the best, possible, real society you can imagine for some real place. In so doing, undertake the following:

1. State the goals of your society — what behaviours or conditions do you want to facilitate? Which do you want to discourage or prevent? Why?

2. Operationalize those goals. For example, if you say you want a society where everyone is equal, what do you mean by 'equal?' Everyone five feet tall? Everyone black? Everyone having the same, or a range of, income or political power (if the latter, how is that operationalized?) or what?

3. Devise alternate institutions that will help you achieve your goals. Remember to consider all forms of technology. While you may of course adapt an existing institution or technology, try instead to invent something 'new.' For example, assuming that you mean by equal, 'everyone five feet tall by age 21,' there are a number of ways you might seek to have this achieved:

—Everyone over or under a certain height (or height range) could be killed.

—People over a certain height could be forced to crouch, or be bound and clothed so as to be reduced appropriately, or live and move in special grooves, or live in height-group communities, or. . . .

—People under a certain height could be required to wear high heels, or high hats, or ride horses, or bicycles, or use stilts, or be stretched, or. . . .

—Groups of people who 'normally' deviate from the required height —for example, Japanese and Watusis — could be required to intermarry.

—Height-enhancing or inhibiting foods and/or drugs could be prescribed.

—People could undergo lengthening or shortening operations.

—Medical service could be encouraged to discover the 'height games,' and to manipulate them accordingly.

—Educational institutions could develop growth-oriented curricula, and grade people according to their limits to growth.

—Religious organizations could exhort people to 'grow right with God' and threaten hellfire to those who disobeyed.

—The national and/or artificial environment could be controlled so that people would be conditioned to 'grow right' without freedom and dignity, according to a schedule or reinforcements which would reward activity conductive to achieving and maintaining a proper height, and punish deviance.

4. Since you certainly will have more than one goal for your preferred society, see that they are mutually compatible. For example, many Americans say they want a society where everyone is 'free and equal.' On the face of it, that seems to be impossible. If everyone is free, they are not likely to be the same. If they must be equal, how can they be free — and different? By defining 'free' and 'equal' appropriately, you may be able to design such a society, but it will take care. Similarly, other goals must be operationalized so as to lessen incompatibility — or else the resulting dynamic tension must somehow be recognized and managed.

5. Since you presumably are designing a world that is not the world of today, what are you doing in your design to assure that it will stay as you want it to be, and not permit it to alter in undesirable ways? Note that I do not intend to imply here that you should prefer a stable world. You may prefer one in considerable flux. But how, then, can you prevent that world from stabilizing in undesired ways? In any event, how will you monitor the future of your world?

6. At one time I would have asked you to indicate how you get from 'here' to 'there'. In the past I have found this requirement to be so severe that many people have decided not to go very far from 'here' in their designs, thus thwarting my intention to get you thinking about clarifying your preferences rather than detailing political tactics.

Plans for a transition period are of crucial importance for actualizing any design for a real world, but at this point, I would be happier if you would dream broadly and clearly, rather than plan narrowly and pragmatically.

7. So far, I have said nothing about design constraints — things in the environment that you must take as 'given' and respond to in your design. Any good architectural or engineering book on design methods stresses the importance of determining such constraints very early in the design process. The exemplary World Order Model Project also has its researchers start out with a statement of their 'diagnosis' of the present and their 'prognosis' of the extrapolated future before it permits them to state their preferred future.

But I am not asking you to undertake a similar exercise here. I thus am in danger of encouraging utopian, rather than eutopian, dreaming. Your design may be so unrelated to the 'real world' of the present as to be totally impossible of attainment in the future.

How, for example, can one design for the future unless one first accepts the reality of incredible population growth, imminent resource decline serious agricultural uncertainties, frightening climatic irregularities, immutable cultural traditions, imperialism, racism, sexism, etc., etc., etc.? Admittedly, one cannot. But my desire here, again, is to get you to think carefully about what you *want,* not about what you fear or what you dislike. While we are a long way from understanding the present adequately, far more people are engaged in that exercise than in attempting to invent the future. While past, present, and future must of course be merged into a coherent and effective political programme at some point if your dreams are to be tested by reality, that is not what I ask of you now.''

And that is not what I will now undertake for myself. Rather, I will do only a portion of what I ask my undergraduate students to do — and what they have frequently done far better than I will.

A vision of a transformational society

In a paper written for the Rome Special World Conference on Futures Research 1973, I stated my basic values and goals for a preferred society. The next several paragraphs are a modified version of that statement:

"I desire a society where every human being is wholly free in every way from unwanted control by any other person individually, or by society as a whole or in any of its parts. The primary unit of my society of the future is the individual person. As a rule, in situations when an individual conflicts with a group of whatever size or significance, preference will be given to the expression of the freedom of the individual over that of the group.

In stating this preference for absolute individual freedom, I will show that I do not envisage as an ideal or as a probability that most or even many persons in my future will become aggressive, 'rugged individualists' in the John Wayne/Ayn Rand image, but I wish to make clear that I emphatically reject the notion that individuals should be pawns who, without real choice, must be subordinated in any way against their will to the desires and directions of any other individual or group, whether parents, spouse, siblings, children, peers, or representatives of society such as policemen, politicians, businessmen, imperialists, modernizers, priests, bureaucrats, teachers, or any one else.

In my world of extended opportunities for personal freedom, I believe that most individuals may seek to actualize a broad range of alternatives in communication, life-styles, social structures, religious or nonreligious beliefs, private and social practices, and so forth which may be, or appear to be, in opposition to the preferences of many — perhaps even most — other people now and at that time. Such a world indeed may appear to be 'chaotic' and 'disorderly' by current — or past — standards. Nonetheless, it is such a world that I prefer.

The primary function of society, and therefore of government at any level in this future, then, should be no more than to provide an environment in which each individual may become self-actualized, self-reliant, and self-determined without unwanted interpersonal or environmental constraints.

Without denying the current and past existence of some socially-conditioned or even biologically-determined human commonalities, I am convinced that because all individuals are in fact unique in both genetic endowment and social experience, they are actually unique and significantly different also in their current attitudes, desires, and behaviours. Individuals are thus not 'equal' in most important instances, and while at one time it may have made sense to treat them as though they were equal (or at least readily classifiable), to do so in the future is undesirable both because it is increasingly unnecessary and because it is contrary to my own basic value preference. As a rule, each individual should be treated the way he or she wishes to be treated.

Thus I take this as the criterion by which we shall judge all political structures and decisions in this future: is the individual enabled to do what that individual wants to do? If not, then my basic preference has been violated, and every attempt should be made to modify the political structure or decision in order to bring it in accord with the basic value preference. I do need to make it clear, however, that I recognize that it may be 'necessary' ultimately (because of our failure of imagination to think up a freedom-preserving alternative) to limit some individual's freedoms — or some individual freedoms — but every attempt must be made to eliminate, or, failing that, to reduce to a minimum even the 'necessary' limits.

Such a condition of individual freedom might be meaningless, if not positively harmful, for individuals without the following conditions also applying:

1. Every individual has an absolute and irrevocable right to food, shelter, clothing, medical and dental care, and any other material goods and services which are available to anyone else. In principle, these things should be made available to each individual's own level of satisfaction. That is, the distributive principle is that of R. Buckminster Fuller's 'bare maximum' rather than current notions of 'minimum standard of living,' 'minimum guaranteed annual income,' or the like. If it turns out to be impossible for each individual to have all of the 'things' that the individual wants, then each individual should be guaranteed a real 'functional equivalent' to that individual's self-determined satisfaction.

Finally, if it turns out that there are items of true and permanent scarcity which cannot be distributed by the principles above, then these things must be permanently owned by no one, but rather made equally available to all by lot or by rotation of use for fixed, brief periods.

I believe that most of the things now considered scarce — housing, food, goods, medical care, and so forth — can be made available in sufficient quantities to satisfy demands either for the specific (or duplicated) item, or its functional equivalent. Moreover, in the society of 'abundance' that I posit, I do not believe that most person's desires for goods and services are insatiable. Insatiable desires are generally a function of relative, rather than absolute, deprivation, and hence seem to be the consequence of specific socialization practices, and not of immutable 'human nature.'

2. Every individual must have the right to be physically mobile or to remain in one place. One of the most important freedom-encouraging and enhancing capabilities of modern times is physical mobility. Most societies now very inadequately cope with this opportunity and its problems by invoking rules and customs drawn from a more stable, sedentary past, and only haphazardly modify them to accommodate certain technologically-forced changes. The ironic contradiction between laws which prevent both migration and loitering is one example.

I believe that everyone should be guaranteed the right and provided the opportunity and means to move about or to stand still. But I do not mean by this that any individual has the right to intrude seriously upon another. Each individual also has the right to be left alone from unwanted interference by any other person. Any actual conflict in these two rights may be resolved in many instances by adding that while each person has the right to be left alone, no person should be so annoyed or offended by the mere presence, acts, or communications of another person that this other person is thereby obliged to move on — or not to move on. While one person's right of mobility ends, as in the analogous classical situation, where the other person's body begins, accommodation and tolerance are first to be sought in situations of conflict. However, if two or more people nonetheless wish to occupy the same space, or to move in the same direction, a solution of functional equivalence should next be sought. Only when this is finally determined to be impossible should the conflict be settled by lot or rotation.

3. Each individual has the right to acquire as much knowledge, information, education, and experience about any topic as that individual wishes. But no one must be forced to learn or receive communication about anything at any time. However, no information about anything shall be denied to anyone who wishes it. This implies an end to many of our recently-acquired notions about privacy to the

extent that no one can deny another person any information that directly relates to that other individual, and all persons should be discouraged from withholding any information from any other person. Still, in the final analysis, a person can refuse to tell someone something of a strictly personal nature that has no significant relation to the well-being of the other. All other communication must be open to anyone who wishes to receive it.

4. Every individual has a right to effective participation in all social decisions which affect that individual. Considering the probable range of behavioural diversity in my future society, I believe the following principle to be conducive to significant decisional participation by each individual:

As far as possible, society should be arranged so that all individuals can act as they please. When collective decisions cannot be avoided, the size of the groups involved in and affected by the decisions should be kept as small as possible so that all persons substantially affected by a decision are able to participate effectively in making it. Genuine effort must be made to maximize the efficacy of the individual's effect in decision-making, both in process and in outcome. In keeping with my basic rule, I believe that an individual should fully understand and positively consent to any collective decision which affects that individual. If the individual cannot consent, and if a collective decision is made which an individual judges negatively affects his or her freedom, then he or she has the right to receive compensation from the collectivity in such a manner as to redress the infringement.

5. Every individual has the right to seek and to receive affection, however and wherever expressed, from any other individual who wishes to display such affection. While any individual has the right to seek affection, any other individual has the right to deny it to that individual, without either person implying offense or rejection.

6. Any individual has the right to join — or not join — with any other individual or group of individuals who wish that person to join with them for the pursuit of any mutually-shared purpose which does not seriously affect any individual not in the group or consenting to its activities. While an individual may accept the consequences of consensual, or majoritarian, or any other collective decision-making rule, each individual also retains the absolute right to resign from the group or to fail to abide by its decision at any time. That is, an individual may subject his or her will to be the will of another individual or group, but may also at any time refuse to accept another's decisions.

The boundaries of my society of the future are not complete without including a minimal set of social and environmental responsibilities:

1. No individual is free to threaten, harm, or kill any other person against the other person's will.

2. No individual is free wantonly to modify the world about.

3. Every human being must be made aware of the probable significant effects, both on other individuals and on the ecosphere in which we all must live, of any specific individual and collective action before he or she acts.

4. Nothing in these three items is meant to prevent a person from doing with him or herself what he or she will, nor to limit the varieties of interactions between consenting individuals, nor to encourage us to become too narrow in our conception of what a 'natural' or a desirable environment is. But there may have to be some limits to behaviour in these areas, if this society is to become and remain an environment where self-actualized individuals are the focus and substance of life.''

Much of the rest of my ''undergraduate assignment'' — the social and technological institutions that would operationalize such values — are indicated in the remainder of my Rome paper. Therefore, I will conclude my ''vision'' of a Transformational Society by showing why I think such a world is preferable, thereby linking the two theoretical assumptions presented in the opening pages of the paper briefly to the values and goals just stated.

For hundreds of thousands of years, humans lived in small hunting and gathering communities of rarely more, and frequently less, than one or two thousand people. Each individual's world was almost totally defined by that small community — its language, customs, environment. Moreover, the members of that community generally formed an essentially closed breeding pool. Hence, to the extent that genetic inheritance determines behaviour or predispositions towards behaviour (and while that extent is a point of controversy at present, I believe it will be found to be significant), to that extent the individuals in the community also shared common predispositions towards behaviour.

Humans' physical technologies were quite simple, compared to those of the present, though their biological and social technologies were formidable, shaping and determining human behaviour and beliefs with much more precision than do similar institutions today. Yet, humans generally were not able to make as much impact upon the physical environment as they are today, though sometimes that impact could indeed rival that of the present.

Many of the social institutions and values of the present are only modestly altered carry overs from those earlier days, and many of the attitudes and predispositions of humans today come from the consistent reinforcement of those hundreds of thousands of years, only occasionally challenged and altered by more recent evolutionary experiences.

The first major challenge to the structures and behaviours of hunting and gathering societies, one which itself is much more recent in time, and also (with the continued existence of some hunting and gathering societies in the world) has not wholly replaced the earlier predispositions, was brought by the invention of agriculture and all the subsidiary social inventions that went along with it: the extended family, the state, organized religion, academia, writing, war and the military, "art", bureaucracy, cities, commerce and all of the other agonies of civilization and its discontents.

There is no doubt in my mind that the technologies of the agricultural revolution made it possible for those who interacted fully with them to become significantly different types of "humans" from those who enjoyed only hunting and gathering-related technologies and institutions. Nonetheless, there were important "life-style" differences between the majority who worked the land and the minority who lived in relation to the subsidiary institutions that the agricultural surplus made possible. The government official, the priest, the scribe, the warrior, the bureaucrat, the merchant lived in a world that was significantly different not only from that of the earlier hunter and gatherer, but also from that of the farming peasant. For one thing, he encountered far more humans in his life, who had quite different values and orientations than did either the hunter/gatherer or the average peasant. For another, if we were of the even smaller minority who could read and write, he had open to him a memory and recall system which made the past part of the present in ways which tribal oral memories could not. The past became much less malleable when it was written down. Now it became possible to colonize time — for some to rule beyond their lifespan. Though interpretations could differ, the words remained the same, while with oral traditions, words were constantly changed to fit changing conditions and needs.

Much of the world still lives in this agricultural condition, or is only recently (in the last 50 to 100 years) beginning to emerge from it. For many people, values and behaviours developed during the agrarian period still seem to be "natural". I believe this is especially the case in a country like the United States where, as a nation of immigrants, so many people are only a very few generations away from having been "forever" peasants.

A great deal of the appeal of the "ecology movement" may lie in the very deep peasant roots found under most Americans. "Life in the Suburbs and the American Way of Life" is only of very recent origin, and an interesting combination of Judeo-Christian guilt, and culture/future shock has been sufficient to turn a resource challenge into The Limits of Growth, if not into a Coming Dark Age in the confined imagination of some Americans. I suspect this may also be the case of some people in the industrial countries of Europe and Asia as well.

Industrial society is not much more than 100 to 200 years old as a major shaper of the folkways of an important part of the world. All of the values and institutions which are used to distinguish a "developed" from an "underdeveloped" country are measures of that change. Although a substantial portion of the alleged attitudinal and behavioural differences between persons in "developed" and "underdeveloped" areas are due to the system of imperialistic exploitation inherent in the present process, there nonetheless seems to be a considerable residue that really is the consequence of expectations and orientations resulting from importantly different experiences of people in the two technological cultures.

And, just as clearly, I believe the dominance of the culture of industrial societies is itself now coming rapidly to an end. This is partly due to the very real aspects of The Limits to Growth, and to the re-orientation of values and preferences on the part of people envisioning and striving for the creation of a "Conserver Society". It is also partly due to the rapidly rising political/economic/cultural awareness and capabilities on the part of the Third World and their ability to envision and move towards a future which is not merely an imitation of the present of the West.

But finally, I believe that a substantial portion of the post-industrial society will be driven by emerging technologies in the area of communication, bio-medicine, space, parapsychology and human management. These technologies, identified as being future-potent by the first "futurists" of the late 1950s and early 1960s, still remain of extreme importance, in my view, although it is no longer fashionable to speak of them. Our silence has not made them go away, however. Many of them are being quietly introduced and are having the "individualizing" consequences that were predicted. Being small, relatively energy–conserving, and generally convivial, they are readily accepted and utilized by ordinary people, although many intellectuals (and here I must say I agree with many of the conclusions, if not the tone, of Herman Kahn's indictment of "The New Class") specifically reject them and — being thus ignorant of their real use and potential — move further and further away from an understanding of what actually is shaping the future and influencing the attitudes and behaviours of many of their fellow human beings.

The technologies I am referring to include presently-existing and further-refining items like portapak video systems, video tape recorders, polaroid movies, CB radio, cable television, satellite communication systems, home computers, computer conferencing networks, electronic newspapers, memory-enhancing pills, recombinant DNA, genetic counselling, cloning, the space shuttle, biofeedback techniques, electronic Yoga, etc.

All of these — and many, many more of a similar nature — encourage individuality and force individual decision-making. They are thus quite unlike industrial technology which encouraged mass conformity and thus fit well into tribal and agrarian expectations of similarity between people. While many humans choose and are choosing to "escape from freedom" and yearn for some form of external "truth" or decision-making process that will deliver them from the responsibility of self-actualization (hence the tremendous renewed interest in religions, old and new), as more and more people experience individual decision-making in their own lives and the fact of their difference from their erstwhile neighbours, then (as age cohort analysis might indicate), subsequent generations of humans should learn to tolerate, then to expect as normal, a situation of individual decision-making and interpersonal difference that we presently might consider to be intolerable anarchy.

That is the world I see as possible and preferable, and that is the reason I present the values that I do for my preferred future.

I must immediately admit that I am focusing on only one facet of a multi-faceted future. It is possible, as so many warn, that humans are not able to stand the fast pace of change and the necessity of individual responsibility that I foresee. It may be chaos indeed — beyond our ability to withstand.

4

Faith and Liberation

ROGER GARAUDY
France

The contemporary crisis within churches and religions is not a crisis of faith but a crisis of the culture in which this faith is expressed.

For almost 2000 years, Christian faith has expressed itself through a culture deeply influenced by Jewish Messianic beliefs, Greek philosophy, both rationalist and anthropomorphic, the organization of the Roman Empire, authoritarianism and, during the last five centuries, by individualism and scientific and technological positivism which have been characteristic of Western philosophy since the Renaissance.

This contamination and perversion of Christian faith over the centuries by languages, cultures and ideologies which were completely to it, lead to the posing of false problems about freedom and grace, human responsibility and the sovereignty of God. These problems had something in common, a very poor image of man and of his freedom, a very poor image of God and of his power, so that all which was granted to man seemed to be taken away from God, and all that which was attributed to God seemed to be taken away from man.

I shall first limit myself to a general presentation of the postulations of our present civilization; then I will demonstrate, of present-day needs, the urgency, of a renewal of faith, perhaps without precedent, based on the daily needs of mankind.

Finally, I shall make some suggestions about actual ways in which to liberate faith, culture and politics, in order to bring about an unforeseen meeting between mysticism and action, capable of transforming faith into a complete source of liberation for each and every human being.

I. The basis of our present culture and the attempts made by "new theologies" to talk of faith in an intelligible way in a century formed by this culture.

Since the Western Renaissance, which was not only a cultural phenomenon but above all the joint birth of capitalism and colonialism, the fundamental objective of our Western societies is what I shall call a

Faustian objective. I refer both to the Faust of Marlowe, a product of the Renaissance, and to the Faust of Goethe, both of whom were contemporaries of the great industrial development of Europe and of the French Revolution.

Faust is a parable of Western culture at the end of the sixteenth century. Christopher Marlowe, in his *Tragic History of Doctor Faust,* spoke of the concept of the new civilization: "By your powerful brain, become God, Master and Lord of all elements".

Half a century earlier, Descartes promised "a science which allows us to be Masters and possessors of nature".

From the end of the sixteenth century to the last quarter of the twentieth century, the development of Western civilization has corresponded to this Faustian model which I shall define by the following three fundamental postulates:

1. First postulate: primacy of action and work, as fundamental values.

In his *Faust,* Goethe presents this programme: "It is by acting relentlessly that man spreads out all his greatness."

All bourgeois revolutions are Faustian: whether they be the struggle for American independence, or those of Cromwell or Robespierre. Both Puritans and Jacobins professed that religion was work. After these bourgeois revolutions, Marxism was born in this Faustian land of the West.

W. Liebnecht wrote: "Faust was the favourite poetic work of Marx." Certainly Marx owes much to German classic philosophers such as Kant, Fichte, Hegel, in his concept of the priority of action as continued by the creation of man by man. From English politic economists, Adam Smith and Ricardo, who only conceived of man as a worker and a consumer, he retains the primordial value of work. Finally, he borrows from Saint-Simon, apostle of the industrial society, a real Faustian conception of socialism, since for him, society was essentially an organization of labour. So, in the West, the unilateral exaltation of work is a bourgeoise concept as well as a socialist concept. Until this last quarter of the twentieth century, the postulate of the primacy of action and work has never again been questioned. It is only since 1968 that the Dionysian value of feasting have been exalted, the value of dance as a symbol of the act of living, that is the attainment of fulfillment by gestures which express more than those of utilitarian work or protocol or etiquette, which are not prefabricated by machine or the product of social conventions, but gestures which express our basic spontaneity — those of poetry, of free creation and of play.

2. Second postulate: the postulate of the primacy of reason, which could be formulated as follows: "All problems can be solved by reason and the only real problems are the ones that science can solve." This view is characteristic of the great rationalists, Spinoza and Hegel for whom reason can even solve the problem of ends, as well as the positivism of Auguste Comte who thinks that reason solves the problem of means and that any

other problem is "merely" theological or metaphysical, and as such is a false problem. It is this positivism which generated scientism and technocracy. Technocracy typified by the question "how" and never "why", the question of means and never of ends. In such a unidimensional concept of the spirit reduced to intelligence, there is no place for love, faith or poetry. For instance, it is impossible to find an aesthetic or to build an aesthetic system upon the philosophy of Descartes, because everything is reduced to concept. Even for Hegel, the greatest aesthete of modern times, the creative moment, as well as the religious moment, is only provisional; the only definitive moment is that of philosophy, that is, the concèpt. The same is true of love: in Descartes' *Traité des Passions,* one finds the mechanisms of passion, but nothing is said about what can make us understand the nature of love as self-improvement, nor of poetry nor of faith.

We have reached a period in our history which is dangerous for us and for all those on whom we have imposed this Faustian concept of the world because we know neither how to give of ourselves nor how to master our means.

3. Third postulate: I shall name the third postulate of this Faustian civilization according to a Hegelian expression: *the priority of the bad infinite;* that is, an infinite which is purely quantitative. For example, for the sake of this postulate, we have been led to believe in an endless increase of growth and above all to define growth as an increase which is simply a quantitative augmentation of production and consumption. Even in the United Nations the development growth of nations is measured by their GNP. It is in the name of this postulate that our societies work, as if this implicit principle were the basis of all our introspection and all our actions: "Everything which is technically possible is desirable and necessary", whether it is a matter of building increasingly powerful nuclear weapons, or of going to the moon. Perhaps the emblem of our civilization is a racing track: cars which go faster and faster, but go nowhere. Another example of this bad infinite is the effort to sustain human life for as long as possible even if this means keeping someone alive who is in a completely vegetative state, thus treating the suffering as objects and victims of a therapeutic performance.

A civilization based on these three postulates and which reduces man to a mere worker and consumer, which reduces the spirit to the intelligence and the infinite to the quantitative — such a civilization is equipped for suicide. Suicide for lack of an aim in life as is proven by the way people escape by means of drugs, and by adolescent suicides which are much more numerous in the so-called more developed countries, such as Sweden and the United States, or suicide by going beyond our means, proofs of which are the menace of the eventual exhaustion of natural resources, and pollution, which is the necessary consequence of the view of nature as a dump or garbage can, both aspects carrying the means of our destruction.

In the name of these postulates, our societies obey the law of the Athenian Sophists, the law of immorality. According to the Sophists: "the good thing to do is to live passions as strong as possible and to find the ways to satisfy them". Today, the functioning of our economic and political systems is based on this fundamental perversion of man.

How might Christian faith be effected by what we might call this "religion of growth", which dates back to the Renaissance, an era whose religion preached resignation and man's integration with the divine order, and which has been replaced by religion based implicitly on the stimulation of desire and in which growth became the hidden God, a cruel god who demands human sacrifices and whose publicity is a demented liturgy?

The fundamental consequence has been a confrontation between this new Faustian man, with his desire for expansion and his Promethean ambitions, and the traditional conceptions of God based on the analogy of a king, of a moral law or a metaphysical concept; for this man desiring to be powerful, the Christian religion represented and still represents a major obstacle to his freedom.

Against the old theocracies Machiavelli proclaims the autonomy of profane values and, notably, the divorce of politics and moral ethics from religion.

The eighteenth century in France links closely the fight for freedom and the fight against religion, considering the monarchy to be based on "divine right" to be "a creation of priests and tyrants", according to the words of Baron d'Holbach.

The nineteenth century transforms this political fight into a scientific fight: Marx is quite right when he says that in a Europe dominated by the spirit of the "Sainte-Alliance", religion is the "opiate of the people"; at the same time Auguste Comte's positivisim refuses to acknowledge the legitimacy of the theological or metaphysical concepts of God except when they are used to describe "positive thought", that is to say when they are of scientific or technical use.

II. The new need of man for faith

From which needs does the demand for faith emerge today? First of all, from needs resulting from negative experiences, both political and economical.

1. In 1850, in his *Economic Harmonies,* Bastiat declaimed the fundamental axiom of the classic bourgeois economy, based on the Faustian individualism of the Renaissance, and of the bourgeois Industrial Revolution in England, America and France:" If everyone pursues his own individual interest, then the general interest will be served." The experience of more than a century refuted this fundamental capitalist law of the jungle called:

"liberalism". The application of this principle led to three consequences radically opposed to the principle: a growing division between the classes in every capitalist country; a growing division in the world between colonizing and colonized countries, perpetuated by the growing division between North and South; a policy of blind growth, with no human ends, the fact that growth has become the law of development for every enterprise, quite apart from its use or its deleterious social effects. From now on, the Faustian postulate of individualism is fundamentally questioned.

2. The claim that only the power of reason, science and technology can form the basis of society is questioned. Capitalist technocracy and so-called "scientific" socialism have revealed, through their own development, that the positivist concept of science, which is the implicit assumption of both, and according to which the question of "how" is always posed and never the question of the consideration of the means and never of the ends has led to the manipulation of men as well as nature, men becoming mere objects, victims of the laws of necessity and fatality. The Faustian postulate of the priority of scientific and technical rationalism and the resulting concept of growth has been fundamentally questioned.

3. The individualistic concept of democracy which emerged from the French Revolution, according to which my freedom ends where my neighbour's freedom begins (as if someone else's freedom were a limit to my freedom and not a condition for it!), led to an attributed and transferred model of statistical democracy: individuals (social automatons) have only a quantitative value, and can only express themselves by attributing and transferring their responsibilities and powers to an elected person or to a leader. The Faustian concept regarding quantitative questions which have as a political consequence the confrontation of only those individuals who have been atomized by the system and who become a mass as a result of conditioning and which are led by all powerful anonymous forces which has been fundamentally questioned.

The most important and significant explosion took place in 1968, amongst young people both students and workers. It was not merely a negative revolution against capitalist technocracy or state bureaucracy, but also against the development pattern known both in the East and in the West. The movement which took the form of utopic, anarchistic and chaotic manifestations, expressed the need for alternatives, and the aspirations of a new faith, which from then on was revealed by the creation of basic communities of many kinds which were rapidly rejected by which are constantly changing. These do not produce a solution but pose a real problem: that of the creation of a new social pattern within our societies which have been disintegrated by individualism; and in the awareness that our socialist revolution would not only be a victory for justice, giving each individual what he deserves (to the slave that which is the slave's, to the master that which is the master's, to the employer that which is the employer's, and to the worker that which is the worker's), but also a victory for love.

It is remarkable that the youth of the day felt the need to discover a new relationship among men different from that provided by the Western Faustian model. In their protest demonstrations they carried the images of Che Guevara, Ho Chi Minh, Mao or Lumumba; there were no European images. They were searching beyond the jungle individualism and organized totalitarianism of Western societies, for a new model of a community, a society which would be based, not on "my" but on "ours".

This did not prevent the "little reason" of positivist science from being attacked by the "little me" of bourgeois society. Slogans such as: "Let us be reasonable, let us ask for the impossible" or "madness is the salt which prevents the reason from going rotten", a basic criticism of the positivist approach of the so-called "human" sciences which borrowed from the natural sciences the appropriate methods for manipulating objects and men considered as objects, led our students to write at the entrance to the Sorbonne: "Faculty of literature and unhuman sciences."

Lastly, the model of representative democracy, attributed, aligned and delegated, was rejected in favour of a model for a democracy which is participative, associative, and self-managing, a democracy based on a concept of man as being a responsible being, creative in all areas of economy, policy and culture. This model took the form of workers councils, at management level, at community level and in the organization of consumption, prices, transport and services, as much as creating centres of initiative in cultural and educational fields, in sports and the arts.

All was finally fully understood in a single act of faith, proclaimed in 1975 by Father Chenu, in his eternally youthful manner, as follows: *The theory of man is based on the same movement by which he denies his individualism whilst integrating himself in the community of the universe.* It is from this that we can grasp the basic problem of our times.

WHICH FAITH?
FOR WHAT SOCIALISM?

I. Which Faith?

The radical criticism of those called by Paul Ricoeur "masters of doubt": Marx, Nietzche, Freud, has rendered a great service to the Christian faith, by freeing it from Constantin's God, from the frigid God, of the philosophers and from the Saint Alliance partner of all dominations. These masters of doubt opened the way to a renewed belief in Christianism.

— It was rightly and clearly stated that the God of traditional theism, conceived in the form of a king and master of morality or as a metaphysical concept, has nothing to do with Christian faith. Christian faith does not require belief in such a god according to which Jesus Christ would be merely a historical manifestation.

— From now on, God is not there to bridge the gaps in our knowledge nor to comfort us in our weakness.

Therefore, it is not possible to confuse faith with ideology, that is, a doctrine for justifying the existing order.

Faith is not a concept of the world but is above all a way of facing the world and acting in the world.

Moreover, faith has to be distinguished from belief. Of belief can one only ask whether it is true or false. Faith, on the contrary, is a vital choice of life over death, of freedom over slavery.

— The alternative is to abandon oneself to the restricting path of one's personal or social history, or to stand up, shed the shackles of one's background and take the risk of opening up new paths.

I cannot speak of God as such, but only about what he means to us: "Whatever I speak of God it is a man who speaks", Karl Barth reminds us. I cannot say anything about God apart from what has been revealed to us by the word, life, death and resurrection of Jesus Christ. Anything else is literature and bad methodology.

So, what is this faith that Jesus Christ reveals to us and inspired in us?

1. First of all, faith is rapture, transcendence and the experience of rapture and liberation.

What is all the more exciting and confusing in the way Jesus acts and speaks is that he is never where you would expect him to be. We always expect a word or an act to be the extension of our biological instincts, our desires, our interests, our individual history, our culture, or our laws.

However, the most striking feature of Jesus Christ's life and death is that these cannot be defined in biological, psychological or social terms. His is a life, beyond routine where nothing is merely the result of the past but where all is free choice, new decisions, the poetic emergence of man, devoid of selfishness or habit.

To live not according to the "law" of Christ, but according to what I would call the "poetry" of Christ is to realise that my nature is to go beyond nature, to realize that each one of my acts, each one of the events that I witness and in which I participate, as well as my personal life and that of society or the history which I live are but links in a chain of cause and effect. They are what they are only in relation to the final end they face and which gives them their meaning; this is the true meaning of the coming of a "kingdom" of Christ.

It is not a question of locating this kingdom somewhere in a distant space or future, as any other utopia, but of being conscious of its strict demands, as if everything that I considered important in the world and in my tasks were to collapse at any moment, as if I were to reconsider all my decisions and all my behaviour according to this more profound and immediate reality because the kingdom is already here, inside and outside us. It is a kingdom which does not have justice as a law, but love as a principle.

Faith emerges only when I stop asking myself "how and start to ask myself "why", when I ask myself about the ends and not only about the means. It is a fundamental requestioning of my personal and social aims.

This act of faith breaks the circle of my habits and my previous certainties.

When a politician stops being interested only in the means which allow him to take or maintain power and begins to ask himself about the aims of the entire society and the possibility of obtaining for each man the freedom to make his own choice of goal and to actively participate in his or her self-realization, then the politician becomes a prophet.

When an artist stops being interested only in the assertion of his individuality and the organization of his career based on his technical virtuosity, and begins to aspire to being the conscience of the community when his work is not just a reflection of reality but an experiment in new possibilities, thus helping a community to become conscious of his project, of his hope, of his future, then the artist becomes a creator.

When a person in love is ready not to take, but to give and also to give not what he has, but what he is, even to give his life for the person he loves, then he learns, as Ruzbehan de Chiraz writes, "to decipher, in the book of human love, the language of divine love". Then the lover becomes a mystic.

But this rapture, this transcendance, is not yet faith.

2. Faith is the act of emptying oneself.

It is the experience of the void and "dark night" of Saint Jean de la Croix.

To reduce to silence the desires which howl in me; to detach myself from the dictates of my social environment; to erase the images that blind me without enlightening me; to separate myself from the words and concepts which have been made to manipulate things.

This act of creating the void, of emptying the "small ego", of depleting myself, this act which Christian theologians called *kenose*, this act to which the "four holy truths" of Buddha in the Benares Sermon, have shown us the road, which in Za-Zen Meditation gives us the experience, this act of despoilment is the only possible introduction to the "awakening" to a "new life". (Buddha's name means "the awakened").

This new life is built on an awareness that I am not self-sufficient, that I only exist in relation to all according to Caliste's great Byzantine formula of the sixteenth century. "I love, therefore I am."

We have come a long way from the Cartesian Sterility of "I think, therefore I am" which reduces man to a mere individual and the spirit to mere intelligence.

An eighteenth-century Musulman Sufi, Cheikh Abu Said, has discovered that which he calls the secret of Satan. Satan says: "If you say I, you become similar to me."

The fundamental experience is that of de la Croix, who breaks with all the traditional images of God: power, beauty, reason, justice.

How can one recognize God in this crucified failure of a man, desperate and weak, abandoned by his fellow men, since no one made a gesture to defend him, whose closest companions denied him, whose own father abandoned him and who before the last painful cry of death asked a last heart-rending question:'' Why have you forsaken me?'' The entire experience of faith is an attempt to answer this last tormenting question which allows everyone to live life in a divine way, that is, to live it with total responsibility for one's own destiny and one's own history. The act of faith is not a meditation upon the cross, it is living out this terrible and liberating experience of the cross.

Only after that the new way begins, after Christ's resurrection. Because Christ is not death. He has been killed. Men have chosen to kill him and he has chosen to die. This act and this choice give the Resurrection its significance. His death was not a natural one, it was the choice of a new life. His resurrection was not the return to a natural biological life, but the start of a new life.

3. Faith is the act of acquiring this new life, the influx of this force and this joy.

Faith is the experience of sources.

Faith is not the experience of limits, but on the contrary, the experience of the unexpected power of overcoming those limits. It is not the experience of a lack, but of a surplus. It is the centre and not the boundaries said Bonhoffer.

Malraux describes the moment of attack when a soldier has left the parapet and is beyond his own life. He writes in *L'Espoir* that it is "the moment when the dead start singing".

Perhaps that is a paradoxical form of the experience of grace and of the Resurrection.

Transcendance is a gift of the other but is not an exterior force: God will never speak if we do not lend him our mouth, he will never act if we do not lend him our hands; but this word or this act beyond Crucifixion is no longer my word nor my act. They have their seed beyond me.

Jesus Christ was not a magician, not a miracle-maker. Each time the unforeseen and the impossible appears, he says: "It is your faith that has saved you."

He does not help or save anyone from the "exterior", as one might save a drowning man in spite of him and without him.

He communicates to us, through a spiritual contact, a force which passes through us without having its source in us.

Christ's Resurrection and ours are not biological or historical events. They are events of faith: The emergence into a new life which is no longer measurable by clocks or astronomers' time. A new life dominated by the joyous certitude that no situation is hopeless. We have heard the Good News: Everything is possible and, at the same time, we have received the force to respond to that call, because Jesus Christ does not live in us only in the manner in which Mozart lives in each musician who plays or listens to his music.

II. What Socialism?

What are the possible effects of this renewal of faith on each level of social life, on the organization of the economy, on politics and the cultural life of our societies?

Today one must avoid the former error of deducing from the Gospel a political programme such as Bassnet's "politics drawn from the Holy Scripture" or a social organization like the ones attempted a century ago in the name of the "social doctrine of the Church", which invariably referred to supposed "natural laws" (for example that of property) which have nothing to do with nature, being products of history, and nothing to do with that faith which is situated beyond nature and history. One must not today render sacred revolutions, régimes or movements which are based on faith, in the manner in which past revolutions and régimes of oppression have often been declared sacred.

The "theologies of liberation" in Latin America, particularly that of Father Gustavo Gutiérrez, did not start from the gospel text and deduce a policy, but on the contrary they began with the struggles of real men in their fight for freedom, and interpreted the way in the light of the gospel.

Gustavo Gutiérrez draws a distinction between three levels of liberation:

1) the struggle for the liberation of exploited classes and oppressed peoples;
2) History as a liberation movement and a permanent cultural revolution;
3) Man's liberation in the face of sin.

These three levels are closely linked, Father Gutiérrez emphasized that sin is not only a personal matter. There is, as Pope Pious XI used to say, "a political dimension to charity". In the countryside and in the city slums of Latin America, there are millions of men whose living conditions are inhuman: Here a man cannot be a man, that is to say a creator in the image of God; while in the cities individuals with health and power confront each other in a jungle. At all levels man and God's images are distorted and trodden underfoot. Man is deprived of the two essential dimensions of his divine attributes: creation and love.

Father Gutiérrez writes: "Our continent lives in a permanent state of 'objective sin'."

This "objective sin", this historical sin, exists not only in Latin America, it also appears to have exploded in those developing countries where large masses are condemned to misery and where the dominant classes are pursuing a Western type of development.

Because of the worldwide domination of the United States and Europe, Society everywhere today is, in different ways, experiencing the same situation of historical "objective sin".

We said that since the Renaissance Western societies have never ceased to fluctuate between jungle individualism and organized totalitarianism and that we are now witnessing a disintegration of the social pattern.

How can we rebuild a social pattern starting from an authentic renewal of faith?

Let us repeat that it is not so much a question of drawing up a political programme as determining the human conditions necessary for the creation of a future with human possibilities.

1. In the sphere of economics where the basic notion is enterprise, until now our societies have only known two types private and state. In both cases a hierarchical system has been imposed which consists of officials with exclusive powers of decision-making and a labour force. Thus for the great majority of workers, work lacks the human dimensions not allowing for a choice of objectives and a choice of the organization of methods and means.

Enterprise is therefore debilitating for every worker but also for society as a whole, for the main objective of an enterprise is its own growth. Such a society is condemned to a blind, anarchic, cancerous growth, one that lacks human objectives.

Tackling the economic world from the viewpoint of faith does not mean promoting this or that kind of enterprise, but in the interest of the human and divine demands of creation and love, it calls for a social experiment which would eliminate the type of society based on a competitive system or on a monopoly in which egoistic individualism precludes the love relationship. Capitalism can never be human. But any system which substitutes one hierarchy for another and which is also to be rejected. In other words, Socialism cannot only be defined by its means, the means of production for instance — this is a necessary condition but it is not enough — but by its objectives which, according to Marx, are the creation of economic, political and cultural structures in such a way that every child who possesses a Mozart's genius can become a Mozart.

The social experiment of new models of management has already been suggested and sometimes even put into practice; the forms are different but the objective remains the same: to create enterprises which are neither private nor public but collective, that is, where the main decisions are not taken by the men who contribute to capital growth or by political officialdom.

An enterprise may be said to be collective when it has considered the following four questions:

— What are we going to do together?

— How shall we organize the work?

— Who is going to manage?

— According to what rules shall we distribute the fruit of our labour?

Are these matters dealt with by all the workers in a particular enterprise?

Such experiments have been made in various forms, either on the initiative of the workers or the demand of the entrepreneur. They all tend to define the enterprise not as a capital association renting men's work but as a men's association renting capital. Such an experiment paves the way for a situation which everyone can eventually become responsible and creative, and where the principle or organization is no longer based on a relationship of power, but one of community from which a new social pattern is born.

Such a concept of enterprise constitutes a transitional phase it is not a socialist enterprise since capital is rewarded, but it is no longer the classical capitalism, since the capital owners no longer have the privilege of managing or appointing directors.

So we move from a shareholder's enterprise to a partner's enterprise.

The aim is therefore to create the necessary conditions for experiment and social innovation, in order to obtain progressively, a state in which each worker, starting from his own economic level, can be responsible for his own destiny.

2. At the political level the problem is posed in the same way: How can we prevent a dictatorship of the decision-making centres over the masses who have no power and are therefore deprived of all responsibility and initiative? This necessitates a radical change in the motion of politics which is generally seen as the art of knowing how to govern and how to keep power, while policy is first of all concerned with the objectives of society as a whole and the performance of the methods whereby the masses can determine those ends and participate in their attainment. The principle remains the same: To allow each man to be a creator.

The first condition to be realized in order to facilitate the emergence of a plurality of projects by which a nation can become the creator-subject of its own history and not an object manipulated object from above, is to abolish all discrimination against movements, parties, trade unions and any men who put forward their suggestions to the nation. No western, eastern, northern or southern country can make use of the most elementary form of this democracy if it does not fulfil this first condition. The criterion by which to judge a system is whether or not it has faith in man and in the divine seeds he has in himself; the type of democracies created by bourgeois revolutions with their parliamentary and party systems is based on the delegation of power and the alienating effect of that power, so that any initiative from below is precluded by parliament and the parties: "vote for us and we shall do the rest".

That is why in all supposedly liberal democracies, where those elected are those whose sole aim to maintain and perpetuate the present growth pattern of the established order, obsolete nationalism and a delirious nuclear strategy the mechanism of what we have called political "entropy" (that is, the difficult distribution of votes where a party or a coalition wins 51% against 49% as was the case in France, Italy, Germany, England, Sweden and the United States) contributes to the blocking of institutions. This is not mere historical chance but a structural consequence of the transfer and alignment of power systems created two centuries ago by the bourgeoisie and which today are unable to resolve our problems and to fulfil our needs.

In order to restore initiative to the people at both the political and economic level, conditions for exprimentation must be created which would allow various voluntary communities to take control of the business of management in districts, towns and regions, as well as in enterprises or universities.

At the political as well as at the economic and social levels, the progressive elimination of bureaucratic decision-making, by means of a multitude of basic experiments, will permit the progressive substitution of legislature imposed from above in favour of contracts arranged at the base.

3. At the cultural level, the need for a freedom whose source is Christian faith, also demands a radical transformation in the definition and aim of education.

Until now, the principal aim of education was to adapt the child or the student to the economic and political needs of the established system. However, in the wider perspective induced by faith, the main objective of education is to prepare youth to invent the future.

This supposes a radical change in the structure and contents of education.

Restricting ourselves to a consideration of the contents and guidelines, let us say that programmes should be conceived in such a way that

— the practice of arts and aesthetics (that is the reflection on creative art) could be as important as the teaching of sciences and techniques:
— a reflection on objectives and the future could be as important as history;
— lastly, and above all, an understanding of non-Western cultures (those of Asia, Islam, Africa and Latin America) could be at least as important as that of Western culture.

For only through this Dialogue of Civilizations could the following be conceived and lived:

1. New relationships between man and nature in which nature is no longer considered as a deposit or a garbage dump, and where the relations is no longer one of conquest but of love.
2. Relationships between humans which do not condemn man to be "one-dimensional" (simply producer/consumer) and which aim at recreating a social tissue which has been disintegrated by in-

dividualism and destroyed by totalitarianism by restoring a communal relationship which is the social aspect of love.

3. Relationships of man with his future and with the sacred which will not be a simple technological extrapolation, but a poetic emergence of man continuing his own creation, and being conscious that in his relation with others and with the whole he acquires the essential, divine dimensions of man; creation and love.

Such are, in my opinion, the first conditions that have to be realized in order to achieve a unity of Christian faith and human liberation and to open the way to a policy of hope.

5

A Humanist Socialist Vision of the Future

MIHAILO MARKOVIĆ

Philadelphia University & Constance University, USA

1. Introduction

Giambatista Vico noticed that society, in contrast to nature, is the product of human activity. Human knowledge and technological power are indeed becoming increasingly more important factors of the historical process; they not only determine the realisation of given possibilities, but also open up entirely new possibilities. History was viewed by Hegel and Marx as a linear process; nowadays we know that it involves several alternative possible futures: from planetary self-destruction or barbarism to various forms of highly cooperative and creative social life.

A greater range of possibilities implies greater freedom, therefore greater responsibility for our generation. Progress is no longer guaranteed, the decline and collapse of present industrialized civilization is quite possible. We no longer have the right to dismiss visions of the future as arbitrary utopian dreams. They may be very real, and in two different senses. First, they may express real potential for change. Second, they may generate decisive new social forces. Consequently while many visions of the future will contain a utopian element in so far as they break with the present, go beyond established structures, involve an element of discontinuity, they need not be "Utopian" in a derogatory sense of that word, reforming to a merely conceivable and desirable but not feasible form of society. It seems to me that our interest should be focused on those visions of the future that satisfy the following two criteria.

(a) they must be practically relevant and take into account existing natural and historical constraints;

(b) they must be preferable from the point of view of general human interests.

We know now more than ever before that the earth's resources are limited, that continuing exponential technological growth is suicidal, that certain traditional institutions arrest any development, that some widespread traditional beliefs are hostile to life, individual autonomy and creativity, that some modern authoritarian movements curb any emancipatory aspirations once they seize political power. One might reasonably ask framework of possibilities there is within such mighty constraints?

Depending on our general practical life orientation we will commit ourselves to the description and practical realization of one or the other of those possible futures. A conformist will make extrapolations which minimally depart from the established social order, a traditionalist will try to direct the course of history in the particular interest of elites that lost power. Our commitment to a certain vision of the future could, however, be guided by some universal human interests. Naturally a claim to universality may be challenged and must be justifiable, both theoretically, by providing sound arguments, and practically, by indicating the beneficial consequences experienced under comparable conditions earlier in human history.

Humanistic socialism is a vision of the future which projects universal human interests and which seems to express the optimal potential of our epoch, at least for developed industrial societies. From the very beginning of its use, in 1833, the term "socialism" has two different meanings. For Pierre Leroux and other Saint-Simonians it meant opposition to the individualism of bourgeois society, therefore a social form in which an individual is subordinated to society. In England the word "socialism" was used by the followers of Robert Owen to designate a new social order which would be constituted by free cooperative associations without the state, after the dissolution of the state. The concept of "state-socialism" developed out of the former, the idea of "liberation", "democratic", "self-governing" socialism out of the latter. Certainly only democratic socialism may legitimately claim to be "humanistic".

The term "humanistic" here presupposes an image of man and of his or her capacities. Thus in contrast to all other living organisms man has latent dispositions: to communicate in symbols; to think conceptually, to solve problems and to realize the hidden structural possibilities of things, situations, other persons and himself; to live in communities and tend to belong, to be recognized and care about the needs of other persons; to act creatively and produce new objects, to learn incessantly from the vastly accumulated experience and knowledge of preceding generations stored in the objects of culture. Those latent dispositions become actualized in the process of socialization. Under unfavourable social conditions they may be arrested and wasted altogether. As a substitute for meaningful productive activities, for rich communal life, closeness and cooperation, human beings tend to develop strong drives to power and property over both things and persons. In the so-called "real socialism" of the present day, the human condition has been improved only in some important material respects, such as the removal of capitalist domination and unemployment, of economic misery and social insecurity. On the other hand, bureaucratic domination is greater than ever in history, labour is hardly less alienated than in bourgeois society, and illusory forms of social life — in authoritarian political organizations and state-controlled cultural institutions — hardly conceal the tendency towards ever greater disintegration and privatization. Humanistic socialism restores an autonomous communal spirit, brings to life the new democratic institutions of a global society, affirms individual creative powers, and, while paying due respect to differences in talents and aspirations, effectively removes any of the social structures that used to generate and support relationships of group-domination and autocracy.

2. Basic contemporary social problems

Humanistic socialism would betray itself if it did not manifest the greatest possible tolerance toward alternative visions of future progress. Naturally it opposes official ideologies that try to rationalize and justify existing unjust and unfree social arrangements. Even more it clashes with those ideologies which are committed to the restoration of the master-slave relationships which have already been abolished. On the other hand, it recognizes the legitimacy of a plurality of alternative visions of the future in different parts of the world where different historical conditions prevail and which have reached quite different levels of material and cultural development.

Nevertheless, there seem to be some general social problems which urgently require solution and which are the causes of human suffering in very different societies in our epoch, although the intensity of their manifestation may vary considerably. These problems are: poverty, the disintegration of communal life, authoritarian decision-making, alienated labour, the destruction of the natural environment. These problems are in their initial stage in some societies, in their critical, terminal stage in others, they are nowhere near solution in some countries, almost solved in others. But everywhere realistic, viable, practically relevant visions of the future must deal with them and try to solve them radically.

1. Poverty still exists in the whole world, in spite of the impressive economic development achieved during recent decades. Its forms are drastic in many Third World countries where productivity is extremely low. However, as a consequence of the unequal distribution of wealth, even in the most industrially developed countries, such as the USA, there are still a considerable number of people living in conditions of material misery — inadequately fed, in slums, permanently unemployed, without a health service, socially discriminated against, especially when they belong to racial minorities. A specific form of poverty is spiritual pauperism, a complete exclusion of workers from the world of culture.

2. The disintegration of communities is a necessary consequence of an economic arrangement that relies on permanent competition and conflict and pushes individuals toward increasing privatisation. As a surrogate,

illusory communities are formed on the basis of shared religious faith, national interest and hatred of ideological enemies. With the decline of religion, and an awakening from aggressive patriotism, and ideological disillusionment, disintegrative forces tend to prevail over integrative ones. Society breaks up into ethnic groups, and these into families, which are, in their turn, being shattered by the conflict between generations and sexes. This all happens in spite of the fact that man is basically a communal being, and that one of his strongest needs is to belong to a community, to share customs, beliefs and experiences with others, to understand and be understood.

3. Another universal human capacity which has been increasingly wasted is spontaneous, meaningful imaginative production. The recent history of labour — for the vast majority of ordinary people — is the destruction of any trace of creativity which still existed in the work of the artisan and the farmer. In modern industry work becomes increasingly mechanical, monotonous and stultifying. Human beings are tied to fixed roles in the process of production and have little chance of escaping from the narrow world of their professional specialty for the rest of their life. Production as a whole is geared to increasing efficiency and profitability rather than to the satisfaction of genuine human needs. The more labour gets alienated, the stronger are the centres of enormous accumulated alienated power — in the state and in the corporations.

4. In spite of the great and very real differences between the political institutions of oligarchic and liberal societies most people are excluded from active participation in social decision-making. In systems of representative democracy civil liberties are better protected than in any other existing political structure. And yet the growing role of the state in economy and public welfare has resulted in a rapidly expanding bureaucracy, in abuse of power and corruption. The existence of big power-oriented political parties, with their own bosses, professional functionaries and ideological manipulation only increases the distance between the citizen and responsible political offices.

5. State-socialism and state-capitalism share an overriding interest in maximising the expansion of material production. In both cases the development of productive forces is seen in purely quantitative terms. At the same time when we know how scarce and irrevocably limited certain natural materials and energies are, and how dangerously disturbed are certain natural harmonies indispensable to life, an exponentially growing industry continues to increase its output, to create artificial needs and to encourage wasteful consumption of those very scarce resources. This is a universal problem although the degree of pollution and depletion may vary considerably. We all live on the same planet, are victims of the same ideology of unlimited expansion, and suffer from consequences which can no longer be localized.

It is possible to begin to attack those problems one by one but not to solve them separately. Material poverty may be overcome within a very authoritarian society but spiritual pauperism will increase. Participatory democracy may be introduced by law but in the absence of social justice will not affect real life. Mindless exponential expansion and ecological deterioration cannot be stopped while these are still monopolies of political and economic power. Therefore piecemeal reforms will not do. A restructuring of the whole society is necessary. This need not mean a violent, uncontrollable, precipitate reversal of all social structures. It may be a continuous, non-violent, well-controlled process. Partial reforms will make sense in stages, phases of a constant overall transformation.

3. The principles of humanistic socialism

Humanistic socialism is based on a belief that each human being has a unique potential of creative powers which are obvious in a child, and which are wasted as a result of the process of socialization carried out by an authoritarian family, school and present day working organization. An entirely different kind of socialization is needed in entirely different kind of living and working communities. The principle of a new humanistic socialization is to bring to life the unique creative potential of each person. Consequently the whole process of production must be thoroughly reorganized and humanized so as to fit both the developed capacities of producers and to satisfy the genuine needs of consumers. From being a mere means, production becomes one of the ends-in-themselves. This presupposes the dismantling of centres of power, the socialization of the means of production and the abolition of class domination. Once the elementary material needs of all individuals have been satisfied, society will be increasingly concerned about needs at a higher level, the satisfaction of which does not require an exponential growth of material output. Material production loses its present importance, the development of productive forces serves, then, the purpose of progressively reducing socially necessary work. Liberated from work all individuals increasingly pursue free creative activities and take part in communal life.

With the supersession of professional politics, bureaucratic state and authoritarian political parties, all social decision-making becomes now thoroughly democratized. Basic living and working communities are now directly run by their members. To the extent to which coordination in economic, cultural and political activities is needed broader regional communities and associations are created, eventually a national or multinational society on a global scale. To decide on such broader issues power is delegated to democratically elected, responsible, rotatable and recallable representatives of the people. The maximum possible autonomy and self-determination of each particular communities, region and branch of activity thus goes together with the minimum necessary coordination, unity and conscious direction of the whole society.

While this society allows ample room for dissent, pluralism, personal and group autonomy, it does not tolerate oppression and exploitation of any sort. The basic value of its culture is not the egoistic power to dominate but power to create in order to satisfy the needs of other members of society.

A plurality of visions is compatible with those principles. Here are some more concrete solutions in the spheres of economy, politics and culture inspired by personal experiences of advanced liberal societies, socialist revolutions and self-government in Yugoslavia.

4. Work in humanistic socialism

The term "work" covers nowadays three entirely different types of activity. For most people inference of both capitalism and state-socialism it is toil, "alienated labour": in order to be maximally efficient and productive, in a purely quantitative sense, it has been divided into as many simple operations as possible and accelerated by the appropriate technology to the limit of human endurance. In this process the producer cannot employ any thinking, communicating, innovating, beautifying potential. He has no say in any decision-making, no relationship with the products of his work. The whole process is meaningless, purely instrumental and a waste of life-force. Alienated labour disappears under humanistic socialism. What remains is work — the socially necessary activity of producing goods and services in amounts sufficient to fulfil the basic needs of all the members of society. Work is still instrumental and must be distinguished from *praxis,* free spontaneous, creative activity which is an end in itself.

Ideally more and more working activities for an increasing number of individuals approaches *praxis.* In practice a distinction always remains. Work is socially organized, disciplined, inevitably achievement-orientated, regulated by some norms which are obligatory once democratically accepted, involving some division of roles and the minimal hierarchy that the technological process itself requires. None of this characterizes *praxis.* Nevertheless the structure and character of work will be profoundly changed under humanistic socialism. Basic changes may be summarized in the following way: (1) the socialization of the means of work; (2) change in the purpose of work; it will no longer be done for profit but to satisfy the basic needs of all the members of society; (3) self-management; (4) humanization of the process of work.

1. The socialization of the means of work has two consequences which are compatible with one another but different from turning private property over to state ownership.

In the first sense socialization of the means of production is the transformation of private property into common social property. That means that land, natural resources, buildings, factories, machines, means of transport and other equipment would no longer belong to individuals with the rights to dispose of them at will, to sell them, or pass them on as an inheritance, or to appropriate all products. But — and here is the basic contrast to all statist societies — those means of production will not become the property of the state, where a bureaucratic elite would, then, acquire the right to dispose of them and to appropriate part of the surplus product in the form of excessively high salaries and material privileges. For it to be social, common, public property it must (a) belong to society as a whole without anyone having the right to sell it or to pass it on as an inheritance and (b) it must be put at the disposal of a working community which would, then, share the income from the results of the work with the rest of society — in order to cover both individual and collective social needs. Socialization in this strong sense is relevant to all those larger enterprises where the process of production is already social but where the appropriation of income produced has been private. And the justification for the socialization of the means of production is the fact that those means were actually produced by social work, by the accumulated, unpaid, surplus of work of hired producers over a long period of time.

There is another, weaker sense of socialization applicable in all those cases where an individual has acquired some property in terms of the means of production saved from his own past work, without exploiting other workers (a small farmer, an artisan, a small shopkeeper). He is free to enter into association with other producers (cooperatives, collectively owned and managed small firms). Such associations would distribute their income (after they had paid their share to satisfy general social needs) according to the rules laid down by themselves. They would be free to lay more emphasis on remuneration according to work or on remuneration according to needs. In the former case they might wish to remunerate proportionately for both actual work and past work, objectified in the invested property. Working communities themselves may decide to distribute all income in strictly equal shares. But this cannot be the principle of the whole society. A genuine equality of individuals who have different abilities and needs, and live under different conditions, cannot clearly consist in simple equality of incomes. Some differences in income may compensate for differences in situations and provide really equal opportunities for life.

2. Once the means of production have been socialized, the whole process of production acquires an entirely different meaning. The aim is no longer production for profit but for the satisfaction of human needs. This does not rule out all competition and all conflict between different particular interests and needs. However, these are conflicts which are not antagonistic, do not involve mutual exclusion and may be resolved by dialogue and consensus. Since the key to power and domination — ownership of the means of work — is socialized, social conflicts must be regulated, and both pro-

duction as a whole and social life cannot but be directed in a democratic way, through negotiation and mutual agreement.

Once the purpose of production is no longer profit, maximization of material output loses its present importance. It may be important only in a state of poverty, where material production is not yet sufficiently developed to meet the basic needs of all individuals. Beyond a certain level it loses any sense. An increase of productivity may then be seen as a means of progressively decreasing socially obligatory working hours. This is not so in the present capitalist form of industrial society. During the decade 1967-77 productivity rose by 107% in Japan, around 70% in France and Germany, 27% in Great Britain and the USA. There was hardly any reduction in working hours and most of the surplus was wasted in over-consumption, armaments and investment in exponential growth — with all its disastrous ecological consequences.

Exponential growth is not necessary in humanistic socialism. Therefore this seems to be the only form a possible future society could take that might put a stop to the rapid deterioration of the natural environment. Three problems may be solved at the same time once human beings get rid of production for selfish, personal interests and begin to rationally regulate production in order to meet genuine human needs: (a) the present destructive, exploitative relationship with nature would be replaced by a search for greater harmony between man and his environment; (b) obligatory work would be reduced and humanized; (c) society would be able to provide more and more facilities for the satisfaction of higher-level communal and psychological needs.

3. Once the power of the big owners of the means of work has been abolished each individual worker gets a chance to become more of a subject in the decision-making process, to reinstate his elementary human dignity and to create a spirit of genuine collective solidarity.

In an economic system of self-management the highest authority in a working organization is a workers' council (or if the organization is very small the collective as a whole). Self-management is a true form of economic democracy and is based on the following principles: (a) Each worker has the right to participate in the process of decision-making, directly or through his democratically elected, rotatable, recallable delegates. (b) One person has one vote and no one can have any power on the basis of property invested, or of past merits, or of whatever political functions he may perform within the working organization or in the wider community. (c) Managers and technicians are responsible for technical decisions but are subordinated to the worker's council, which takes basic policy-decisions and has the right of overall control over the executive management and the administration. (d) The economy as a whole must be considerably decentralized in order to allow a sufficient measure of autonomy to each basic working organization. But in all those matters where higher-level coordination and direction are indispensable, decision-making power is delegated to self-governing bodies of larger associations of enterprises of whole economic branches and of the economy of the whole society. The system rests on a synthesis of decentralization and delegated, democratic central decision-making power.

This kind of economic system of integral self-management transcends both *laissez-faire* economic liberalism and rigid authoritarian state planning. A really rational, long-range direction becomes possible here, but it is flexible, democratic, and takes place at all levels of the organization of the economy.

Basic policy decisions will be rational (and not eventually manipulated by the technostructure) to the extent to which workers' delegates acquire the necessary minimum of economic knowledge and general culture. They have a chance to do so since (a) under humanistic socialism they will get a far better and essentially different education than under either capitalism or state-socialism; (b) the reduction of obligatory working hours allows sufficient leisure time for study; (c) workers' councils need not depend for information on management but may organize their own critical study groups to get necessary objective data; (d) a prolonged active participation in decision-making in all spheres of social life provides remarkable political and economic experience that may well surpass that of specialists and technicians.

4. Once the entire society is restructured in order to create ample room for emancipation the process of work itself can be substantially humanized. Except in a few advanced countries — especially Norway and Sweden — the problem has been generally neglected. Workers still suffer from the extreme dullness of their work and the underutilization of their abilities, from complete dependence on the machine, from exposure to poisonous materials, noise, dirt and dust, from the humiliating control of foremen, from the impersonal nature of huge modern factories. Such problems are not automatically solved by the mere socialization of the means of work or even by the introduction of self-management. However, these are essential preconditions for a radical reorganization of the whole process of work. This radical reorganization involves the following changes in approach:

(a) The renunciation of dehumanizing technology, the choice of some alternative technology which allows more individual and group autonomy, more collaboration and communication among workers, more complexity of working operations, more self-control.

Sometimes, at least in some areas, this kind of change may be the consequence of the technological process itself, e.g. of automation. For example, in some industries night shifts could be entirely eliminated using automata which can be programmed to work for hours without any human control. Contrary to expectation, work with fully automated machines may turn out to be more interesting than that with semi-automated ones. For example, the work of an operator in an automated chemical factory is no longer steady and does not have any regular, predictable rhythm. It consists of periodical monitoring (which requires great care and responsibility), of long periods of relative inactivity (which can be filled by reading or talking to other workers), and of occasional dealings with crises. The latter, as in any problem-solving, requires the full mobilization of all the intellectual forces of the worker, and considerable ingenuity in order to locate the trouble and repair it as quickly as possible. However, this level of automation is not possible in many branches of material production, let alone in services.

An essentially different approach which is always possible is a return to small, though less productive, enterprises. They offer a better chance of being democratically run, self-reliant and evenly distributed (avoiding huge pollution concentrations). Above all, they offer a more interesting and more complex kind of work. Even from the point of view of present-day economic thinking (the axioms of which will become irrelevant soon) it is clear that modern technology does not exclude smallness. A good deal of recent progress lies in the transformation of huge, complex instruments and machines into small, simple ones. A future source of energy for a whole country, even for several countries, could be a small nuclear fusion plant. For a country that is just beginning its industrialization programme the most rational policy might be to build small enterprises, which would be able to use local raw materials, local labour forces with limited skills and inexpensive "intermediate" technology.

For entirely different reasons the need for small enterprises will emerge in the advanced society of the future. An ecological need to slow down production will coincide with a purely aesthetic need for beautiful hand-made goods. Highly productive automated plants will saturate the markets for uniform industrial goods. Elementary needs could be fully satisfied, poverty could disappear entirely. Then the beautiful would slowly begin to prevail over the functional. Craftmanship would be revived; huge scale industrial production would tend to lose its present importance because the need for it would begin a relative decline.

(b) Another facet of the humanization of work is the reorganization of the process of production. Big systems will be split into smaller units without loss of necessary coordination. For example, assembly lines will be eliminated, productive tasks will be given to relatively autonomous groups of workers who will divide them among individuals, rotate roles and determine their own rhythm of production. Control from above will be replaced by self-control and self-regulation.

Another possibility is to abandon too narrow and specialized a division of work and to design jobs which are much more complex and interesting, employing a considerably larger proportion of a worker's mind and imagination. For example, instead of repeating the same simple operation time and again a worker might be responsible for assembling a whole engine on his own.

(c) This presupposes that the whole concept of the division of work will undergo profound change. Division of work will become increasingly free and flexible, avoiding rigid professionalization as much as possible. One of the basic tenets of the new education will be the choice of work according to ability and other subjective dispositions. This will involve free access to all jobs regardless of sex, race, nationality or age. Instead of being tied to one single role in the process of socially necessary work for the duration of his whole life, each worker will have the right to demand variety in his work and to get the necessary additional knowledge and skills that would qualify him for a change of roles.

(d) The physical environment in which people work could be substantially improved. The present rate at which workers are exposed to poisonous substances, to likely accidents, to noise and dust will be regarded as unbelievably barbaric. Recently in a comparatively poor country, Yugoslovia, the workers of the textile factory *21 of May* in Pirot have, on their own initiative, turned their factory into a place of beauty, art and culture.

All this, however, relies on the assumption that class domination and exploitation would be abolished throughout society. Otherwise, "job enrichment", a negligible measure of worker's participation, alternative technology, beautification and personalization of the working place essentially serve the purpose of conserving an inhuman, unjust system by making small concessions and introducing harmless inexpensive modifications. This explains why many of those small reforms are being pushed by technocracy in its efforts to cope with absenteeism, and are sometimes being imposed on workers against their will.

Furthermore, there is nothing essentially liberating in a small enterprise as such. The very fact of smallness does not exclude the possibility of the master–slave relationship. Personal, visible masters may be more cruel and oppressive than abstract institutionalized ones. The road to emancipation and justice is longer when one has to get rid of hundreds of thousands of individual masters than if one has to transform a couple of abstract master institutions. This is why state capitalism is historically progressive with regard to early entrepreneurial capitalism. And that is why the slogan "Small is beautiful" may express not only a progressive anarchist or socialist idea but also the romantic, retrogressive attitude of dispossessed small landowners, small businessmen or an enlightened technocratic optimist's desire to preserve the status-quo.

In spite of all these limitations present-day attempts to humanize work without changing the existing structure of power have the great merit of examining a real problem which has been neglected by many movements for social change and workers' liberation.

5. Communal life and participatory democracy

The present division of society into a political sphere, in which an individual is subordinated to the state, and a civil sphere, in which he is free to pursue his egoistic interests, will be replaced by a distinction between public life regulated by democratically adopted communal rules and personal life regulated only by ethical rules and by autonomous, individual intentions. Once the only social obligation — work — is met, an individual will freely decide how much seclusion he wants and how much he will participate in the activities of various working, political, cultural, sportive and entertainment communities.

The elementary community — the family — will exist in a variety of forms: not only nuclear but also extended, embracing several generations; including any number of members and not only heterosexual but also homosexual relationships. All this flexibility will be limited only by a minimum of humanistic requirements: the equality of partners, the communal care of children, freedom from the tyranny of the stronger.

Tensions and conflicts cannot be eradicated from human communities. Nevertheless, domination, tyranny, master–slave personal relationship will be treated as pathological phenomena. Society will fight them with appropriate education, and guaranteed, practically feasible freedom of choice among alternative communities.

The need to coordinate, direct and rationally cope with large-scale public problems, naturally gives rise to larger associations of communities, and eventually to a global social organization. Issues of different natures and different levels of general relevance will be dealt with at different levels of social organization. A good deal of education will be taken care of in the family and local community. Issues such as those to do with transport, energy policy, global economic coordination, and ecological protection require unique decisions affecting the whole society. The general principle is that as much decision-making as possible (depending on the nature of the problem) should take place at the lower levels of society — in enterprises and local communities, in individual regions and in integrated, relatively autonomous branches of activity. Only when a problem causes conflict, or danger, and transcends the limits of a given community, should it be placed in the hands of a higher public authority, where it will be solvable. The example of such issues are; reducing economic inequality among relatively autonomous and self-reliant regions, society joining forces as a whole to make a break-through in a new, labour-saving, better-quality, less-polluting production; securing certain minimum requirements of health protection, culture and education for the whole of society, switching to new sources of energy (solar, geothermal, nuclear fusion); improving the quality of the natural environment throughout the country. Thus a tendency towards decentralized decision-making (concerning particular local and regional needs) is quite compatible with a necessary minimum of centralistic democratic regulation (concerning the needs of the whole society).

Under humanistic socialism the organs of public authority at all levels have an entirely different character from that of liberal capitalism. These are no longer organs of the state but organs of self-government. This means the abolition of alienated political power, of the professional political structure which disposed of it, and of the coercive function that distinctly characterized the state of a class-structured society. The practical meaning of this transformation may be spelled out in the following way:

1. The members of a self-governing body of any level of society are directly elected by the people or delegated by a lower level organ of self-government. The procedure of election is fully democratic: it puts an end to the privilege of any candidate due to his greater wealth, professional political role or his backing by a ruling political organization.

2. The members of a self-governing body are elected for a limited period; the principle of rotation must be strictly observed and it excludes the perpetuation of power and the creation of an elite of professional cadres.

3. The members of a self-governing organ are directly responsible to their electorate (and not to any political organization). They are obliged to give a regular account of their work to the community which they represent. In case of an unresolved conflict they may be subject to recall.

4. Representatives of the people must not enjoy any material privileges and will return to their normal professional activity after the expiration of their mandate. While they serve in a self-governing body they may only be compensated for their work as for any other creative public activity. Anything beyond that level constitutes a concealed form of exploitation, produces undesirable social discrimination, lowers the motivation of the representatives as well as the morale of the community, and eventually leads to the creation of a new alienated social elite.

5. An organ of self-government constitutes the supreme authority at a given level. In this it differs from analogous organs of participation, co-management, or workers' control, which have only advisory, consultative or controlling functions and, at best, only share authority with political bureaucracy, capitalists or techno-structure. Self-governing institutions presuppose the elimination of all ruling classes and elites; professional technical management must be subordinated to them. They create basic policy, formulate longe-range goals, establish the rules, decide about framework issues, control the implementation of adopted policies.

6. All the power of self-governing bodies is delegated to them by the people from the given area and not allocated from above, from the centre. When social power is alienated, all transfer of the collective will goes from the top to the base of the social pyramid. When it is not, it is always the lower level of social organization, closer to the base, which decides how much regulation, coordination and control is needed at the next level. A

decision having been reached, the appropriate amount of power is then delegated to it. In such a way the authority of the central federal assembly rests on that of regional assemblies and all of them are ultimately authorized to decide on certain issues by the councils of the basic working organizations and local communities. Experience gained in a quickly changing world occasions changes in the whole structure: where there is a growing sense of ethnical identity, the cultural life will be increasingly decentralized; on the other hand, a scarcity of energy requires the joint efforts of the whole society and a considerably higher level of coordination and overall control.

Clearly, the problem is not the central character of decision-making but the source of its authority. In a bureaucratic state classical liberalist doctrines of "social contract", sovereignty of the people and "majority rule" serve to legitimize a situation in which all power stems from a relatively small central oligarchy, even when it is considerably diffused and decentralized. In self-governing socialism all power really originates from the councils in the atomic social communities, even when a part of it has been delegated to central self-governing institutions.

Such a dependence on the will of the community does not exclude the possibility of a democratic leadership. A person temporarily becomes a leader when he or she has the ability to articulate and explicitly state the real needs of the community and to reconcile them with the general interests of society as a whole. Authoritarian leadership is excluded since it cannot be backed by any alienated power and the route by which it was possible to become a career politician is banned. On the other hand, no community can expect that a representative of ability, conviction and personal integrity will blindly follow every twist and turn of its will. In the case of conflict he will win a consensus due to the strength of his arguments, or will resign or will be recalled.

One of the most difficult problems facing any democracy is how to preserve a unity of purpose and protect the general interest without itself becoming overwhelmingly strong. The classical liberalist solution has been to separate legislative, executive and judiciary power — and this is an achievement of lasting value. However, at a much higher level of social organization public institutions assume new powers: the regulation and planning of work, the overall control of the implementation of adopted, programme, and policy. All these powers should be separated.

Self-governing assemblies could, then, be organized on a double principle. They would be composed of several kinds of delegates who represent different interests; delegates of all workers would naturally constitute one chamber, delegates of all communes another, directly elected representatives of all citizens a third one, the latter would mediate between the two former in the general interest of society as a whole.

On the other hand, assemblies at all levels — regional, national, federal would then be divided into councils responsible for one of the separated powers: legislation, planning, control, judiciary, etc. Each member would participate in the execution of a particular power in corresponding self-governing agencies.

All improvements in the structure of self-government do not make much real difference if the whole political process is fully controlled by one or more political parties. The party in the proper sense is a political organization that struggles to win power and rule, that is hierarchical and authoritarian, manipulative and ideological. Such a party naturally struggles to assume the role of a tutor over self-government and to turn it into one of those attractive displays that serve to legitimize its own monopoly of power. Since the existence of such parties is incompatible with humanistic socialism the alternative is a pluralism of political organizations that aspire to educate but not to rule. They can play a variety of useful social roles: expressing and articulating specific group interests, preparing rational proposals for the solution of important social issues, mobilizing people to support them. Under such conditions the pluralism of political life will no longer be the pluralism of entrenched class interests struggling for domination but a pluralism of visions, of options, alternative imaginative approaches in a really free society.

Conflicts in such a society can rarely be resolved by the parliamentary rule of the majority vote. The majority vote is often the political instrument of the domination of the stronger, more powerful interests. The majority vote is only really democratic when the various particular groups exist in conditions of homogeneity and perfect equality. But in a humanistic society there are still groups of different size and power (larger and smaller national groups, industry versus agriculture). Conflicts among them must be resolved by negotiation and consensus.

Special institutions comparable to Scandinavia's "ombudsman" protect the rights of individuals against the organs of public authority. They would have the power to give free legal advice and the power to investigate and to alert higher-level organs of self-government in any case where human and civil rights have been violated.

6. Cultural praxis

People will spend much more time outside the public sphere of the global society in smaller freely elected communities and in individual spontaneous self-expressive activities.

Humanistic socialism is anything but a uniform highly regulated society of blue ants. This is a more personalistic society than any in human history — certainly more than in a liberal bourgeois society, in which *real* individual freedom was greatly restricted by the uncontrollable forces of the state and the market. On the other hand, a person in a humanistic socialist society is not only a unique being but also — in contrast to the selfish isolated bourgeois individual — a communal being, deeply concerned about the condition of other people.

There are two factors that account for this process of progressive liberation from the necessities of global life. First the amount of obligatory public work decreases with the fast increase of its productivity. Throughout historical variability and uncertainty one constant may be reliably established and extrapolated: the growth of knowledge, the increasing wealth of scientific information, the progressive development of productive forces. It follows that the same level of satisfaction of the human needs of the same number of people will be achieved with a progressively decreasing amount of working time. People still work insanely long hours because production is geared to profit and not to the satisfaction of real needs and because governments need soldiers and do not care enough about a reasonable population-growth policy. And even in the initial stages of the new society when it emerges from an insufficiently developed bourgeois society some excessive work may be needed in order to eliminate material misery and to satisfy the elementary needs of all members of society.

But then, instead of the wasteful exponential growth of material output, a switch toward higher level cultural needs becomes possible and indeed necessary. It becomes possible because under given social conditions there is no longer any social force that has either interest or power to push toward a surplus of material goods, and toward the creation of artificial needs for them. The switch toward culture becomes necessary for ecological reasons and as a consequence of a radically changed anti-consumerist consciousness the anti-consumerism that we are witnessing today especially among youth is still inconsistent. The excessive consumption of material goods has been replaced by the excessive consumption of cultural and pseudo-cultural goods. But it is not enough just to positively consume cultural goods (often of doubtful value) one also has to take an active part in creating culture, in performing cultural activities — in the same way in which one will freely participate in the political process, in meaningful communication of all sorts, in play and love.

There are three conditions essential to the mass flourishing of cultural *praxis.* Cultural performances of the best quality must increasingly become free. Society must provide the necessary material facilities for mass cultural activities: theatre halls, musical instruments, exhibition halls, printing equipment. And most important of all: education must be totally and radically reorientated. Nowadays the main goal of education is a preparation for a specialized role in the division of socially necessary labour — this will increasingly become a matter of secondary importance. The primary goal of education becomes self-understanding, the discovery of one's creative potential, the preparation for a basic life-project, building correspondingly necessary skills for autonomous, self-development and self-expression. This does not mean that everybody will become Einstein or

Bartok, but one will have a chance of actually becoming what one dispositionally is.

7. Concluding remarks

Even a limited fantasy suffices to ascertain that the way of solving present-day urgent problems as described above does not lead to a perfect society without any tension, conflict and personal unhappiness.

Any free action involves a risk of failure and frustration. The higher the aspiration, the higher the risk. Society may only create conditions and provide facilities for one's self-development, it does not guarantee success. It will respect hard work, it will recognize effort but cannot reasonably be expected to appreciate and praise results which are objectively failures.

One important inequality remains: inequality in gifts, talents, inherited capacities. This kind of inequality is partially expressed in present-day social arrangements which tend to produce and preserve inequalities in wealth, power, education. Money transforms the impotent, boring, colourless person into a powerful attractive superman. The abolition of social institutions that equip a minority with apparently supernatural powers while depriving a majority of inherent natural powers — does not give rise to a totally egalitarian society. On the contrary, for the first time in history real natural differences will find full expression and they will produce differences in statues and in communal recognition. The point is that in a society organized on the lines above there is no way in which natural differences could produce class differences. The essential difference between status and class power is that under given circumstances the former relies exclusively on talent and top-quality performance; the latter relies on the accumulated and appropriated labour of others.

A corresponding problem arises in political life. A person with the qualities of a real charismatic leader will enjoy high status and could be very influential within a self-governing body. Excellent orators may turn into dangerous demagogues. But a number of restrictions built into the very political fabric of society could effectively prevent the emergence of new dictators and omnipotent bureaucracies. Once power is adequately decentralized and separated, once the principle of rotation is strictly observed, once it becomes customary to criticize and recall leaders rather than to glorify and deify them — there is indeed no way in which a new dictatorship could establish itself — unless through an unexpected genetic mutation a whole people becomes feeble-minded.

Humanistic socialism is not a perfect society that removes all causes of human suffering. It resolves only the crucial, most painful social problems. We are not yet even aware of the new riddles and conflicts that would emerge in a new society: those are beyond the horizon of our epoch. Deepest metaphysical doubts, despairs and quests for measuring will always remain with us, as universal constituents of the human existential situation.

Consequently, humanistic socialism is not an absolute ideal, an ultimate eschatological end of history. It is only the expression of the optimal historical potential of our epoch.

6

A Humanistic Vision in an Age of Liminality

E. MASINI
World Futures Studies Federation, Italy

Premise

Many of us who are interested in the future have been discussing the urgency and the possibility of creating visions which go beyond the present age of change and which at the same time are acts of awareness of those changes, awareness of ourselves as part of the process of history as well as awareness of living in a world of transition. I believe that we must live the changes, the aspirations, the tensions of our time hoping for their realization, maybe not in our generation, but in the next. I also believe that if we live the period we are living through intensely and consciously as individuals and as social beings, as well as social actors, we cannot but understand the flow of changes that are traversing this specific moment of history and be compelled to make an effort to gain a deeper understanding that in time may generate a vision. What else is a vision but the fleeting crystallization of the movements which traverse and make our age dynamic?

The human being is central to the vision not as an abstraction but as a concrete builder, as a liver of the historical moment which is in the movement, in the process.

1. The humanum principles

The vision of the future is not a fantasy, an abstraction divorced from "real" life. It is the conscious thinking, the deep listening to the historical moment which is in each of us as part of the flow of history, and at the same time it is the building of an antithesis to the present; from both the future is born. It is the awareness of the seeds which are in the process of change in the present to which must be added our "different" perspective. It is the sensing of the Tao (flow of life) to which we must become accustomed in order to receive a vision which is not an abstract tomorrow but one that is imbedded in the present as potential future and at the same time has a specific bearing on a person, a society, a culture.

In the flow of life through history we can detect principles which E. Jantsch[1] calls principles of order. They may be grouped into three categories:

(A) At *the level of the individual* such *principles* of order geared to the development of humankind are "aesthetic" principles in the sense that they direct the human being who is thinking consciously towards that which makes explicit what he/she implicity is in every movement of the human heart.[2] The more men and women think explicitly about their implicity, the closer they come to being truly themselves "aesthetically".

Two elements are to be stressed here: (a) the seeds as universal principles, basic to the vision[3] the consciousness of the person and (b) the person. In fact to get closer to the principles of order a person has to develop capacities of consciousness and perception extended to many cognitive modes, to many creative processes. He has to experience from the analytic to the holistic, from the intellectual to the intuitive, and must abandon the lopsidedness which is typical of Western societies, always expressed in linear terms, and search for the non-linear dimension. He must search for complementarity in the mode of organization between the biological, the psychological and the spiritual elements of the human being, between the active part of the human being, he which tends to manipulate others and nature, and the receptive part which he tends to become part of.[4]

One must search for different levels of consciousness. At different levels of consciousness we can in fact perceive reality beyond the "common-sense reality"[5] towards the "scientific reality" and/or towards the "mystic reality". The first denotes the aspects of reality that the individual perceives, responds to, interacts with; the second and third are different levels of perception which both try to understand how the cosmos works. Neither of the last two is perceived through the senses, but through other, different levels of consciousness. The scientific level is commonly accepted, the mystical not; and this is the difference between the two over and above their difference with the first, the "common-sense level". Through these levels, especially the second and third, one can reach a synthesis and this is where and when the vision emerges. These are the levels of perception which have to be developed and which are more often present in some women and in some men but which in 'my' vision have to be developed in *all* men and women.

[1]E. Jantsch, *Design for Evolution,* George Braziller, 1975.

[2]G. Hegel, *Lectures on Aesthetics,* 1935, as well as Plato and Plotino.

[3]Of these we shall discuss more further on.

[4]Arthur J. Beikman, *Bimodal Consciousness in the Nature of Human Consciousness,* Ed. R. Ornstein, Freeman, 1973.

[5]Philippe Lee, "Does Consciousness Make a Difference?" In Symposium on Consciousness — Penguin Books, 1977.

Some studies describe moments "at the peak of experience" in art, creative thinking and love[6] as self-validating, and self-justifying. Other works describe perception in meditation (the creative meditator).[7] We have to develop and search for ways of understanding, feeling, being aware of the seeds of change that are linked to the principles in the flow of life, the flow of history and indicate, at the same time, ways of building the antithesis to the present. These kinds of awareness are linked to each other culturally and psychologically. Some people, such as children, women, victims of persecution, artists, etc., are more able than others to perceive the seeds, the principles of order in the flow and are capable, at the same time, of adding to and transcending the present.

(B) *At the social level* there are social ethics, principles which justify men's and women's behaviour in their relations with other men and women in society. These are the principles on which men and women act according to a specific social character. The social character is defined by E. Fromm[8] as "the internalized mechanism of each individual to maintain the system, the group, the nation, the culture". The social character is extremely important as it determines at what level principles are chosen, it determines priorities in a specific space and at a specific time.

(C) *At the environmental level* are environmental ethics, the principles that guide relationships between human beings and nature. Principles which, in a specific hierarchy, can lead either to exploitation, where man is the proprietor of nature, or else to participation where human beings and nature complement one another.

All these interrelated principles, when perceived in a specific hierarchy, create a vision of the history of man and woman. Already as I write I fragment even if I do not wish to and I do not see the whole, the totality of which we are part. The totality is difficult to perceive and the problems arising from that difficulty create more and more fragmentation and more and more contradictions. But it is only through the perception of the principles which make up the flow of life as a whole and by transcending this perception in a personal, cultural way, in a moment of innovation that visions can emerge. For this we must strive.

2. Needs

As Erich Fromm says,[9] social organization has two legs: the social character, which I have defined and described above, and human needs. Human needs are the spur to action; the non-answer to the needs, not meeting them, hampers realization/actualization whether at the biological level, the psychosocial or psycho-environmental level or at the spiritual

---

[6]Abrahm H. Maslow, *Towards a Psychology of Being*, Van Nostand Company, 1968.
[7]Patricia Carrington, *Freedom in Meditation,* Anchor Books, 1978.
[8]Erich Fromm, *The Sane Society,* Routledge & Kegan Paul, 1959.
[9]Erich Fromm, *op.cit.*

level. These levels together constitute the three dimensions of the human being, the totality.

Given the difficulty of grasping the totality, needs can also be defined as
material and non-material, but the border-line again is fluid and fuzzy. I
prefer to define non-material needs as those:

(i) Material needs which have a non-material component in their
satisfaction, like the need for nutrition which depends for its
satisfaction on the food exchanged in a community. The symbolic,
even religious meaning of food is in this context.

(ii) Non-material needs which have a material component in their
satisfaction like the need for communication that is linked to the
satisfaction of seeing, touching, etc.

(iii) Non-material needs *per se* such as needs for a meaning in life, needs
for a meaning in work, etc.

I therefore define as material needs all those that do not fit the previous
definitions.

S. Marcus and C. Mallmann[10] define needs in terms of their non-
satisfaction the result being illness, and while acknowledging the difficulty
of generalization, they seem to accept Johan Galtung's categorization of
illness into violence, misery, alienation and repression as responding to four
categories of needs: security, welfare, identity and freedom. This leads to a
universal definition both of needs and of illness but to a distinction between
needs and desires which are for their part related to space, time and culture.
A distinction is also made between the satisfaction of needs and desires
which also are related to space, time and culture.

I prefer to speak of needs as humanum principles rooted in the human
essence and of hierarchies of needs which are different in different moments
of manifestation.

In this vision, needs are embedded in the humanum as the totality but are
continuously changing in their manifestation and in their priorities, as
related to space (geographical and cultural) and to time (historical and life
span). In this vision priorities do not generally follow a fixed pattern as has
been postulated by A. Maslow.[11] In fact, needs for nutrition emerge even in
a situation of high spiritual satisfaction (in prayer). Needs for love emerge
in a situation of high satisfaction of biological needs (in nutrition, housing,
etc.).

3. Needs and social character

Needs interact with the social character as the two legs of the social
organization described by E. Fromm. Needs are thus perceived in terms of

---

[10]S. Marcus and C. Mallmann in *Empirical Information & Theoretical Construct in the
Study of Needs,* GPID Project, 1978.

[11]A. Maslow, *op. cit.*

the vision a particular society has of its goals, its well-being, its quality of life, its growth in economic terms, its development in holistic terms. So needs and social character continuously interact and influence each other, i.e. in an urban community, and will influence the participation, communication, identity needs of the people involved. The satisfaction or non-satisfaction of those needs will change according to the social character of that urban community tending towards anonymity and solitude or towards self-actualization.

In other terms we may say that a social group, community, or country will offer actual or possible satisfaction to the needs of its constituents according to its specific social character through its social structures. But as social character interacts with emerging needs, it will change too, and the fact that very often the social structures do not follow the change in the social character rapidly enough provokes tension, stress and often revolt and revolution.

Using the urban community example, when the social character changes because the need for security through work is not satisfied any longer and security is searched for, i.e. in voluntary associations or groups (whether for leisure or of a religious nature), then other needs require satisfaction (need for experience in art, need for privacy in the family, need for religious meaning). If the social structures do not adapt accordingly (if there are no theatres, no churches, no houses that allow for the need for family privacy, etc.) While the movement of the social character interacting with needs goes on, i.e. if the society is far ahead of the social structure, then reactions take place whether of revolt (the masses) or revolution (the elite).

To conclude, needs are rooted in the humanum and play a central part in the individual's drive for survival and self-actualization, but different needs emerge differently according to the specific social character of that group, community, country, or culture and in their turn influence the social character in a continuous process which is the process of human history.

The dynamics of this are extremely complex because many social characters coexist in a concentric pattern. The social character of Europe as related to individualism, to a specific family structure to a dichotomizing logic coexists with Italy's social character, with Calabria's social character, with a fishing village's social character and the interaction of all these with needs changes continuously. But how do we get a glimpse of the visions in this complex context from which visions eventually emerge?

4. The age of liminality

I have been discussing visions not as fantasies but as awareness of the seeds of human history in the flow of life, coupled with an innovatory antithesis to the present. The seeds are linked to the humanum principles understood as principles of order in the flow of life (E. Jantsch[12]). Such

---

[12]E. Janstch, *op. cit.*

principles are aesthetics, social ethics of a social environmental and spiritual kind. They are based on the needs which emerge as needs or desires in different ways and priorities according to different moments and spaces. Needs together with the social character determine the social organization. This constitutes the passage from the vision to the social organization and eventually to the social structure.

The flow of life in Taoist terms[13] is made of processes which contain the principles of order. At some specific moments of history, the processes crystallize around principles and social structures emerge based on the needs (principles first, desires second) and social character dynamics. Hence the social structure of the family (a specific family structure) emerges in the flow, in the processes involving the principles of aesthetic and social ethics (the need to be together and to preserve the species, etc.); but it actually is centred on a specific priority of needs, of desires (of authoritarianism, of participation, of openness, of defence, etc.). But the processes go on in the flow of life and a specific structure is eroded and eventually dissolved while other potential structures in the processes lie dormant, capable of emerging and blending with actual structures.

Nothing is completely new in the flow, nothing completely old or outdated. Both innovation and completion are there as these are the two complementary concepts of the Tao, this we must search for the seeds of change in the flow and at the same time add to it, transcend it to create the future (innovation). What we have to develop is the capacity of perceiving the seeds of change in the flow which respond in different ways to human principles.

We do not know much about this awareness. We need to develop philosophical approaches and reach different levels of consciousness. An awareness of the growing of these seeds is in fact not an individual endeavour, but a part of one's capacity to belong to the process, to be part of the flow of life. It is a collective effort where we both grow and are aware, are aware and grow at the same time.

Many people perceive the seeds of change in the processes of human history: children not yet hampered in their awareness by superimposed games and terms of reference; artists, painters, poets capable of a sudden glimpse of the totality — probably as has been suggested to me, the victims of persecutions and of repression, and people who refine existentially their consciousness, straining towards the desperation and hope of humankind.[14]

Perhaps also we have to develop a receptive state coupled with the present feeling for the future, receiving and growing in an effort towards the totality. It may be man's need to overcome what Jean Houston calls the

---

[13] J. J. L. Duyvenda, *Tao Te Ching;* Milano, 1973.

[14] This is the fruit of a discussion at the WOMP meeting in Poona, July 1978, with Richard Falk.

crisis of consciousness, in his search for greater perception for alternative cognitive modes, for creative processes.

"We should learn to think in images as well as in words; we could experience these levels of the psyche where the images are archetypical, mythological and possibly transpersonal. To turn to these things is to restore the ecological balance between the inner and outer worlds . . . it is to extend the position of inner space which unlike outer space has inexhaustible resources"[15]

The processes are ever-moving and the structures discernible in them are, as we said, crystallizations around principles which both emerge and dissolve. When the time of dissolution and, simultaneously, of other possible structures, dormant structures, has come, then one must agree with Victor Turner[16] that we live in a time of "liminality". The structures are not yet there but they are so to speak preparing by crystallizing around the symbols of principles.

1. The nuclear structure of the family is only now dissolving and the structure of an open family where children live with more than two adults lies dormant. Equally dormant, but presenting an alternative, is a family structure where the grandparents again play an important role (not a patriarchal family again, but one where the older people also are of service).

2. The structure of work as a life-span decision is dissolving, a structure with individual mobility between professions and in geographical (and other) spaces is emerging.

3. The structure of a centralized nation state (in the north) is dissolving, the dormant structure of regional decentralized units is emerging.

4. The structure of women's role in society as an object of power is dissolving, the structure of women as subjects of power emerging.

What are the symbols of the principles around which these dormant structures are beginning to crystallize?

In the case of the family: eating together in communes where children are not alone with their parents where other adults including grandparents sit around the same table is a symbol.

In the case of work: the symbols are the additional activities like the construction of tools, crafts, acting, singing, etc.

In the case of decentralized units, the rejection of centralized decisions in Italy about the financing of political parties, and the new police law during the last referendum are important symbols.

In the case of women, their refusal to be of desire as they are encouraged to be in advertisements is a symbol. The alternative dormant structure

---

[15]Jean Houston, "Romethus Rebound: An Enquiry into Technological Growth & Psychological Change". In *Technological Forecasting and Social Change*, Vol. 9, No. 3, 1976.
[16]Victor Turner, *The Ritual Process: Structure & Anti-structure*, Aldine Publishing Company, 1969.

would be one in which the two sexes equally sometimes considered each other as objects of desire.

These may be simple examples whose significance and potential as symbols can be discussed. But they nevertheless represent examples of the seeds of change which preceded the structures which emerge in the processes in an age of liminality like the one we seem to be living through.

As Victor Turner puts it: "liminality implies that high cannot be high unless the low existed, and he that is high must experience what it is like to be low. High and low, structure and communities, homogeneity and differentiation, equality and inequality."[17]

Liminality implies the possibility of the emergence of the high and the low, of equality and inequality. All possibilities are there and those who are aware must search for the ones that will emerge, the new dormant structures in a time of dissolving old structures, transcending them in an antithesis to the present.

At a personal level it can be seen as living in the Tao, at a social level as living in the Communitas. But this state is not permanent, the structures crystallize around some principles, low, high, or unequal. Let us search for them and let us also participate in this choice of potentials with the aid of those better equipped: children, artists, women, etc.

5. A humanistic vision

How do we build a vision? We do not build it, we search for it within the processes in the flow of life, as part of the Tao, the ever-present possibility of completion and at the same time the ever-present possibility of innovation.

The seeds are there and we have to search for them in a participative way but also we have to build on them, transcend, capture the antithesis with the present which will, together with the seeds, build the future. This awareness has guiding lines in aesthetic, social ethic and spiritual principles.

The aesthetic principles are those by which one makes explicit to oneself that which implicitly one is in every movement of the human heart. At the biological level, ones needs are to do with security, health, nutrition, etc. The social ethic principles are those (including environmental ethics) by which the individual guides his/her interaction with others and with nature, the psycho-social needs — needs of equality, communication, participation, love as well as of interaction with nature.

As for the spiritual dimension it is difficult to define the principles, I can only say that they are related to the meaning of life which is rooted in the history of all men and women. They could be the principles of the Yogi Philosophy which requires compassion towards those who are miserable, towards those who are joyful, rejoicing, towards those who are in sin or forgiveness.

---

[17]Victor Turner, *op. cit.*

They could be the principles of Christ, "love (your neighbour) as you love yourself".

This could be the law of being instead of having as developed by Fromm.[18]

The Tao stresses the need to go beyond dualism to the flow of life where the mind and matter are not two, where the soul and body are not two as the soul is part of the soul of all times, where there is no separation between the past, the present and the future. But the Tao that can be told is not the absolute Tao. This is what Lao-Tzu says (better than I):

> "When the people of the Earth all know beauty as beauty, then arises ugliness; when the people of the Earth all know good as good, then arises evil. Being and not being, interdependent growth, difficult and easy, interdependent in completion, long and short, interdependent in contrast, high and low interdependent in position, tones and voice interdependent in harmony, front and behind interdependent in company"[19]

This is the flow of the Tao, this is the time of liminality which I was trying to describe in which men and women live out their contrasts in understanding the completion. This is the difficulty of the vision but also the only way, I believe.

6. Women in an age of liminality

Women historically have had to live as low and high, as beautiful and ugly — throughout history they have out of necessity created alternatives. An example of this are the beguines who, in a time when women could either be married or become nuns, created alternatives in religious groups; other examples are the wives of the pioneers in North America who encouraged spiritual values; the women of Japan fighting for peace for their children after Hiroshima (and fighting pollution after that); the women of Warsaw building schools and places for their children to play after World War II; the women of Nigeria fighting for better working conditions in rural areas. Women today are often the animators of communes, of alternative ways of life. Women have had to be conflict resolvers, understanding different values in their families and also in different situations. All these are signs of the invisible history which women have built but which has not as Elise Boulding says,[20] been seen or acknowledged. The structure of society in which women are objects of power is dissolving, the structure of society of women in which are subjects of power is emerging. What are the symbols around which, as symbols of principles, these dormant structures are beginning to crystallize?

---

[18] Erich Fromm, *To Have Or To Be,* Harper & Row Publisher, 1976, Bhagwan Shree Rajneesh.

[19]Tao — *The Three Treasures,* B. S. Rajneesh, 1978.

Again, as Elise Boulding says, women are more adapted to horizontal structural situations — as shown by the examples given than to the vertical structural situations which have dominated the social life of humankind. Maybe this is the great alternative, the great "revolt" of the masses of women for the future, from a vertical managerial attitude, to a horizontal, receptive, communitarian way of life. This is the liminality in which women seem to be able to live with their tendency towards an understanding of the totality; the being and the not being, the tones and the voices, the high and the low of the Tao directed towards growth and harmony, position and identity.

If this is an age of liminality, if we are aware of the seeds in the processes of human history in the flow of life and can add to them, maybe the time has come to recognize women as highly aware, able to contribute as creators of visions which are, however, already in the processes, in the Tao.

---

[20]Elise Boulding, *The Underside of History,* West View Press, 1976.

7

Exploring Alternative Social Visions

JOHN McHALE and MAGDA CORDELL McHALE

Centre for Integrative Studies, College of Social Sciences, University of Houston, USA

Preamble

A discussion of alternative visions of society presupposes both the visions and the possibility of alternatives. The theme itself assumes a level of individual and social consciousness involving a particular sense of history, an awareness of change, of the existence of alternatives and of the possibilities for realizing some desired and alternative human condition.

These are not universal. They are time-bound and culturally specific ideas which may be identified as the product of particular social and historical moments.

The alternative visions of an earthly utopia, of the perfected form of society, for example, have their origins largely in Western ideas of material progress and improvement in the human condition — in the perfectibility of society and human institutions.

In other cultures and times, the vision of the perfected form has tended to be restricted to the religious and the metaphysical. For lack of alternative ways of improving one's material lot in this life, most visions were turned towards the after-life.

The historical lineage of the utopian vision runs, summarily, from Plato and More through Marx and Engels. Most of our contemporary alternatives derive from this lineage. The irony of its recent diffusion and dominance, be that just when the developed world has become less certain about various elements of that vision, the developing world has come to embrace many of its ideological commitments.

The central problem, however, may be that many of the traditionally utopian alternatives are, even if viable, no longer so promising or interesting. Perhaps it is not that the utopian vision has been betrayed but that it is not good enough anymore. There is an underlying paradigm change in our period to which it does not fit very well.

To explore other alternatives we may need to free ourselves from the constraints of some aspects of the utopian ideal — from its apparent universality and collectivity and from its eventual tendency to be authoritarian.

Our alternative visions may not be those of a perfected homogeneous form of society but of a number of imperfect, heterogeneous and coexistent social alternatives. These would also be less oriented to universal and ideological prescription but depend more on particularistic, open and flexible frameworks emerging from individualized preferences rather than collective aspiration.

Accommodating such socio-cultural heterogeneity, in a world which requires a high degree of homogeneity and interdependence to maintain its stability and survival, may be one of the most crucial aspects of any set of alternative visions.

The Dream Denied

Although the decline of the utopian vision, of the belief in progress, seems recent, elements of this reaction may be found even during the ebullience of the nineteenth century.

William Morris in his version of the small handicraft guild revival is an early precursor of Gandhi and Schumacher. The intellectual malaise and disenchantment with "modern life" was a strong theme in the nineteenth century. Romantic Movement in its rejection of the growing rationalization and dehumanization of the human through the machine, and its incipient unease and distrust of science and the emerging industrial society.

In our own period, many of the "alternatives" expressed in social thought stress that we may only find renewed security and meaning through allegiance to the older solidarities — usually those of earlier social orders.

The vision of the Enlightenment, of the human as a self-conscious, freely choosing and rational being was largely abandoned for one which,

> ". . . agreed that the basic characteristic of human experience was the limited nature of its freedom. Men were masters of their fate . . . only for limited periods and in strictly limited segments of their activity. . . . Some such conviction of the inevitable limitations on human freedom — whether by physical circumstance or through emotional conditioning — has become the unstated major premise of contemporary social science."[1]

Though it continues to reverberate in contemporary discussion, we may ask how far these kinds of reaction have led to any positive alternatives. The loss or denial of the dream which it expresses may well be confined to the intellectual. Others in society may still be more directly concerned with securing freedom from want via a more equitable share of industrialized affluence.

---

[1]H. Stuart Hughes, *Consciousness and Society: The Reorientation of European Social Thought 1890-1930*, New York, Alfred A. Knopf, Inc., 1958.

The more profound shock to the utopian vision and to the idea of the inevitability of progress within that vision is the occurrence of the set of events characterized by an Hiroshima and an Auschwitz. Here the dream of perfectibility is denied not by intellectual reservations about the quality of industrial society but by the physical demonstration of human predilections for destructive atavism.

The symbolic transition is to a world in which the ideas and ideals of the recent past — of reason, progress and perfectibility — become oddly tenuous and lose their inevitability.

A new and more sober assessment of the human condition seems to have emerged since then in which optimism regarding human aspirations and potentials is more tempered. The quality of humanity and of human society are viewed less as given "natural" and universal constants but rather as requiring self-definition, vigilance and reaffirmation.

Our current alternatives have a feeling of stasis. At the revolutionary end of the spectrum, though productive of greater social equality, there is less emphasis on social justice and individual flexibility. At the small-scale end of social innovation there is often a Rousseauesque fascination with the primitive and pastoral, turning nostalgically towards the replication of earlier communitarian efforts.

As ideological directions, many of these alternatives take their theoretical premises from the last century without benefit of the changes in scale, attitude and implementation made possible by the scientific and technical developments of our own period.

While drawing upon these developments, the systems approach tends to be preoccupied with an underlying search for security and the authority of systemic absolutes. In this approach to alternatives, computerization replaces individually fallible reason with the value neutrality of instrumented process and a systems mystique which supplies both moral force and infallible truth. Systems alternatives await a more human face.

All Change?

1. *In the classical concept, change was a temporal and material aspect of life: the good and the valued were immutable and unchanging.* Utopian alternatives embraced both the classical and the progressive ideas of change. They projected unchanging human values into the cumulative development of a fulfilled future and were essentially non-dynamic and "surprise-free" models.

2. In certain respects this notion is questionable. As conditions change, so do human values, goals, institutions and behaviour.

Change itself may not be cumulative and continuous but discontinuous and abrupt. Nor is it linearly progressive in all sectors of human activity. In the social, economic and technical realms there is evidence of progressive change where things are better or more efficient than in the past; in the cultural realm, things are essentially different but not cumulatively better, worse, or more efficient.

3. *Alternatives imply choices and costs.* Though choices need no longer be made in either/or terms, they incur costs — if only the cost of foregoing some other alternative. Social alternatives imply social costs and whoever pays the greater cost must consider whether the change is worth that cost.

4. *Views of the direction of change in alternative visions have been either utopian or dystopian* — either visions of material and spiritual progress or "scenarios of decline and catastrophe". Recent ideas of uncertainty, ambiguity and relativity temper this dichotomy with a more provisional and operational view of change.

For example:

> " a. What things can neither bring about change nor be changed in themselves?
> b. What things can make change but cannot be changed?
> c. What things cannot bring about change, but can be changed?
> d. What things are continually being changed, or continually bring change, or both?
> e. What things can both bring about change and be changed?"[2]

These categories may be usefully considered in the exploration of alternatives.

5. *Questions about alternative societies and ways of life arise from the sharp consciousness of change in our own period.* Two critical aspects are salient in this regard:

> (i) The explosive growth in our actual and potential capacities to intervene in the larger processes governing our collective survival. Our ongoing change patterns now constitute a social and ecological transformation of unprecedented magnitude. The scale of these changes has already altered many of the ground rules which have previously governed the human condition.
> (ii) On the other hand, there is a severe lag in the conceptual understanding of this transformation and in the cognitive and affective understanding of how we may manage change more humanely and more effectively.

These factors give rise to a climate of uncertainty, unease and dissonance in which the search for alternatives societies is but one aspect of a larger set

---

[2]Heinze von Forester.

of questions about the purpose of human life, which more people are querying than in any other period.

Considering alternatives

Any consideration of alternative societal directions is essentially normative, coloured by personal preferences and the social and cultural value contexts from which they are considered. The following proposals flow from such a view — from the Particular to the Universal.

A. From the Particular . . .

The first charge that any alternative society might satisfy is that it meets the needs of its people — that it provides a quantitatively and qualitatively better and more satisfying life.

Widespread concern with the *quality of life* is a characteristic of richer rather than of poorer societies. More attention to life-quality probably occurs more deliberately and self-consciously when the majority of the citizens of a society has achieved an adequate quantitative standard of living.

Before that level is reached, people tend to be more preoccupied with *life-quantity,* i.e. with the material means necessary to exist. Dire poverty breeds apathy and passivity. Alternatives and aspirations are circumscribed by the struggle for sheer physical survival. There is a lack of awareness of possible alternatives engendered by the incapacity to improve one's lot.

1. Basic needs. The *a priori* consideration, therefore, for creating more alternatives for more people would be *meeting their basic survival needs —* in terms of food, health, education and livelihood. These cannot, of course, be considered in isolation but in relation to the larger psychosocial needs for security, mobility, self-identity, affection, respect, and so on, which go further in determining self-realization, growth, and full access to and participation in the social and cultural life of one's society.

Access to such needs may be viewed as a two-fold social right.

One: the right of the individual to have the freedom and opportunity to define to be responsible for, and be able to meet his or her own needs.

Two: the right to call upon the support of the society where individual efforts fail due to overriding circumstances. Given the present inequities in the system, there is then an implied responsibility for the world society that the meeting of the basic needs of the world's poorest should, in some sense, be a first charge on the world's resources and facilities.

The numbers of people in the world who are in need of such basic alternatives may be summarized approximately as follows:

THE WORLD'S POOR, 1976 (in total world population of 4 billion people)[3]

Undernourished (below suggested calorie/protein levels)	570 million
Adults illiterate	800 million
Children not enrolled in school	250 million
Without access to effective medical care	1500 million
With less than $90.00 income per year	1300 million
With a life expectancy of below 60 years	1700 million
With inadequate housing	1030 million

Meeting the basic needs of this number has considerable implications for any other set of alternatives we might consider. These implications extend to the global quality of life, to alternatives in reorganizing the international economic order, to changes in the economic and social growth directions for both rich and poor societies.

While the specification of basic survival needs may tend to be universalistic, the meeting of such needs, at the individual and societal level, is obviously more particular and variable according to the social and cultural differences and preferences of a given society. Many different alternative strategies may be generated locally according to circumstances and according to the ways in which people decide to meet their own needs.

2. Beyond the basics. The range of alternative visions of societies capable of providing a satisfactory quality of life is highly variable and ways of meeting life-quality needs are less amenable to operational definition.

"Quality of life" is the perceived well-being of people, individually and in groups, conditioned by their perception of the quality of the social and physical environment which sustains this.

Targetting specific alternatives for enhancing life quality is difficult as, (a) the sensed or felt needs and aspirations comprising life quality are more subjectively determined and (b) ongoing changes in attitudes, values, roles and life-styles also change perceptions.

Quality of life alternatives need to be reduced, therefore, from universalistic prescription to particular social contexts in terms of specific cultural needs and experiences, i.e. quality for who, where and when.

This is true for considering alternative societies as well as for individual alternatives.

For one society, collective religious practices or communal life pursuits may be primary. In others, individually oriented work or recreative pursuits may rank higher. Some societies prize tradition and continuity as important aspects of life quality while others may place a higher premium on innovation and modernity. Emerging societies may give highest priority to the assertion of their cultural and political independence as a prerequisite for qualitative development.

---

[3] John McHale and Magda Cordell McHale, *Basic Human Needs: A Framework for Action,* A report to the UNEP, Transaction Books: New Brunswick, New Jersey, April 1977.

Rather than assume the lockstep of the conventional economic developmental paradigm this suggests a more open set of alternative directions.

Given these caveats one may consider some of the qualitative social trends which may be indicative of social alternatives — which lie "beyond the basics" — on the other side of affluence.

(a) *The widening of individual roles and choices.*

The freedom to choose personal alternatives and to exercise a wide range of social and cultural preferences may be a key measure of the quality of life for individuals, groups and societies.

The trend towards an increased range of such choices may be seen in the expanded range and differentiation of life-style alternatives taken up at different stages in this life cycle in present societies compared with past traditional societies — and in the decline in role, gender and racial stereotyping as people become less limited by sex, minority or occupational roles in seeking more individualized sets of social roles and commitments.

(b) *Increase in the scope of social life.*

Here one might emphasize the emerging alternative directions and capacities for organizing life in more personal terms. These are less constrained than previously by the collective demands of the group or society.

(c) *Better standards of living.*

"Better" does not necessarily mean higher material standards. This has two aspects whose relationship may seem paradoxical:

1.   It is only when some level of material sufficiency is reached by a society that more individuals can exercise a greater range of qualitative preferences.
2.   As standards of living improve, materialism as a life objective tends to decline. Most exploration of quality alternatives is concerned with reorganizing life and society around non-material (and non-economic) ends and purposes. It is expressed in concerns with environmental quality, with the quality of work-experience, with morality, with discrimination and so on. There is a shift in value perspectives from things to people.

We move from socio-economic conditions where material possessions were often the only justification for a lifetime's labour to those in which the moral significance of such possessions is less likely to serve as motivation for striving in its own right.

In further exploration of alternatives, one may also advance the following normative prescriptions for emphasis:

(a) *A reorientation of society.*

From serving itself as a collectivity to serving the individual ends of its members. In essence this means a re-emphasis on respect for the human and the humane more than for the abstracted or institutional embodiment of the human. It also means a reorganization of social arrangements to accommodate the variability of human nature and response better, rather than the administratively convenient categories of the collective institution.

(b) *The expansion of social life in more personal and less collective terms.*

This is not an anarchic goal denying the role of the society and the social order but recognizes that one of the key changes in our period is the potential release of human beings from the socio-economic constraints as they emerge from previous marginal survival conditions and its necessary conformities — which placed the survival of group life over the more idiosyncratic preferences of the individual.

(c) *The creation of new social roles and challenges.*

Even given the widening of social roles, options are still restricted. Many people are excluded from socially meaningful activity and commitment, among them the aged, the young, the female and the racially discriminated against. A wider range of viable human options needs to be explored via more deliberate social innovation.

(d) *The role of work and non-work in society needs to be recast.*

1. Routine productive employment, as we have known it, may no longer be feasible for large numbers of people, e.g. where technically advanced processes do not require such large labour forces in various productive sectors. What are the meaningful ways of rewarding non-economic activities or non-productive pursuits which have other values both to the individual and the society?

2. Coupled to this is the problem not only of work but of education. Most of our education is still in how to earn a living, in how to be economically productive. We have not yet evolved patterns of education for living or for living more fully and more meaningfully.

(e) *The reconceptualization of the locus of wealth and powers in society.*

Our concepts of wealth and power are still economic and physical, as reflected in our allocations of power and social prestige, when patently most of the real wealth created in our period is more clearly based on "ephemeral" conceptual knowledge, i.e. intellectual wealth. The largest source of untapped real wealth is social wealth but, trapped in our older conceptual habits, we have few means of using our potential capacities in this area to more direct advantage and more humane purposes.

(f) *The redirection of social and economic growth.*

For poorer societies there may be no alternatives to a continued emphasis on economic growth simply to provide their peoples with essential goods and services. Meeting the basic needs of people in such societies implies growth in economic terms and in increasing effective social demand.

For the more affluent, the redirection and diversification of growth may not emerge from considerations of physical limits but from desirable preferences and changed economic and technological realities. Economic growth has been pursued abstractly for its own sake — often to the neglect of growth in social, cultural and other realms. It is not a question of alternatives to growth as such but of alternative ways of growing.

Continued technological growth, for example, need not entail greater resource use or greater environmental and social deterioration. The new ranges of electronic and biotechnologies afford new modes of wealth generation which are relatively parsimonious and more in harmony with the preferred quality of life alternatives.

B. To the Universal . . .

The alternative directions considered suggest a wide spectrum of heterogeneous societies. Accommodating this heterogeneity will require a more stable world system — within which context the following universalistic goals need to be reaffirmed both at the local and world society level.

1. *Reduction of global tensions and crises — military, economic, social and environmental.* This implies in turn strong attention to the problems of the basic needs of the world's poorest, of more vigorous arms control, of the reorganization of the international economic order towards greater equity and more rational control of global resources and the environment.

2. *The redesign of our technological and economic systems.* Many aspects of our technological systems even in the so-called advanced nations are obsolescent, poorly organized, and inefficient in their use of both physical and human resources.

Our economic systems barely deserve the term as they are hardly economic in human terms and certainly not systematic. New relationships between private and public enterprise need to be explored. Many of our vital social products and services, in the areas of health, housing, transport, etc., can no longer be provided at satisfactory levels by the economics of the private sector — but the performance of the public sector, in many cases, is even less satisfactory.

3. *The redesigning of a more equitable and secure social order.* This deals with both the problems of government and the redesigning of social institutions. In both senses it underlines that the major factors militating against

the attainment of quality of life — even in affluent societies — are not pollution, urban disorder, work alienation, economic crises and deterioration of amenity but the *sets of institutional arrangements through which these disfunctions occur, i.e. the pervasive institutional crisis.*

C. The institutional challenge . . .

The traditional "institutional" problem in organizing social, economic and political life was how to optimize homogeneity and conformity. This was a necessary function imposed by the marginal survival constraints of earlier societies.

Societal life was essentially a zero-sum game. The resources for social and economic maintenance were limited. If one group won the other lost. The rules of the game generally emphasized physical competition for survival involving access to scarce resources and power struggles over their allocation.

Social cohesion was paramount for survival and the claims of group survival tended to take precedence over those of the individual. An individual's area of choice was limited and constrained — either conform or be censored, exiled or killed; either marry or burn, and so on.

To a certain extent, in the past century, we have changed many of the physical ground rules upon which this kind of social reality was based and reduced many of the constraints which have formerly defined the human condition.

At least one-third of the world's people live well above marginal existence. We have acquired the knowledge and techniques to *potentially* circumvent the traditional constraints of resource scarcity and competitive survival.

Indeed in terms of future sustainable growth directions we are no longer faced either with the problem of a limited fixed pie to be divided up nor of a finite resource pool to be exhausted. There are many possibilities for new and alternative directions based upon sets of renewable and regenerative resource systems.

The overall social and economic situation is more clearly that of a non-zero-sum game. Global survival is now clearly predicated on all winning — in such a way that the gains of one society do not necessarily result in loss or less for another.

The collectivity need no longer be so constraining upon individual ranges of choice. Many choices are no longer so exclusively either/or but may offer both alternatives without excluding others.

The new problem and challenge for the design of societal institutions is how to optimize heterogeneity and diversity — with emphasis on individually, rather than collectively, determined choices as ultimately determining social existence.

Concluding note

To a large extent we already possess the physical means and the technological and resource capabilities (1) to meet basic human needs at world level in the near future and (2) to pursue a wide range of social, economic and cultural alternatives within various kinds of societies.

What we lack more specifically are the requisite sets of alternative socio-economic, institutional and political arrangements through which we may use our means to more human and humane advantage.

The exploration of such alternative arrangements and of the visions of alternative forms of society which they accompany, emerges as one of the major tasks for the study of the future.

8

How is a Vision of a Desirable Society Possible Today?

ANDRZEJ SICIŃSKI
*Institute of Philosophy and Sociology,
Polish Academy of Sciences, Poland*

FIRST of all, I want to state explicitly that the following remarks are purely personal. They represent only my own views and are not derived from any "school of thought". In addition, I should point out that they have been formulated *ad hoc,* for the purpose of the Mexico conference, that is to say, they are not based on any systematic analyses or studies.

Selected methodological problems

1. I would like to point out the difficulties involved in formulating any meaningful social visions nowadays. One could even argue that the development of such visions today is impossible.

The main reason for such difficulties lies in the fact that contemporary visions should be much more comprehensive than any previous utopias for at least two reasons:

(i) Any contemporary vision of a desirable society must be to some extent "democratic": it should embrace all the people of a given society, without those distinctions characteristic of many earlier utopias, such as: master vs. slave, citizen vs. non-citizen, etc; no kind exploitation may be assumed to be the basis of any social organization.

(ii) Such a vision should be satisfactory for people of different cultures. In the contemporary world with all its interdependencies, it would be unreasonable to propose a concept valid for one nation or one culture exclusively. However, we are aware of significant differences between cultures, differences in behaviour patterns, living standards, accepted values, images of the world and of man himself, etc.

2. Besides the problems connected with the complexity of social reality, I see other sources of difficulty. The main one is the crisis in contemporary social thought, with its eclecticism and its critical rather than constructive approach.

So, by and large, I would say that the difficulties I have encountered in trying to formulate a coherent vision of a desirable society are not simply the result of my personal lack of imagination, but have more general causes.

3. Alternative visions of desirable societies may be worked out from at least two points of view:

(i)   as a kind of criticism of an existing situation, i.e. as suggesting some alternatives to contemporary societies;

(ii) as more abstract alternative visions of societies, i.e. societies without any negative aspects and/or which present desirable features.

In the following sections I will consider the second point of view.

4. Visions of desirable societies could relate to different, but interdependent, "levels" of social life:

(i)   the macro-social level: with such problems as power, production, etc., and their respective counterparts, oppression, exploitation, etc.;

(ii) the micro-social level: with such problems as interpersonal communication, social bonds, the role of the individual in society, etc.;

(iii) the individual level: with such problems as personality development, creativity, etc.

This proposal will concern mainly the first two levels.

A search for the requirements for a desirable society

5. Although I think no meaningful, coherent and general vision of a desirable society is possible today, I still believe one may undertake a more modest task, namely, to reflect upon some ideas or principles which would be essential in a desirable society.

Such ideas, if sufficiently general, could materialize in many diverse forms in different cultures and nations. On the other hand, there is the obvious danger that being too general and too abstract, they will have no chance of exerting even a modest influence on social reality. Being aware of such a danger, I want, nevertheless, to specify basic ideas of that type, and to discuss, in brief, some of their general implications.

6. Let us start, however, with some basic assumptions:

(i)   Contrary to many utopias, the following comments will relate to the human being, not to an idealized superman, or to a hypothetical post-human being, the result of some future evolution.

(ii) The main point of reference for an evaluation of a desirable society is, to me, the human species, its development and evolution.

(iii) I do not intend to analyse here the practical problems of the implementation of my suggestions. First of all, the very question of the nature of the basic requirements of a desirable society seems controversial. Secondly, their possible implementation would take different forms in different cultures and societies.

7. The main principles which, I believe, should underly a desirable society will probably seem obvious or banal. They are: freedom and *equality*. However, I think that from time to time one should return to some issues which have been extensively discussed and appear to have been fully explained.

8. There is a basic difference between the two concepts mentioned above, as seen from the point of view of a desirable society:
— the first of them — freedom, as understood in a positive way
— is treated as an *autothelia* value, whereas
— the second, equality, is an *instrumental* one.

In other words, I assume that:

(i) a desirable society is one which secures the human being a maximum of freedom;

(ii) however, one particularly important limitation and condition of the freedom of each individual is the freedom of other individuals; this being implicit in the idea of equality: my desires, my development and my self-expression are both restricted and stimulated by the freedom of others, individuals, groups;

(iii) thus the main problem confronting a desirable society is the relationship between freedom and equality, which could be solved in a practical manner suited to each culture;

(iv) assumption (i) implies — and this should be clearly stated because of its controversial character — that securing the freedom of individuals, groups and societies, with a minimum of limitations resulting from a desire for equality, is in the interest of the human species and favours its development.

Some ideas concerning a balance between freedom and equality

9. Since every society in order to exist must: (1) be organized in a certain way, (2) cope with its surroundings, and (3) have some general rules by which to evaluate its members, I see the following three areas as being crucial to a society of free and equal people:

(i) that aspect of societal organization which is usually labelled control or power, particularly the nature, distribution, etc. of this control;

(ii) work;

(iii) the criteria of social position.

The first two considerations belong to the macro-level, whereas the third relates to the micro-level. I would like to speculate a little about each of them.

10. As far as the problems of control are concerned, I want to refer to the rather old concept of the *cooperative*.

I believe it is necessary to recall today some old cooperationist ideas, such as a system of sharing the delegation of power to elected members for a defined period of time, and the possible recall of those members, etc. In my opinion, the cooperative is, from the point of view of reconciling freedom and equality, the best type of organization ever invented.

Clearly, in this context the concept of the cooperative could and should be extended beyond its traditional scope. It can be applied not only in the sphere of the production and distribution of goods and services, but also to living quarters. A desirable society run on the lines of a cooperative society would introduce cooperative principles into the administration of society in towns, regions, and finally, on a global scale. To a great extent this system would be similar to such concepts as "communalism", or a "multi-level federalism", in the terminology of one of the leading Polish theoreticians of the cooperative movement (Wolski, 1948).

A cooperative organization of this nature should be governed by some general rules:

(i)   it should have a structure of functional, and not hierarchical inter-relationships, e.g. a "global cooperative" would not be "above" others, but would deal with problems which could not be solved at other levels;

(ii) the basic principle of that organization should be that the scope of activity (competence) of a cooperative would not depend on what could be done by the smaller units, but on what could not be solved on a smaller scale.

One of the problems which arises in connection with this system of control and administration, is the question of how to make people avail themselves of their rights as cooperative members and how to prevent their tendency to cede those rights to any kind of "experts". Such tendency is well known today, and it appears in many societies at many levels. However, it is obviously a result of the type of societal organization prevailing nowadays. Many years ago Karl Mannheim pointed out a discrepancy between "mass society", which alienates people from more general social problems, and the idea of the plebiscite. He wrote:

> "If we consider the plebiscitory element in democracy we are justified in saying, after the experiences of the last epoch, that of all democratic institutions, it has made the largest contribution to the destruction of the system. The plebiscitory principle drives people towards what we have described as crowd psychology . . . . a modern plebiscite treats the individual as a spectator, whereas in the smaller democratic groups he was an active and cooperative member of the commune" (Mannheim, 1940).

So, the first condition for rendering meaningful cooperative types of control and administration is a more general change in the organization of society (e.g. in the direction of the "beta" type of society as defined by Johan Galtung or, in traditional terminology, the "Gemeinschaft" type of organization, or "primary" vs. "secondary" groups).

The second condition for bringing about the active participation of the people would be to make use of technical devices whereby to secure reliable information about the current problems of a given cooperative (assuming the full accessibility of all information), and also to demonstrate the consequences of alternative solutions to the often very general, problems of day to day life in the present and in the future, and the impact of those solutions on the development of a group or society.

In such circumstances, a refusal to try and influence the course of events would mean the renunciation of freedom, and as such, would be reprehensible in a desirable society. To determine appropriate attitudes and aspirations would be one of the main objectives of a policy of "education for freedom", indispensable in a desirable society and, particularly, also, training in the "art of decision-making" (Siciński, 1972).

And finally, I want to point out the fact that in a desirable society of the cooperative type it would be possible to realize the ideal of "planning for freedom" (to use Karl Mannheim's term. Such planning could be effective, because it would embrace all spheres of human life, from the individual to a global scale, but, at the same time, would allow for the autonomy of individuals, groups and cooperatives of different types and what is more, would allow for diversity.

11. Let us start a discussion of some of the problems of work in a desirable society with a rather long quotation from an interesting German novel, *März* unfortunately, in my rendition of a Polish translation:

> "Behind the fact that people agree to work in factories, mines, or offices, there is obviously violence. Would anybody agree to gut fish in abominable, slimy rooms, putting up with the stench of the fish, as do workers in canning factories, if it was not a question of survival? Would anybody willingly have bones crushed by pieces of machinery or have their hearing destroyed by the noise of a car factory, their lungs by mining, and their skin by working in a chemical plant? Who would voluntarily type idiotic business letters, and suffer the bad temper of office nitwits? The housewife is under pressure to do her chores, the children are brought up, people even make love under pressure of violence and dependence. If we look at interpersonal relationships we always see some element of violence in them, so we may speak of the social character of violence. The chief, the foreman, anyone in a superior position at work makes use of it. It is the job of experts and mystifiers to camouflage this violence and suggest to a subdued individual that he has chosen his work of his own free will. They present force as something inherent in the nature of things.
>
> "Perhaps we will approach an understanding of this psychosis, when there is a breakdown of social bonds and we will see a fierce, irrational protest against this intolerable violence" (Kipphardt, 1976).

So the main aim of our desirable society would be:

(i)   to eliminate particularly unhealthy, as well as to eliminate intellectually idle work.

Until now a great deal of effort has been directed towards increasing work efficiency; this being the underlying principle of the development of technology. However, in a desirable society the elimination of "inhuman" and uninteresting work will be a crucial issue;

(ii)   since it is reasonable to assume that even a technological development of the type would not eliminate all undesirable work, in a desirable society such work would be treated as a kind of "public service" and carried out according to a system analogous to the present military service, or performed on a rotary basis; in any case, it would not be "assigned" — as a "job" — to any individual ("Gastarbeiters" included);

(iii) on the other hand, it is assumed that there will not be any "obligation to be creative" in a desirable society, as suggested in some futurogical proposals; there will always exist people of different abilities, different psychological dispositions; for instance a job which would seem monotonous to some people could be a source of happiness, engendering a feeling of usefulness in others; certainly the type of work undertaken, or a person's abilities and skills would not be a criterion of social position in a desirable society.

12. No type of social organization will maintain a balance between freedom and equality if the criteria used to evaluate the individual and the group are not changed.

Many kinds of criteria for determining social position operated in the past: seniority, wealth, social origin, merits, etc. In a desirable society the most important criterion of social prestige should be the "attractiveness" of an individual (and of a group) to other individuals and groups. And this attractiveness could stem from such attributes as: benevolence, the readiness to help others, the ability to co-operate, trustfulness, an ability to empathize an attractive personality, etc., i.e. such attributes, as are usually looked for in a friend (at least, in the Polish usage of that term), particularly in the ideals of youngsters. In sociological jargon, one could say that in a desirable society the sociometric method would be the best one to apply in establishing somebody's social worth.

It is reasonable to expect that within a desirable society there would be differences in the dominating orientations of people's behaviour, such as (to use the typology of a Polish psychologist): ipso-centric, allo-centric, socio-centric, i.e. orientations towards optimalization of the actions of the subject itself, of the actions of other people, and of the functioning of groups and institutions, respectively (Reykowski, 1975). So the said "attractiveness" could reveal itself in many different ways.

In any case the main role of social and interpersonal relationships within a desirable society would be to generate a feeling of security, in contrast to the present situation, where they very often pose a threat. It is obvious that human beings will never be free from different kinds of danger, starting with the danger of death which accompanies one from the very moment of birth, to dangers coming from the non-human world. So why must social life be an additional threat to a man or woman?

13. The desirable society discussed here would be much more varied than any society hitherto. The variations in people and groups would be the result of differences in abilities, skills, interests, emotional dispositions, etc. They would also reject cultural difference. Such differences would be given far greater opportunity for development than in any previous societies.

I think that the influence of mass production, mass marketing, mass media, etc., results in the complete unification and standardization of people's ideas and values, unless they are treated solely in an instrumental way.

I want to repeat, what an eminent Polish sociologist, Stanisław Ossowski, wrote 35 years ago (during the Nazi occupation): ". . . the processes of universalism and processes of differentiation would be characteristic of a new democratic culture. The processes of universalism would ensure social equality. . . . The processes of differentiation, on the other hand, make human culture colourful and versatile. . . . Among plans and calculations the differentiation processes are there to preserve the charm of the undetermined and the unpredicted" (Ossowski, 1947).

14. One must consider whether the above proposals would not commit the error common to most utopias of delineating a completely static society. I do not believe that this is the case in the desirable society discussed here.

The ideal of a balance between freedom and equality, the basic principle of that society, would always be a source of tension, and would maintain it in an alert state. What is more, it would probably never be fully realized at any level of social organization from the family to a global scale. One for this would be that unforeseen problems would arise, needing new solutions, thereby maintaining momentum and balance.

The pursuit of a balance between freedom and equality would provide the dynamics of our desirable society.

Closing remarks

15. Looking over my ideas for a desirable society, I see that in fact they go no further than that famous device of 200 years ago, "liberty, equality, fraternity", probably the most wonderful slogan ever formulated. However, the main problem lies not in the finding of a formula, but in its interpretation, and above all, in its implementation in social life. The present interpretation of that device is certainly different from the former one, and, what is more, that device has never ever been realised anywhere.

16. One could consider the problems of a desirable society from the point of view of the popularized notion of the "quality of life". This notion has been interpreted differently by different people, e.g. some time ago, for the purposes of a Unesco project, I defined it as "the level and interconnections of two aspects of human existence: (i) the possibilities of a full development of the human individual, (ii) one's satisfaction with one's life".

One could discuss, too, the problems of a desirable society from the point of view of satisfying *needs*. Here, I would suggest accepting a rather general meaning of the term "need", and would consider one of the most important problems, that is the coordination and fulfilling of the different needs of biological and social life, e.g. in terms of the cell and the molecule, of the organism, of the population, of the biogenesis (Siciński, 1978).

I believe both points of view are implicit in the comments presented above.

17. Finally, I would like to answer briefly questions formulated by Eleonora Masini in her circular letter concerning our conference:

— "Do these alternative visions exist in people? Can we foresee the transition of them into existing reality, the processes of implementation and hence the strategies? What social movements are potentially supporters of such visions?" — My answer to all these questions is, unfortunately, negative.

— "How can we make such visions visible to the people of the world and catalyze the enormous energies which are striving to find ways which are alternative to the present? Which means would be adequate, useful for such a catalyzing process? Drama, TV, films, books, etc.?" — Here, I would answer; "I am not sure. However, I believe the main problem is not the means, but big, attractive, and dazzling visions."

References

KIPPHARDT, H. (1976) *März* (my rendition of a Polish translation).

MANNHEIM, K. (1940) *Man and Society in the Age of Reconstruction,* London.

OSSOWSKI, S. (1947) *Ku nowym formom życia społecznego.*

REYKOWSKI, J. (1975) *Osobowość jako centralny system regulacji i integracji czynności, in: Psychologia* (ed. T. Tomaszewski).

SICIŃSKI, A., *Training in the Art of Choosing, PHP,* No 21, June.

SICIŃSKI, A. (1978) The Concepts of "Need" and "Value" in the Light of the Systems Approach, *Social Science Information,* **17,** 1.

WELSKI, J. (1948) *Zbiór materiałów do nauki o spółdzielczości pracy.*

9

Shaping the Future:
The World in the 1980s

B. F. OSORIO-TAFALL
El Centro de Estudios Economicos y Sociales del Tercer Mundo, Mexico

1. Opening Remarks

I wish to state from the very outset that the views I am about to express are neither my own, those of the organization I serve, nor of my government or any other government on earth. Therefore, the announcement that the Special Representative of the Secretary-General in Cyprus is to lecture here tonight is definitely incorrect and should be deleted accordingly from the invitation card. Instead, it is a common — nothing special — citizen who will address you.

Furthermore, I wish to warn you that this lecture is based on a little personal experience and knowledge, on a lot of curiosity about the immediate future of the world, and on extensive and intensive perusal of the copious literature on the subject matter. I decline personal responsibility for any factual error in my exposé. The authors of the books I have read, the editors of the magazines I have consulted and the men of art and science who were interviewed for this lecture should be blamed for all my blunders.

2. Introduction

Men have since the very beginning shown a preoccupation with the future. From the cave men of Paleolithic times up to the present technetronic age, interest in the future has gone through ups and downs. At one time or another, the Greek oracles, the charting of stars or the reading of animal entrails were fashionable means whereby men might know their fate. There have always been scholars who tried to write history in advance, describing imaginary worlds and sponsoring the desirable organization of human societies. This was the subject of the utopian writing in which excelled satirists like Jonathan Smith and Aldous Huxley (in his *Brave New World* Huxley expresses his concern over the dangers of scientific progress) and social reformers like Sir Thomas More (*Utopia* is his most famous work: it was written in Latin).

Anticipators like Jules Verne and H. G. Wells popularized science fiction and achieved greatness as prophets and spokesmen for progress.

It was possibly Wells who inspired a notable effort undertaken more than 40 years ago by Kegan Paul in England and E. P. Dutton in the United States. They published a series of small books, about 80 in number, under the general title *Today and Tomorrow*, in which some outstanding minds of the epoch made predictions about the future. As Daniel Bell says, "the titles were romantic and metaphoric and this provided a clue to the style and content of the series".

Almost all the volumes used a Greek name — a figure of myth or speech — to personify or typify their subject. J. B. S. Haldane wrote *Daedalus, or Science and the Future*; Bertrand Russell, *Icarus, or the Future of Science*. The spectrum of the series ranged widely from Bonamy Dobree on *Timotheus, or the Future of the Theatre*, to Vernon Lee on *Proteus, or the Future of Intelligence* to R. McNair Wilson on *Pygmalion, or the Doctor of the Future*. Some volumes were squarely at the heart of the enterprise, such as *Sibylla, or the Revival of the Prophecy"* by C. A. Mace and the *Future of Futurism* by John Rodker.

What is striking about these volumes — many of which I enjoyed in my youth — is their fanciful character, the airy and even comical tone, as if the idea of speculating about the future had a somewhat absurd but pleasant quality. In effect, the books gave the impression of a "lack of seriousness". However, some books were much more successful than others. Russell's volume on the future of science, for example, was deeply pessimistic, for he refused to believe that the progress of science must be a boon to mankind. Haldane, writing in 1923, made the stunning prediction that the centre of science would pass from mathematical physics to biology. And in his projections for the future Haldane specified that progress in medicine would practically abolish infectious diseases; that new discoveries in nitrogen fixation and the use of genetically improved seeds would multiply crop yields; and that "by 1951" biologists would be able to produce "ectogenic" children through artificial insemination and the maintenance of female ovaries in the laboratory. (It is clear that Haldane's persuasive "scenarios" were the source of Aldous Huxley's frightening vision in *Brave New World*) H. Stafford Hatfield, in his *Automation, or the Future of Mechanical Man,* published in 1928, brilliantly anticipated cybernetic mechanisms that "perceive a change in conditions, such as size or composition of material, and immediately adjust the tool so as to meet correctly the changed conditions" and sketched an automation that read manuscripts of different sizes and type faces, automatically regulated traffic, and the like.

Daniel Bell, reviewing the prophets of the past, finds that almost all of them — at least in their sociological predictions — "lack any notion of how a society hangs together, how its parts are related to one another, which elements are more susceptible to change than others, and, equally important any sense of method. They are not systematic and they have no awareness of the nature of social systems: their boundaries, the interplay of values, motivations, and resources, the levels of social organization, and the constraints of custom and privilege in change.

"If — as we shall soon see — there is a decisive difference between the studies of the future that are now under way and those of the past, it consists of a growing sophistication about methodology and an effort to define the boundaries — intersections and interactions — of social systems that come into contact with each other."

The recent interest in the future is quite novel. During the twenties, as I have already indicated, the idea of prophesying the future was a rather amateurish undertaking. Then for about 30 years there was little interest in the future. Men were preoccupied with a worldwide depression, many of them suffered the horrors of nazism and fascism, the concentration camps, and were battered by the onslaught of war, first in Spain and thereafter in the Second World War. It could be said that men were too much obsessed by the twentieth century to spend time speculating about the twenty-first. There were indeed the apocalyptic fancies of Spengler (*The Decline of the west*), Toynbee (*A Study of History*), and Sorokin (*Social and Cultural Dynamics*), as well as the recent popularity of the Jesuit Teilhard de Chardin, with his vision of mental evolution replacing physical evolution. But in the past 6 or 7 years there has been a lot of thinking and writing on the future, and, more important, half a dozen institutions have been created to deal seriously and consistently with problems of the future. So Futurology has come of age. Possibly the man who contributed most to this subject is the Frenchman, Bertrand de Jouvenel, who directs the group *Futuribles*, and who, with the initial financial support of the Ford Foundation, has published many studies of the future. Mr. de Jouvenel's organization, S.E.D.E.I.S. continues to publish, without the Ford Foundation's financing, a monthly journal, *Analyse et Prévision,* devoted to the subject. Jouvenel, in his *Studies on Conjecture*, has borrowed the word "futuribles" from the sixteenth century Spanish thinker, Luis de Molina, remembered for his emphasis on free will.[1]

Another French group, called *Perspectives*, was founded by Gaston Berger. In England, the Social Science Research Council, under the chairmanship of Mr. Andrew Schonfield, has set up the Committee of the Next Thirty Years.

---

[1]Luis de Molina (1535-1600), Spanish Jesuit theologian. His book *Concordia*, issued in 1589. He said that the condition of grace was dependent upon the free consent of the will. He defended the freedom of man's will. Dominicans attacked Molina and his doctrine. Jesuits defended him. Dispute grew extremely bitter. Molina taught at Coimbra and Evora Universities. Francisco Suarez (1548-1617), Jesuit theologian. The best of the old scholastic theologians. His "congruism" is a middle course between the teaching of Molina and the Dominican predestinarian teachings.

Futurism, it should be pointed out, did not have in the twenties the contemporary meaning (1967 and onwards) of organized and systematic studies of the future, but derived its name from the radical movement in literature and art initiated in 1909 by the Italian poet and novelist Filippo Tommaso Marinetti. His *Manifeste du Futurisme* (1909) called for a revolutionary attitude towards life and art in general, exalting such aspects of contemporary life as speed, machinery and war. His special manifesto on literature (1912) insisted on courage, audacity and rebellion as the essential elements of poetry; it advocated freedom for the word (*parole in libertá*); the abolition of syntax, and similar anarchic, "liberating" tendencies.

More recently, Futurology has become very much an American subject. The organization called "Resources for the Future" has undertaken, with the help of the Ford Foundation, a notable series of studies (principally, *Resources in America's Future* by Hans L. Landsberg, Leonard L. Fischman, and Joseph L. Fisher); the Rand Corporation has sponsored the *Delphi Prediction Studies* of Olaf Helmer and T. J. Gordon (available most readily in the volume *Social Technology* by Olaf Helmer). The American Academy of Arts and Science has created the Commission on the Year 2000, under the sociologist, Daniel Bell, and the Hudson Institute, directed by Herman Kahn. The Commission on the Year 2000 has prepared five volumes of mimeographed material, and Herman Kahn in collaboration with Anthony Wiener and other members of his Hudson Institute have published an ambitious exercise in systematic speculation called *The Year 2000: A Framework for Speculation*. Other American institutions, notably among them the Stanford Research Institute, have also plunged full scale into studies of the future.

Here in this island of Aphrodite, Mr. Clerides and Mr. Denktash, in more or less cordial collaboration, are also engaged in the difficult task of looking — and certainly not through a crystal ball — into the future. It is expected that their target will be much closer to next year than the year 2000, so I can claim tonight to be in the good company of outstanding futurologists.

Daniel Bell asks, "How does one explain this resurgence of interest in 'the future'? Some of this is due, undoubtedly, to the lure of the millennial number of the year 2000. . . . But 2000 is still 30 years away. Nevertheless, two-thirds of all people in the advanced countries now alive will probably witness the turn of that *khiliastic* year. Some is due to the romance of outer space, man's conquest of the moon, and the possibility of reaching out for Venus and Mars."

This upsurge of studies of the future arises also from the simple fact that every society today is consciously committed to economic growth, to raising the standard of living of its people, and therefore to the planning, direction and control of socio-economic change. What makes the present studies, thus, so completely different from those of the past is that they are oriented to specific social-policy purposes; and along with this new dimension they are fashioned, consciously, by a new methodology that gives the promise of providing a more reliable foundation for realistic alternatives and choices. We are learning to regulate change for specified ends. With the growth of modern communication and transport, and the impact of radio, television and movies, we are more quickly aware of the linked consequences of change, the need to anticipate these and to plan for them. But the recognition of the need for planning involves an added dimension as well: the nature of time. To give only an illustration, the expansion of medical services involves a 15-year plan — approximately the time it takes a young man to enter college and *complete* his medical degree. In fact, especially in a post-industrial society, planning necessarily involves long-term commitments and requires long-run forecasting.

But planning, by its very nature, is not a mechanical process. Central to it is the problem of choice — both of the ends desired and of the allocation of resources. All this puts us on the threshold of an ancient and persistent human quest: to choose our future. And what is central, therefore, to the present studies on the future is not an effort to "predict" the future, but the effort to sketch "alternative futures" — in other words, the likely results of different choices, so that we can understand the cost and consequences of different alternatives.

Now some words of caution. No futurologist pretends that single *events* can be predicted. These are often contingent and even irrational. Nor can one predict what historians call *turning points* in the lives of men or nations — those events (for instance, the success or failure of a revolution) that can move nations in new directions. But all such events are constrained by various contexts: of available resources, of customs and lores, of willpower. And they are shaped, as well, by basic trends in human society, the advance of science and technology, literacy, economic interdependence and the like.

In order to be fair in the presentation of this subject matter, I wish to warn you that there are many critics of the futurologists who find their methodology and conclusions wrong. Outstanding among them is Andrew Schonfield, who, in a lengthy article (*Encounter,* February 1969), attempts to demolish Kahn and Wiener's views on the "year 2000". For Schonfield, current Chairman of the British Social Science Research Council, Futurology remains allied to fantasy. "It cannot be turned into a respectable hard science merely by getting the economists and the technologists to put some numbers on it."

3. Shaping the future

I do not pretend to have any *knowledge* of the future, which would be foolish, but neither do I pretend to have no opinion at all about it, which would be evading my responsibility as a man.

I belong to the group of people who definitely take the view that what shall be depends upon our choices now and tomorrow. It is precisely because the future depends upon our decision and actions, and these in turn upon our views and opinions regarding the future, that the latter so much need to be stated, weighted and tested.

Any decision we are now taking, any action we are now undertaking, can bear results only in the future, be it immediate or distant. Therefore, any conscious activity, of necessity, implies "looking forward".

However, a complex society like ours cannot be changed suddenly. The basic framework of day-to-day life, mainly in the developing countries, has been shaped during the past 50 years or so by the way the aircraft, the automobile, instant telecommunications have brought the peoples closer together, increasing interaction among them and shrinking the planet. It is highly unlikely that — at least in the next 15 or 20 years — the impending changes in technology will radically alter this framework. I think it would be safe to forecast that the world will not change drastically and that many of the present problems and difficulties will remain with us for many years to come. It will be a certainty that public authorities will face more problems than they have had at any previous time in history. The main difficulties derive from the magnitude, frequency and complexity of the outstanding problems, to such a degree that they will possibly exceed the capacities of governments to control and eventually to solve them. For this and other reasons, it has been predicted that the society of the future two or three decades will be more fragile, more susceptible to hostilities and polarization along many different lines. Yet to say this is not — as Bell has said — to surrender to despair, for the power to deal with those problems is also in our hands.

The great changes will undoubtedly take place in the Third World, in the recently emerged independent countries of Africa, in the developing nations of Southeast Asia and Latin America, where the revolution of rising expectations is being superseded by a concerted effort for those countries to share in the wealth of the world.

I agree that our main task now concerning the problems of the future consists of defining — on a global rather than national basis — our priorities and in making the necessary commitments. I believe the paramount aims of the next two decades will be concerned with protecting environmental and human values. The major challenges and problems already confronting our present society — such as a livable physical and mental environment, effective urban planning, the expansion of education, the pressures of population density and the reduction of privacy, the consequences of the population explosion, the fragility of political institutions beset by many pressure groups — will extend to the end of the eighties and beyond.

This does not mean that substantial changes will not take place as they have been doing since the end of the Second World War. But I think that the nature and magnitude of most of these changes are already known to us.

Man does not live in a vacuum. He is closely linked to a Mother Earth by an umbilical cord of air, water and plant and animal life. As the concept of natural resources — both living and non-living — does not make sense without man, it is not possible to conceive of man's existence without his environment. If man has to adapt himself to the various and changing physical, chemical and biological conditions which make his environment, the human environment itself is profoundly affected — more often than not for the worse — by man's multifarious activities. The industrial and technological development which the world has seen has been achieved at some high cost to man and to the harmonious relationship which must exist between man and his environment. In years ahead it is imperative to prevent further deterioration of the human environment. Fortunately, man is today in possession of scientific and technical knowledge and resources which are truly spectacular. It can be safely assumed that further progress will follow year after year.

We can predict without error the dangers to which mankind would be exposed if he further neglects the preservation of the human environment and if the present steady deterioration continues. I believe that in the next decade man will accept, perhaps for the first time in his history, that clean air, fresh water and clean soil are to be considered on the same economic basis as food, clothing and electric power. I would submit, therefore, that the time is coming when developing and developed countries will take into account in their development plans the possible implications for the human environment.

4. Sources of Change

You may realize that it would be beyond the boundaries of possibility for me to deal — even superficially — with this extensive subject. A whole course would be needed. For that reason I will refer only to a few selected illustrative topics — about which I can claim a certain degree of scholarly authority. Indeed, this arbitrary selection is coloured by the twin effects of my academic formation (or should I say deformation) and my personal likes and dislikes. However, I am confident that my menu will satisfy your tastes. To start with, you will notice that the fascinating topic of Western and Eastern relations and their relations with the Third World, particularly in the political field, is not being dealt with in this lecture. This in spite of the tremendous interest of the subject of trying to examine the possible different forms of association between the Western powers that could develop in the next decade or so.

The omission is deliberate, notwithstanding my interest in the theme, and for obvious reasons, is being left out. However, as I am sure of your great curiosity in the topic I recommend two publications. The first is a study prepared by Professor Lincoln P. Bloomfield of the Center for International Studies, Massachusetts Institute of Technology, entitled *Western Europe to the Mid-Seventies: Five Scenarios.* And the second is *Europe's Futures, Europe's Choices.* Models of Western Europe in the 1970s', just issued this year under the editorship of Alastair Buchan, with the participation of various members of the British Institute for Strategic Studies, outstanding among them my good friend Peter Ramsbotham, the present High Commissioner of the United Kingdom in Cyprus. I strongly recommend to the Directors of this Centre to request H. E. the Hon. P. Ramsbotham to lecture here. He would do so with much more knowledge and authority than I could claim.

The futurologists distinguish — in general — four main sources of change. The first source of change is the impact upon society of science and technology. According to Brzezinski, we are entering a novel metamorphic phase in human history. In his opinion the world is on the eve of a transformation more dramatic in its historic and human consequences than that wrought either by the French or the Bolshevik revolutions. Compared with the approaching transformation, these famous revolutions merely scratched the surface of the human condition, while the revolution which is taking place will have deeper consequences for the way and even perhaps for the meaning of human life than anything experienced by the generations that preceded us.

Brzezinski maintains that America is already beginning to experience these changes and in the course of so doing it is becoming a *Technetronic* society: a society that is shaped culturally, psychologically, socially and economically by the impact of technology and electronics, particularly computers and instant communications. The industrial process no longer is the principal determinant of social change, altering the mores, the social structure and the values of society. This change, Brzezinski claims, is separating the United States from the rest of the world, prompting a further fragmentation among an increasingly differentiated mankind, and imposing upon Americans a special obligation to ease the pains of the resulting conflict. The work in progress indicates that men living in the developed world will undergo during the next decades a mutation as basic as that experienced through the slow process of evolution from animal to human experience. The difference, however, is that the process will be telescoped in time — and hence the shock effect of the change may be quite profound. Those interested in the technetronic age may consult Brzezinski's article entitled *America in the Technetronic Age*, printed in the January 1968 issue of the British magazine *Encounter.*

In the next 20 years great advances will be made through changes growing out of the so-called biological revolution, biomedical engineering the computer, water desalting, and possibly weather control and modification. I will refer later in more detail to the biological breakthrough.

The impact of the computer will be vast. By the beginning of the eighties, the world is likely to look quite different, particularly to young people. Herman Kahn, the co-author of *The Year 2000*, in an article for *The Times* of London, presented some views on how computers and technology might change our way of life in the next 10 or more years. In this article Kahn put together a preliminary list of trends and issues of the early eighties. According to him, it is almost certain that computer-assisted instruction and computerized retrieval systems for information will begin to be ubiquitous in schools and other institutions frequented by the young, at least in the more developed nations. For many children the computer will, literally, play a role less than, but close to, that of parent and teacher. Kahn says that it is interesting to note that in many schools in the United States children have developed an intense respect and affection for their computer teacher. This is not surprising. The voice of the computer has been chosen for its warmth, friendliness, clarity and pleasantness. Thus, the computer-teacher is always friendly and understanding. It never loses patience; it never gets angry; it is never sarcastic, indifferent or inattentive. I wonder what the present teachers think of this unpersonalized competitor.

By the eighties we will probably see in the United States and perhaps in other advanced countries, a national information-computer-utility system with tens of thousands of terminals in homes and offices connected to giant central computers providing library and information services, retail ordering, billing services and the like. At least in wealthy families computer services will be utilized as a convenient method of regulating temperature, humidity, operating various cooking devices, etc. They may even have the ability to begin to play surrogate mother — or at least surrogate baby-sitter and playmate as well as home tutor and/or teacher. Such household computers might well have access to a very large variety of games, amusements, entertainments and a number of alarm-type circuits to inform the parents or the grand-parents or the neighbours when they should look in themselves to see what the youngsters are doing.

Contrary to what appears to be a popular belief, it does not seem likely that the society of the eighties or even of the year 2000 will be one in which most of us are condemned to leisure while only a privileged few will be permitted to work. If anything, it seems quite likely that there will be an extreme labour shortage in the developed nations — certainly a shortage of certain kinds of competent personal services and perhaps a general and overall shortage which will tend to drive up the price of labour. Doubtless, the average number of hours worked per year will go down but for those of you who want to work longer there will most likely be plenty of opportunities. This does not mean that there could not be a considerable amount of unemployment, mostly of unskilled labourers, but simply that the skills and/or desires of the unemployed will not be matched by the opportunities of the job market.

Weather modification, still only on the horizon, would make possible a control of the environment men have dreamed of for millenniums. However, the futurologists' view is that the working out of the economic and social arrangements would pose some difficult problems for human civilization.

In reaching this point I agree that a critical examination of science and technology is in order. We are asking whether our scientific and technological endeavours are sufficiently focused on solving the problems facing society today and tomorrow and whether we are sufficiently alert to the possible dangers to society inherent in some technological advances.

The second source of change evidenced by the most developed countries — as exemplified by the United States — is the wider dissemination of existing goods and privileges throughout society. This is indeed the realization of the promise of equality. What the few have today, the many will demand tomorrow. Thus wrote Alexis de Tocqueville in his summation of American democracy (*De la Démocratic en Amérique*). What this French liberal politician and writer said in 1935 can be said now about the HAVE and HAVE-NOT countries. The underdeveloped world, stirred by the conviction that poverty is a scourge that can be eliminated from the face of the planet, refuses to accept its fate and defends its right to a decent, healthy prosperous life.

A third source of change involves structural developments in society. These changes have been excellently described by John Kenneth Galbraith in his *Affluent Society* (1958), but more emphatically in his *The New Industrial State* (1967).

In the most advanced countries the weight of the economy has shifted from the production sector to services; more important, the sources of innovation are becoming lodged in the intellectual institutions, principally the universities and research organizations, rather than in the older, industrial corporations. As Daniel Bell says, "the consequences of such a change are enormous for the modes of access to place and privilege in society. They make the universities the 'gatekeepers' of society. They make more urgent the husbanding of 'human capital' rather than financial capital, and they raise crucial sociological questions about the relationship of the new technetronic modes of decision making to the political structures of society."

Finally, the fourth source of change — a very important and perhaps the most important one, but unfortunately the most refractory to prediction — is the future behaviour of the two super-powers and the evolution of their respective relationships between themselves and with the rest of the world.

The problem of *détente* in a nuclear age, the widening gap between rich and poor nations, the threatening role of "colour" as a divisive political force, the re-emergence of narrow nationalism; the possible emergence of China as a third super-power, as well as the changing balance of forces — both technological and moral — are all questions that reach from the present into the distant future.

5. Biological Revolution

Mankind is on the threshold of a unique revolution — a biological revolution that, together with the current biological assault on the environment, requires a unique solution.

Just as physics and chemistry did in the past hundred years, biology will steadily bring about a totally new pattern of existence. Whether it will be a happier and more satisfying pattern is by no means obvious, and it is not even clear whether society, in its present form can survive the strains which will be imposed.

A number of scholars of repute, from various cultures and civilizations, are "seriously doubtful as to whether mankind will last more than one century". Aside from the nuclear threat, there is widespread suicidal pollution affecting the air we breath, the water we drink and the land we till, for which our whole technology is to blame. Superimposed on these stresses, the social stresses created by the new biology may prove a sizeable final straw. Of course, many other scholars of equal repute dismiss these Cassandra's voices.

Eugenic and genetic manipulation will possibly be one of the most controversial aspects of the biological revolution. Geneticists are so confident of being able to tamper with heredity that they have begun to warn us to beware of them.

Artificial insemination; extended use of contraceptive devices; legality of abortion and/or sterilization; control of the sex of unborn babies; decrease in numbers of defective children because of genetic intervention before birth — all these are practically already with us.

In the field of ageing, gerontologists foresee both an extension of the lifespan through organ transplants and regeneration, and the preservation of a degree of youthful vigour into old age.

Neurologists and others are exploring the brain, and already hint at raising the level of intelligence, at improving memory, and the control of human instincts, behaviour, drives, emotions as well as physical and psychological characteristics by means of "genetical engineering".

Biochemists have seriously proposed an attempt to synthesize lower forms of life from inorganic materials. All these so-called "advances" will have profound ethical, ecological and social implications.

There will also be noisy debate about the ethical connotations of our individual right to live as well as the right to die with dignity. This has to do with the use and abuse of experimentation with hospital patients. New attempts will be made to solve problems in the largely unexplored field of psychosomatic disease, as well as the question of a clinically precise and both ethically and legally acceptable determination of death.

Some biologists have even prepared a list ranging the "achievements" and possibilities of biology into three groups: Discoveries which are going to affect us within the next 5 to 10 years, if they have not already begun to do so; those which should become practicable within some 50 years; and those which are more remote.

The group which affects all of us (Phase One — by 1975) and on which no delay can be brooked, includes, in addition to transplantation techniques, parthenogenetic birth, prolonged storage of human eggs and spermatozoa, arrested death, choice of sex of offspring, and the mind-conditioning or mind-modifying drugs. Surely enough to cope with.

In Phase Two (by 2000) it is forecast that we shall see (I am not included in the "we") all these problems become more acute, with hibernation and arrested death for prolonged periods; unlimited transplantation possibilities with the problem of rejection solved; and a very wide range of mind-modifying techniques, not only drugs but electric effects, imperceptible odours, gases and the like. If the artificial placenta has not been perfected in Phase One, it now will be, and naturally produced offspring will be brought to term on it. In addition, we shall see the start of life-copying. Living organisms will be produced, putting together units of life derived mainly from breaking down living systems; into these organisms a steadily increasing proportion of fully synthesized material will be incorporated. An impact will be made on the problem of prolonging youthful vigour. The first cloned animals will be produced.

Not until Phase Three (well after 2000) can we expect synthesis of living beings from abiotic or inorganic material, in the same way as that in which primeval life started on our planet; the control of ageing or keeping alive a whole, disembodied human brain would also be achieved.

All these experiments should reach fruition, unless war or politics or disaster drastically change the present curve of development, within the lifetime of those now young, and a few of those who are not so young.

I suspect that the immediate reaction of many people to such forecasts is that, if not downright impossible, they lie so far in the future as to be of no practical importance to people now living. Nothing could be further from the truth. While some of the possibilities hinted at by biologists may lie — as I have already said — a century or more in the future, it is certain that much of what they are doing will begin to bear fruit in the lifetime of most now living.

The burning question is: Who will guide those who claim to possess the scientific skills needed to steer mankind?

The dangers involved in the scientific advances so far quoted were discussed at the beginning of November during a week-long conference on the biological revolution and its technical fall-out, organized by the Centre for the Study of Democratic Institutions, an independent American educational body in Santa Barbara, California.

At that meeting, most of the criticism was addressed to the medical profession at large or its failure to meet or even discuss the proliferation of the new moral problems it was facing. "We simply have an absolute void in the whole area of medical ethics", said Dr. Michael Scriven, Professor of Philosophy at the University of California. Several calls have been made for a law to protect people from science and technology. A group of American scholars have suggested — for America at least — that the Constitution should be amended, if not completely rewritten, to encompass an "environmental Bill of Rights". This would be designated to ensure an individual's right to a *livable* environment and his right to individuality and identity. It should enable him to prevent any action which would adversely affect the environment and also guard him against the threat of genetic or other bodily interference that would challenge his individual integrity.

6. Impact on Human Societies

Bell has admirably summarized the impact of foreseen changes in the society of the future and on the kinds of social arrangements that can deal adequately with the problems humanity will confront in the eighties and beyond. Although his remarks refer to the United States, many of his "predictions" could be applied to other advanced countries.

John Fischer, under the heading "Planning for the Second America" in the November issue of *Harper's Magazine,* commenting on the same theme, says that "within the next thirty years, the U.S. can expect to double the physical plant of all its cities. To take care of the predicted growth of population it needs to build a new house, school and office building for every one that now exists. It will need twice as many parking lots, universities, bus lines, jails, garbage dumps, airports, and bars. For the number of Americans will almost certainly rise from about 200 million to 300 million before the end of the century; and virtually all of the new people will live in cities. . . . What our forebears did in 300 years, we have to do (continues Fischer) in 30. Such is the inescapable arithmetic of the population explosion." One can build and rebuild cities only by making long-range plans and commitments.

Have you ever thought of the Nicosia of the future?

Bell, from whom I draw extensively, predicts that the problems of social choice and individual values, that is, the question of how to reconcile conflicting individual desires through the political mechanism rather than the market, becomes a potential source of discord. He believes that the relationship of the individual to bureaucratic structures will be subject to greater strain. The increasing centralization of government creates the need for new social forms that will allow citizens greater participation in the process of decision-making. The growth of a large, educated professional and technical class, with its desire for greater autonomy in work, will force institutions to reorganize older bureaucratic patterns of hierarchy and detailed specialization.

The individual will live longer and face — as he grows older — the problem of renewed education and new careers. Academic titles and diplomas will have limited validity, particularly in Medicine, Physics, Electronics, Engineering, etc., restricted — like a passport, for instance — to, say, 5 years. Retooling and re-education through refresher courses will be compulsory.

In this respect Brzezinski states that "the expansion of knowledge and the entry into socio-economic life of the intellectual community has the further effect of making education an almost continuous process. By 1980, not only will approximately two-thirds of the United States urban dwellers be college-trained but it is almost certain that systematic 'élite re-training' will be standard in the political system. It will be normal for every high official both to be engaged in almost continuous absorption of new techniques and knowledge, and to take periodic retraining. Otherwise, it will not be possible either to keep up with, or absorb, the new knowledge."

If the word "absorb" is replaced by "assimilate", I would endorse that view. This is because it is not the knowledge absorbed but the knowledge assimilated which counts. Absorption, although a prerequisite, does not necessarily imply total or even partial assimilation.

The family as a source of primordial attachment may become less important for the child in both his early schooling and his emotional reinforcement.

The world of the eighties will be a more mobile and more crowded world, raising problems of privacy and stress. The new densities and "communications overload" may increase the potentiality for irrational outbursts of violence and crime.

7. Final Comments

The problems confronting the future decade and beyond are enormous both in complexity and dimension. They are also enormous in their importance to the present and the future economic and political stability of the world — as well as in their prime importance to human welfare.

Those which are purely physical problems, problems of science, engineering and technology, as well as those which are economic in character, can and will be solved. Of this we can be reasonably certain.

However, these physical problems carry with them sociological, political and cultural problems which are even more staggering, more difficult to identify, more nearly impossible to quantify and, perhaps, more drastic in their effect on our civilization. There is not now, at least not yet, a basis for an equal faith that their solution can or will be found.

Selected Bibliography on the "Future"

AMERICAN ACADEMY OF ARTS AND SCIENCES (1967) "Towards the Year 2000: Work in Progress" *Daedalus,* summer edition.[1]

ARMYTAGE, W. H. G. (1968) *Yesterday's Tomorrows.* Routledge & Kegan Paul, England.

AYRES, R. U. (1966) "On Technological Forecasting". In *Selected Papers from the Hudson Institute, USA.*

BELL, D. (1966) *"Twelve Modes of Prediction."* *Daedalus,* American Academy of Arts & Sciences, USA.

BELL, D. (1967) "Notes on the Post-Industrial Society", *The Public Interest,* Nos. 6 and 7.

BELL, D. (1968) "The Year 2000" *Dialogue,* Vol. 1, No. 1, US Information Agency, Washington, DC.

BISHOP, J. and DAVID, D. M. (1966) *New Horizons in Medicine.* Dow Jones & Co., New York.

BLOOMFIELD, L. P. (1967) *Western Europe to the Mid-Seventies: Five Scenarios.* MIT, Cambridge, Massachusetts.

BOULDING, K. (1960) "Expecting the Unexpected." In *Prospective Changes in Society by 1980.*

BRADY, N. C. (1967) *Agriculture and the Quality of our Environment.* American Association for the Advancement of Science Symposium Volumes, No. 85, pp. 467, Washington, DC.

BRZEZINSKI, Z. K. (1968) "America in the Technetronic Age." *Encounter,* Vol. XXX, No. 1, pp. 16-26, London.

BUCHAN, A. (Ed.) (1969) *Europe's Futures, Europe's Choices — Models for Western Europe in the 1970's.* The Institute for Strategic Studies, pp. 167. Chatto & Windus, London.

CALDER, N. (Ed.) (1965) *The World in 1984.* The Complete New Scientist Series, 2 vols. Penguin Books, Harmondsworth, England.

DE JOUVENEL, B. (Ed.) (1963, 1965) *Futuribles. Studies in Conjecture,* Vols. I and II Droz, Geneva.

DE JOUVENEL, B. (1968) *Arcadie, Essais sur le Mieux Vivre.* Futuribles, S.E.D.E.I.S., Paris.

GALBRAITH, J. K. (1967) *The new Industrial State,* pp. 427. Houghton Miffling Co., Boston.

HAEFELE, W. (1968) "The International Implications of Modern Technology." *NATO's Fifteen Nations,* Vol. 12, No. 6.

KAHN, H. (1966) "On Alternative World Futures." In *Selected Papers from the Hudson Institute, USA.*

KAHN, H. and WIENER, A. J. (1967) *The Year 2000. A Framework for Speculation on Next Thirty-Three Years,* 431 pp. The Macmillan Co., New York, and Collier-Macmillan Ltd.

KRECH, D. (1966) "Controlling the Mind Controllers." *Think Magazine,* July-August issues. IBM, USA.

MINSKY, M. (1966) "Artificial Intelligence." *Scientific American,* New York.

PARFITT, T. (1969) "Agriculture 1980" *The World Today,* April issue, pp. 178-184. Chatham House, London.

PREHODA, R. (1967) *Designing the Future. The Role of Technological Forecasting.* Chilton Books.

SCHMEK, H. M. Jr., (1965) *The Semi-Artificial Man.* Walker & Co., New York.

SCHONFIELD, A. (1969) "Thinking about the Future." *Encounter,* Vol. XXXIII, No. 2, pp. 15-26, London.

SOROKIN, P. A. (1962) *Social and Cultural Dynamics,* 2 vols. Bedminster Press, New York.

TAYLOR, G. R. (1968) *The Biological Time Bomb,* 240 pp. The World Publishing Co., New York.

WESTIN, A. (1966) "Science, Privacy and Freedom: Issues and Prospects for the 1970's." *Columbia Law Review,* June and November issues, pp. 1003-1050 and 1205-1253.

YOUNG, M. (Ed.) (1968) *Forecasting and the Social Sciences.* Heinemann, London.

---

[1]This Summer 1967 issue of *Daedalus,* the magazine of the American Academy of Arts and Sciences, is devoted entirely to "Towards the Year 2000: Work in Progress". The introduction by Professor Daniel Bell, Chairman of the American Academy's Commission of the year 2000, summarizes some of the principal literature on the subject.

Annex I

Table of developments

The dates are those of technical achievement, not of general availability, which depends on social and economic considerations.

Phase One: by 1975

> Extensive transplantation of limbs and organs
> Test-tube fertilization of human eggs
> Implantation of fertilized eggs in womb
> Indefinite storage of eggs and spermatozoa
> Choice of sex of offspring
> Extensive power to postpone clinical death
> Mind-modifying drugs: regulation of desire
> Memory erasure
> Imperfect artificial placenta
> Artificial viruses

Phase Two: by 2000

> Extensive mind modification and personality reconstruction
> Enhancement of intelligence in men and animals
> Memory injection and memory editing
> Perfected artificial placenta and true baby-factory
> Life-copying: reconstructed organisms
> Hibernation and prolonged coma
> Prolongation of youthful vigour
> First cloned animals
> Synthesis of unicellular organisms
> Organ regeneration
> Man–animal chimeras

Phase Three: after 2000

> Control of ageing: extension of life span
> Synthesis of complex living organisms
> Disembodied brains
> Brain–computer links
> Gene insertion and deletion
> Cloned people
> Brain–brain links
> Man–machine chimeras
> Indefinite postponement of death

10

The Frugality Society:
A Future Design for the First World

BART VAN STEENBERGEN
The Netherlands

Introduction

In this paper a vision is developed of the future of the first world. This may sound strange in a time like ours when much emphasis is laid on a *global* perspective. One might query the need to divide the world into a first, second and third and (for some) even a fourth one. Are we not living in one spaceship, earth?

In my opinion this disaggregation is legitimate if in the vision of that specific "world", the problems of the other "worlds" and of the globe as a totality are taken into account.

What do we mean by the first world? Different interpretations are possible in this respect, the broadest one being the industrialized non-communist world. My interpretation is somewhat narrower; I will define first world societies as welfare state societies, that is to say, societies which are "tamed" capitalistic in the economic sphere, democratic in the political sphere and which have a high level of collective social welfare. Within the first World — in my view — Northwestern Europe is most typical of this type of society. The other parts of the first world (North America, Japan, Southern Europe) differ in one way or another from the above described "ideal type", but all these parts have a tendency to develop in the direction of this kind of welfare state society.

This paper consists of four sections. In the first section a number of remarks are made on the title of the project: Alternative visions of desirable societies. In the second section I will describe three developments, one on a global level, one within the third world and one within the first world, which are essential for my vision or design as I prefer to call it. (In this paper the second world will not be under scrutiny). In the third section a design of the future of the first world is developed and finally in the fourth chapter a number of empirical trends and developments are described which point in the direction of this design.

I. Alternative visions of desirable societies

A few observations can be made about the title of the project "Alternative visions of desirable societies".

1. The word "vision" is used. In this respect we can talk about a revival of the utopian tradition. Sometimes other words are used like model, scenario, design and blueprint. Personally I prefer the word "design". It combines the somewhat "soft" utopian and vision dimension with a more systematic (and even scientific) approach, which is so typical for the model. The designer is like a social architect: creator, artist and scientist at the same time. He creates something new but he knows the limits within which he has to stay.

2. The word alternative refers to two things. In the first place it emphasizes something which is different not only from the present but also from the dominant trends. In the literature on scenarios a distinction is made between trend and contrast scenarios. The latter are in one way or another in contrast with the dominant trends, the main stream, the surprise-free future, etc. Alternative visions more resemble contrast scenarios than trend scenarios. Secondly, "alternative" in combination with "visions" refers to pluralism. It is not one alternative vision we are looking for, but a number of those visions, reflecting different ideological outlooks.

3. The word "desirable" may create problems, for one must ask, desirable for whom? We can distinguish at least three levels. In the first place within a society we are dealing with different groups of people, ideologies, etc. Some consider an egalitarian society desirable, others are strongly opposed to it. By means of vivid and open discussions and a democratic decision-making procedure, this problem can to some extent be solved (Habermas would call this a "herrschaftsfreier Dialog Mündiger Menschen".) Secondly, we are often confronted with the tension between the desires of individuals (and groups) and those of society as a whole. This may sound odd (how can a society have desires?). Let me give an example. From the point of view of the individual it is legitimate to have a vision of a desirable society in which everyone has a private car. However, in densely populated areas in particular, this would be highly undesirable from a societal point of view. This is an old problem, the tension between desirability on an individual and on a collective level. However, in my opinion, even this problem can be solved to some extent. The greatest tension, however, may not be within a certain society but between different societies. Society A may have a vision of a desirable future based upon a great deal of consensus between all members of that society and with a well-balanced give-and-take between individual and collective desires, preferences, etc., but this society may cause great damage to other societies, often without being aware of it (since I am not thinking primarily of an aggressive society like Hitler's Germany). Let me try to make my point clear. If we nowadays look at the utopian visions of the future of the first

world as written during the sixties, we are struck by the fact that everything seemed to be possible in that period. In some ways this may have been the happiest period in the history of mankind, because the material basis for the real welfare and well-being of society was present. At the same time, new social movements worked towards the realization of the old values of the French revolution: freedom, equality and brotherhood. Nobody in the first world sensed that their visions would in any way damage the development of other societies. One of the most interesting examples of such a vision in which everything seemed to be possible was Johan Galtung's post-revolutionary pluralist society based upon "individualism" and "horizontality" (I refer now to an earlier version written for a conference of futurists which took place in 1970 in Kyoto. Later versions have been considerably modified.) Galtung's desirable society offers the individual a maximum of variety and freedom of movement. In this society everyone has a guaranteed income and anyone is free to withdraw from a work relation. The line between work and leisure tends to disappear, education is free for anyone at any level at any time, politics is not a matter for professionals but should be brought back to the people, etc. Galtung's vision is to a great extent the vision of a society from the point of view of the individual. The individual would have a great life there. Whether this vision creates a desirable society is not certain. However, this tension between the desires of individuals and those of society as a whole probably can be solved. More problematic is the relationship with other societies. In many ways Galtung's society reminds me of the ancient Greek city-state in which the free citizen had much time to devote his energy to politics, art, philosophy, literature, education, etc. This was possible because the Greeks had slaves to do the hard work which was necessary to keep the (economic) system going. Nowadays we consider the institution of slavery as inhuman, but fortunately we are developing new slaves in the form of machines, computers, etc. Karl Marx already foresaw that industrialization and modern technology would solve the problem of scarcity and hard labour and that this would mean ultimately that the objective conditions would be created which would allow man to enter "the realm of freedom". (The main problem which still had to be solved was the abolition of obsolete socio-economic structures.) Almost all visions of desirable societies as developed for the first world during the sixties (and as mentioned before Galtung's pluralist society is one of the most interesting examples) are implicitly or explicitly based upon a highly industrialized, highly automated type of society. The machine has replaced the slave and this machine creates the necessary wealth to make it possible for human beings to travel around, spend much time on education, art, politics, personal relationships etc. Until the beginning of the seventies it was generally believed that the envisioned future of this rich and wealthy first world would not harm others. The historical meaning of the limit-to-growth message is that we may have to do here with a zero-sum-game, that is to say that since the production and absorption capacity of mother earth is limited a development of the first world in the direction of an even more automated and industrialized society is probably harmful to the third world and to the globe as a whole.

4. Finally the word "society". What interests us is how people will live with each other in the future. Excellent designs have been developed on the relationship between nations, states and societies. Richard Falk's book *A Study of Future Worlds* is an interesting example of that type of design. Here we are primarily (but not only) interested in the internal dimensions. What does such a desired society look like from the inside, how will people live, work, spend their free time, what values will they have, etc.

II. Three relevant developments

My vision of a desirable future for the first world is based upon three developments:

1. Whether we like it or not, the discussion on the future of the first world has entered a new stage since the limits-to-growth report. The message of this report and similar ones is clear: mother earth has limitations both in her production and absorption capacities and this must influence the economic policy of the first world in particular, since this is the part of world society which is to a great extent responsible for this explosive situation. It means that in one way or another, the first world will be forced to limit its material growth. How much it should limit its growth is a matter of debate.

2. Concerning the relationship between the first and the third world the following alternatives can be described: the traditional (and still prevailing) relationship is one of the economic dominance of the first world over the third one. Recently two new relationships models have been discussed, in particular in the context of the New International Economic Order.

The first one can be described as the *interdependence* model. A good example is the RIO (Reshaping the International Order) report. This model is based upon an international division of labour, that is to say, the advanced, capital-intensive industries will be concentrated in the first (and second) world, the labour-intensive production (agriculture and some industrial sectors like textile) will be concentrated in the third world. According to Tinbergen this is a non-zero-sum game, that is to say it is in the best interest not only of the poor but also (in the long run) of the rich countries. This model means an increase in international trade (and in particular North–South trade), and is based upon a form of global Keynesianism.

The second model can be described as the independence model. The participation of the third world countries in a global market with international agreements and some form of indicative planning may be acceptable in a first phase of the New International Economic Order period. Some experts, however, foresee in a not too distant future a second phase in this process of economic emancipation. In this phase a number of third world countries will break through this global interdependence model, by emphasizing their national and regional self-reliance.

This will have the following results:
— the third world countries will become primarily interested in the fulfilment of the (basic) needs of their own population;
— there will be less emphasis on the cultivation of export products like coffee, tea, tobacco, sugar, bananas, etc., and more on the cultivation of rice, wheat, corn, etc., for internal use;
— there will be less interest in the exploitation of minerals and other resources, since most of these resources are mainly for export to the rich countries and rather irrelevant to the fulfilment of basic needs.
— there will be less interest in an international division of labour. For the first world this would mean that one could count less on the import of food, minerals (and other resources) and industrial products from the third world countries. The first world also will have to be self-reliant to some extent.

3. To develop a vision of the future of a society based only upon the external pressures on that society is not a very rewarding task. It would be extremely difficult if not impossible to convince the members of a society that from then on "frugality" would be the watchword if it was generally felt that this watchword was forced upon them by outsiders. The second problem connected with this watchword is that frugality for most people has a somewhat negative connotation. If external pressures pointed in the direction of an increase of wealth, this would be more acceptable. So if it were true that frugality is the result of external forces alone and is disliked by everybody, we might have to give up. However, this is not the case. There are tendencies, forces, developments and movements within the first world countries which point in the direction of a growing criticism of material growth. If we make a distinction between the concepts of welfare and well-being, whereby welfare refers to material wealth and well-being to a more general existential feeling of harmony with oneself and with the surrounding social and natural environment, the traditional view was that these two go hand in hand, that is say that increased welfare is not only a necessary but also almost a sufficient condition for well-being. There was never any disagreement between liberals and socialists on this point. Marxists also believed (and still believe) that the realm of freedom (well-being) is based upon material abundance. It is fair to say that until recently welfare and well-being were linked together, for, in order to have well-being, poverty had to be abolished, the basic needs had to be fulfilled and society had to be wealthy enough to permit more leisure, to make an extended social security system possible, to pay for the (from an economic point of view) non-productive groups in our society, etc. In short no well-being without welfare.

However, here we face a dialectical turning point since there is increasing awareness that more wealth is not promoting well-being, but on the contrary is becoming "counter-productive". Some of the values which are nowadays often associated with well-being like human scale, self-determination, ecological awareness and personal growth, are explicitly threatened by more welfare. If we look for a material value which is congruent with the above-mentioned values it would be something like material simplicity, that is to say, "a non-consumerist life style based upon being and becoming and not having" to use the definition of the American Friends Service Committee.

In this context the concept of over-development is enlightening. In many ways the development of the first world has led to a form of over-development in a number of areas, that is to say that this development by its one-sidedness, its emphasis on material growth has suppressed the development of other elements of our culture. To give an example, the welfare state has created huge institutions in the field of schooling, health, social security, etc. Originally these institutions were meant to abolish ignorance, illness, poverty and social insecurity. Supported by economic growth these institutions could flourish to such an extent that they become over-developed and a threat to other (more informal) social institutions. Our modern health system is a good example of over-development. It does not make our society more healthy any longer, and as Illich has pointed out, it has also suppressed other social institutions in this field through its monopolistic position. The notion of "self-help" (as an individual or as a group, neighbourhood, community, etc.) has disappeared, and other modes of medical treatment have not had a chance to develop. Moreover, a great deal of the activities in the field of health care, but also of social welfare, can be described as curative, that is to say, first, society makes people sick, helpless, alienated, dependent, etc., and then builds institutions to cure them.

III. The frugality society

In this section a picture will be drawn of my vision of a desirable (first world) society. As a sort of general "leitmotiv" the following phrase is used: "outwardly simple and inwardly rich". The founder of Walden, Henry David Thoreau, formulates it even more strongly when he says: "Most of the luxuries and many of the so-called comforts of life are not only not indispensable but positive hindrances to the elevation of mankind." In this chapter we shall describe the general economic, political and socio-cultural characteristics of this frugality society as well as its place in the global scene.

1. General characteristics

This design is based upon two basic elements.

The first basic element is: frugality on the material level. In many respects this society is a negation of the industrial society in which we are now living. This shift towards frugality is partly the result of external pressures as described in the preceding chapter, and partly the outcome of a shift in the orientation of values within the first world.

The second basic element is: a more equal and just distribution of material wealth. On a global level this means a floor, a social minimum, or — as the Bariloche research group has formulated: a decent standard of living for the poor countries, or better, for the poor in the poor countries, and at the same time a (material) ceiling, a maximum for the rich countries (and in particular for the rich in the rich countries). Within the first world it means among other things a drastic income redistribution. A frugal society is not only ethically unacceptable but also politically unfeasible if this new scarcity is not distributed in a more just and equal way.

2. Place in the global system

This design is based upon a regional self-reliance model. That is to say that the different regions are to a great extent independent and self-sufficient. There will be much less international division of labour as proposed in the R.I.O. report (the interdependent model). The first world can no longer count on the import of food products, raw materials and (labour-intensive) industrial products from the third world.

3. The socio-economic structure

3.1. Economic growth. One of the starting points of this design is negative (material) growth until a new balance has been reached; the balance of the sustainable society. It is difficult to say what exactly the material level of a sustainable society is. This is partly a matter for more research, partly a matter for political discussion, but for the time being we assume a level which is considerably lower than in most welfare states nowadays.

Recently there has been discussion about "zero-growth". In some respects this design is more radical, since we are proposing a negative growth. On the other hand we refer to a negative material growth which is not the same as the GNP, although we may assume that in our design the GNP will also go down.

Secondly, this negative growth is an average, since we are concerned here with selective (non) growth. Some parts of the economy will have a strong negative growth rate, but others may remain at the present level or even grow (see the paragraph on work). The criteria are such that in general:
— the more a product is considered a luxury product, the less its growth;
— the more the production and the consumption of certain goods (and services) make use of scarce resources, damage the environment, etc., the less growth in that sector.

It is often argued that in such an economy the entrepreneur (or the manager) would have no incentives, would not be motivated to work hard for his enterprise. However, as indicated, not all sectors will have a negative growth. Moreover, a number of enterprises will be socialized. Most importantly, however, there will be new incentives; challenges for the entrepreneur in the field of recycling, social benefits, a frugal way of dealing with scarce means, etc. It is true that an entrepreneur needs a challenge; it is a myth that the only challenges he is interested in are growth and profit.

3.2. Market or planned economy? The economic production system will be based upon new goals. Traditional goals like profit and the expansion of the enterprise will move back stage. The following are the new goals:
— production should fulfil the real needs of the population;
— production has to be ecologically sound;
— production should be economical in its use of scarce means (energy, etc.).

It is clear that these goals cannot be reached in the context of a market economy. So some forms of central guidance (by national and/or regional governments) and of planning will be necessary. In particular those economic areas which are related to basic needs, those which are dangerous for the environment and those which use a disproportionate amount of scarce resources, will be socialized, that is to say, brought under public control. Socialization may mean "nationalization" but also "localization" and "regionalization", depending on the level which can best serve the public interest.

In addition to this the remaining "free" sector will be subjected to a number of restrictions. This can be done by means of negative sanctions (all sorts of prohibition orders) but also (and preferably) by positive sanctions like subsidies for those companies that apply themselves to recycling, alternative sources of energy, a frugal and small-scale production, etc.

Here we may have to do with some contradictory elements in the design. On the one hand, we need a strong central guidance and planning system, in particular in the transition phase, since the internal dynamics of the market system will not move the economy quickly enough in the direction of negative growth. It is possible that the price mechanism — in the long run — will point in the direction of a frugal society (scarce means will become very expensive), but this mechanism always works at the expense of the poor, the powerless and the weak both in terms of people and societies. But on the other hand, as will be shown later, this design is to a great extent based upon decentralization, small-scale units etc. So we face here a tension between centralization and decentralization. An attempt to solve this problem would point in the direction of a basic needs sector which will be centrally planned and guided and put under public control, and more decentralization in other areas, with more room for private initiative also.

3.3. Work and technology. The position of work in this design is different from most future designs for the first world. During the sixties most futurists predicted the emergence of a leisure society, and nobody seemed to care any longer about the problems of work. This changed drastically during the seventies when the first world countries were suddenly confronted with unemployment. Moreover, this unemployment seemed to be a structural (and not a temporal) phenomenon, that is to say, it is caused by a process of automation or in general by the development of modern technology. In short this work presents two types of problems:

The first has to do with full employment. In most industrialized Western countries this is an official goal of socio-economic policy. However, nowadays one hears an increasing number of people saying that in an age of automation we should abandon this goal. This means that one can distinguish between those who have a positive and those who have a negative attitude towards full employment. The second problem area lies in the relationship between work, capital and technology. During the last centuries technology has become more and more automated, capital intensive and labour extensive. Should this process be allowed to continue in the future, that is to say do we have a positive attitude towards this type of capital intensive and labour expelling production or not? If we combine these two problem fields we get the following picture:

		Labour *extensive*/Capital *intensive* production	
		Positive	Negative
Full employment	Positive	A	B
	Negative	C	D

On the basis of this we can develop four (alternative) scenarios.

Scenario A is in fact a trend scenario. It represents the dominant trends of the socio-economic policy in most industrialized countries. Since this policy promotes both full employment and automation it is primarily concerned with the creation of new jobs.

Scenario B accepts full employment as a goal, since it is convinced that work gives a meaning to life, but it is to some extent opposed to modern technology.

Scenario C has a positive attitude towards automation, modern technology, etc., but is prepared to give up full employment. There will be less work for man in the future. We should not (artificially) try to create more jobs but we should all work less, that is to say, divide the remaining amount of work more equally.

Scenario D is the scenario presenting the most extreme contrast since it challenges two pillars of our modern society; full employment as well as capital intensive production based upon modern technology. It presupposes a somewhat non-materially oriented ethos.

What is apparent nowadays is that Scenario A combined with elements of C forms the main trend and the most acceptable alternative. Our design, however, is based upon Scenario B and to a lesser extent Scenario D.

This means in the first place that we do not accept a further development of labour expelling technology. Technology should be a servant to society and not its master, that is to say that in a society in which work becomes scarce, we are not in favour of promoting this type of technology. Moreover, work is not only a means of acquiring an income but also gives meaning to one's life in one's particular job is considered meaningful both for the individual and for society. Moreover, this process towards less automation and a more labour-intensive production in the first world is a necessity for reasons of pollution, environmental damage, the limitation on growth, resource depletion, etc. On the other hand, we do not want to go back to an earlier stage of the industrial revolution. A more labour-intensive production is only acceptable if it goes hand in hand with creative and meaningful jobs. More important than full employment is employment of full value. So a de-automation process should be planned in such a way that the new vacant jobs promote human creativity. In those sectors where de-automation creates unpleasant, dull, monotonous jobs, this process should be restricted. In short, one can say that this type of society is based more upon crafts. It means a revival of the artisan.

3.4. Consumption. There will be a new consumption ethos and a non-consumerist life style. Some characteristics of this life style are:
— The consumption goods one buys promote activity, self-reliance and involvement.
— The consumption pattern should be devoted to the fulfilment of one's real needs. One is more or less immune to pressures from the outside to buy things (advertisements).
— The individual considers the impact of his consumption pattern on other people and on the earth.
— The "throw-it-away" principle is rejected and there is much emphasis on do-it-yourself and on a healthy life-style.

Although living simply implies consuming quantitatively less, it should not be equated with living cheaply. The handcrafted, durable aesthetically-pleasing products that appeal to frugal consumers are more expensive than mass-produced items. The durability of products is very important, also the fact that they will be used until they are worn out. Quickly changing fashions will be less important. Secondhand shops, auctions and repair shops will flourish. The emphasis on a healthy life style will create a different vacation pattern (the bicycle and the tent will replace the bungalow and the car) and a different food pattern. The vegetable garden will replace the lawn, small-scale bio-dynamics farms where no pesticides are used will emerge, health food shops and restaurants (reform, bio-dynamic, etc.) will to some extent replace the supermarkets. There will be more awareness of the serious global food problems which will lead towards a moderate form of vegetarianism. The use of stimulants (tobacco, coffee) will decrease, partly because these products will be imported less (the third world countries will use their cultivated land primarily for basic needs products like wheat and rice) partly because this does not fit into a healthy life style. There will be one exception, the interest in good wines will increase.

Needless to say, energy-consuming products like dishwashers and electric toothbrushers will slowly disappear. Other machines more necessary for the household (like the refrigerator, the freezer and the washing machine) will be made more durable, used more collectively and repaired (not thrown away) if possible. Here we may face a conflict with the emancipation of women. In our present-day society the emancipation of women is strongly linked to the possibility of having a job outside the house and this is only possible in an automated household. It is clear that in our future society the household will demand more time than nowadays (fewer machines, more repair work, more do-it-yourself activities, the care of the vegetable garden, etc.). So this might be a step backwards in the process of the emancipation of women. However, in our design we assume that this emancipation process takes a step forward, that is to say that these household tasks will be divided equally between the different members of the small unit (the nuclear family, the extended family, the commune, etc.). Nevertheless this is a problem one should be aware of.

3.5. The redistribution of wealth. A society in which material growth will be negative for some time is only acceptable if at the same time the new scarcity is distributed more equally. There are several possibilities:

(a) A redistribution of incomes in such a way that there will be a maximum income. At the same time the minimum income existing in most welfare states will remain at the present level or even increase somewhat. There will be no complete levelling; the maximum net income will be something like four times the minimum income. In addition to this, new criteria for the distribution of income will be developed. Income according to need will not be a dominant criterium (however, it will be more important than nowadays). Society is simply not rich enough for this, although there will be a (rather small) guaranteed income for everybody.

(b) In addition to income redistribution, there will be a distribution system of certain consumption goods. This distribution system will be under public control, which makes it somewhat independent from the price mechanism. Such a distribution system has two advantages:

1. It can promote a policy of frugality where scarce means are concerned.
2. It is an instrument to promote a just distribution throughout the population. In particular basic needs can be fulfilled on a low price basis.

An example. Each individual (or small unit) has a non-transferable energy card. This energy card is based upon two principles:

(a) the more energy one uses, the more expensive the unit;
(b) there is a maximum (a ceiling) for the different energy-consuming activities (private transport, public transport, heating, etc.) expressed in petrol, oil, miles, etc.

There is some room for manoeuvre, which means that somebody who travels a lot by plane and exceeds his maximum allowance will not have to freeze in winter without heat or hot showers. In order to make a just distribution system every individual (unit) receives a free or very cheap basic amount.

This distribution system may have two possible so-called unintended consequences:

(a) a gigantic black market (a negative consequence);
(b) a preventive effect in the sense of an energy-saving life style. One saves energy just as one saves up money in the bank, in order to be able to use more of it later (to make that plane trip to Mexico, for example).

4. The political structure

In addition to what has been said in section 3.2 we come up here against a possible internal contradiction in the design. All the above-mentioned characteristics of the socio-economic structure require a strong government on a national and/or regional level, since these developments will not take place in a natural way, that is to say through a price mechanism or a market system. On the other hand, this design is to some extent based upon decentralization, that is to say the basic units are relatively small and self reliant. The design is also a critique of (negation of) the modern welfare state in so far as that type of state has a tendency towards bureaucracy, giantism, technocracy, etc. We have no final solution for this fundamental problem, but a few remarks can be made:

(a) It is not necessary that the power of the state should increase on all levels and in all areas. The national or regional government will be strong in fields related to energy, production and consumption, distribution, the environment, transport, agriculture and industry. In other areas like education, health and culture there will be more room for decentralization, that is to say more power for local governments and more room for private initiative.

(b) a strong government is acceptable if it is supplemented by a strong citizen, otherwise we will have to face the danger of a totalitarian state. This presupposes an emancipated and politically conscious citizen, who can be described as a "gesamtgesellschaftliches Subjekt" (Adorno), that is to say, a societal subject who is aware of the problems of his society as a whole and who is prepared to let his individual (or group) behaviour be guided by these problems. In our case it means a subject who has internalized the necessity for a frugal society and who makes this visible in his concrete behaviour. So on a general level there is a consensus between government and citizens on the basic principles, but at the same time we have to do with a citizen who permanently controls his government through formal democratic institutions like parliament, political parties, trade unions, etc., but also through civil disobedience, what the Germans call "Bürgerinitiative" (initiatives of the citizens, action groups, anticipatory experiments, etc.) in its concrete policy-making. Here again we may have to do with an internal tension in the design. This is mainly a time tension, since a day has only 24 hours. As indicated above, this society is not a leisure society, on the contrary people will have to work hard. At the same time they will be politically active and well-informed about national and international affairs. So, in short, this is a typical active society (Etzioni) with very little time for just sitting in the sun and doing nothing. Another solution is to abolish sleep.

5. The socio-cultural structure

5.1. Values and norms. As I have already mentioned before the "leitmotiv" of this design can be described as outwardly simple and inwardly rich. Under certain circumstances the increase of (material) welfare is a necessary prerequisite for the increase of (non-material) well-being. However, in the first world we are increasingly aware that the opposite is the case, which means that the increasing abundance is becoming a hindrance to a better society. In that sense frugality is not just a must because of external pressures (resource depletion, pollution, third world claims, etc.) but also a must if one wants to surpass the existing society which is based upon competition, self-interest, rugged individualism, etc.

We can distinguish seven values related to this "leitmotiv". These are:

1. Material simplicity. The American Friends Service Committee have for a long time led the way in demonstrating a life style of creative simplicity, which they define as a "non-consumerist life style based upon being and becoming, not having".

2. Ascetism combined with aesthetism. To some extent this non-consumerist life style is an ascetic life style but at the same time it is an aesthetic life style. Frugal consumers are interested in handcrafted and aesthetically enduring products.

3. Human scale. There is a preference for human-sized living and working environments, in other words "Small is beautiful". The smallness theme touches on many facets of life. It implies among other things that living and working environments should be decentralized as much as possible into more comprehensible and manageable entities. The gigantic scale of modern institutions and living environments creates anonymity, alienation and incomprehensibility. A reduction of scale is seen as a means of getting back to basics by restoring to life a more human sense of proportion and perspective. A potential danger of this value is that it leads to parochialism and/or a retreat from the "big bad world". This danger of parochialism can be decreased if we add:

4. Solidarity at a local, national, regional and global level. This means that there is only one race (the human race), only one earth (mother earth) of which we all are a part and for which we are responsible. This value presupposes political consciousness and a "gesamtgesellschaftliches Subjekt" as described above. This solidarity is also the basis for the acceptance of an economic system based upon frugality, the redistribution of income, etc.

5. Self-determination. This means being less dependent upon large complex institutions. An important aspect of this value is a tendency towards material self-sufficiency. For our frugality society it is relevant that a person may seek to grow his own, to make his own, to do without and to exercise self-discipline in his pattern and level of consumption, so that the degree of dependency (both physical and psychological) is reduced.

6. Ecological awareness. This refers to a new attitude of man towards nature. Nature is no longer something which can be exploited (the concept of the dominance of man over nature). This value emphasizes that man is part of nature, that he should live with nature and listen to nature, or to use the terminology of Marcuse: man should be in dialogue with nature.

7. Personal growth. The traditional Left (and even to some extent the New Left) has often neglected the more subjective and personal values such as the exploration of one's own life. In our vision the liberation of society should go hand in hand with the liberation of oneself. We must aim to free ourselves from overwhelming externals so as to provide the space in which to grow — both psychologically and spiritually.

5.2. Education. The Western educational system is mainly devoted to the promotion of cognitive and intellectual abilities. This is a reflection of our professional status hierarchy in which the university professor has the highest and the unskilled worker the lowest status. In this design we see a revaluation of craftwork. This means that within the educational system more emphasis will be placed on handwork, handicrafts, and the training of artisans, and that work in these fields will have higher status. Secondly, education will be less the monopoly of specific institutions, that is to say, the sharp dividing line between education and non-education will diminish. In this respect Illich's concept of "de-schooling society" is relevant for our design. The importance of the professional teacher and the school as an institution for educating people will decrease. The small unit and the place of work will have a more important educational function. Thirdly, there will be more emphasis on an all-round education, in which the rational and emotional, the cognitive and the intuitive, the intellectual and the artistic, the creative and the reproductive, the technical skill and the critical attitude will have an equal place in the educational process. Fourthly, an important function of education will be to encourage a political and societal consciousness.

5.3. Health. Here too the monopoly position of the institutionalized health service will diminish. In this design man is more conscious of his own body and more inclined to take care of himself (self-determination). There will be much emphasis on a healthy life style or, to use the expression of the ancient Romans, *mens sana in corpore sano.* Naturally there will be some form of institutionalized health-care system. This system will be characterized by:

— less emphasis on highly specialized medical technology (de-medicalization); there will be fewer specialists;
— more emphasis on simple medical centres, which are at the same time social centres for the community for social, psychic and somatic problems, information, instruction and advice, etc;
— more emphasis on prevention and on self-help.

IV. Societal support for a frugal society

A few words could be said on whether we here have to do with a pure utopia, or whether there are tendencies, developments, signals, movements, etc., in the present welfare state societies which point in the direction of a frugal society as described in the preceding chapter. We will describe more or less at random a few of these signals. Much more research needs to be done in this area. We will limit ourselves to internal tendencies and leave external pressures out.

1. In April 1977 the Harris bureau carried out a survey among a cross-section of the American population on questions related to economic growth. In his comment on the results Louis Harris writes: "The American people have begun to show a deep skepticism about the nation's capacity for unlimited economic growth and they are wary of the benefits that growth is supposed to bring. Significant majorities place a higher priority on improving human and social relationships and the quality of American life than on simply raising the standard of living." The survey was done in

such a way that people had to choose between two alternatives the US should place more emphasis on.

A few interesting results:

— By 79–17 per cent, the public would place greater emphasis on "teaching people how to live more with basic essentials" than on "reaching higher standards of living".

— By 66–22 per cent, the public would choose "breaking up big things and getting back to more humanized living" rather than "developing bigger and more efficient ways of doing things".

— By 59–26 per cent, a majority feels that inflation can better be controlled by "buying much less of those products short in supply and high in price", than by "producing more goods to satisfy demand".

— By 76–17 per cent a majority opts for "learning to get our pleasure out of non-material experiences", rather than "satisfying our needs for more goods and services".

Although each social scientist knows how much difference exists between the opinion of persons and their actual behaviour, these results are striking and show that there is a potential willingness to change direction in favour of a more frugal and non-material oriented society.

2. Concerning the question of a redistribution of income, with minimum and maximum limits, in my home country the Netherlands, as in most welfare states, a minimum income has already been in existence for some time. Two years ago the (former) Dutch government accepted the idea of a maximum net income of five times the minimum as an official policy in all areas the government can influence (mainly the collective sector).

3. Duane Elgin and Arnold Mitchell have done a study for the Business Intelligence Programme of the Stanford Research Institute on a recent American movement called the movement for a voluntary simplicity. The values of our design are influenced by this movement in particular. Elgin and Mitchell are very optimistic about the present size and growth potentials of this movement. They claim that nowadays some 4 to 5 million adults are voluntarily living according to a wholly simple life style that about twice as many are living simply in a partially voluntary way and that a very large group of one-third of the population sympathizes with the ideals of this movement. Within 10 years Elgin and Mitchell expect that 25 million Americans will be among the full and 35 million among the partially voluntary supporters of the simple life style.

In our view the empirical support for these figures (both in the present and in the future) is rather weak, but nevertheless it is interesting that the idea of a frugal society on a voluntary basis is spreading around.

4. In Western Europe a number of church groups (supported by the World Council of Churches in Geneva) is promoting the idea of a new style of life. This new life style refers to a different way of dealing with money, goods, the earth and people.

As far as I can judge we have to do here with a rather powerful social movement, which is effective in particular in the field of a different and more frugal consumption pattern (the Protestants and in particular the Calvinists may have been the founders of capitalism as a production system, but the necessity of an increasing consumption in order to keep that capitalistic sytem going has never appealed to them) and in the field of a growing awareness of the poverty and misery of the third world and the relationship between that misery and our abundance.

Naturally many more of these signals and indicators can be found, but these few are only meant as an illustration of the idea that the concept of a frugal society as an alternative for the first world is not a pure chimera.

PART II

11

Introduction

IAN MILES
Science Policy Research Unit, University of Sussex, UK

1. Introduction

This second meeting on "Visions of Desirable Societies" involved some twenty-five participants, about one-third of whom were women, and about two-thirds of whom came from Third World countries[1]. Both the constitution and content of the meeting reflected attempts to build upon the achievements, and to overcome some of the limitations, of the first meeting on this topic. In introducing the present meeting, *Eleonora Masini* reiterated the common aim of both meetings: the promotion of images of the future going beyond mere extrapolations to the identification of actions and actors that might help to bring about more desirable futures. Thus a focus on ends as well as means is required: one of the problems of the earlier meeting was that there had been a tendency to dismiss the question of processes of transformation from the present to the desirable future altogether. Further, while the visions presented had been of evolving societies, rather than static, "perfect" ones, and while there had been much concern with the possibility of diverse cultures co-existing in the future, there was some feeling that the discussion had been too dominated by Western perspectives, and, also, overemphasized criticism of the visions produced by established future research as compared to the development of original images of the future.

So the present meeting was explicitly designed so as to promote dialogue between researchers from very different backgrounds (and "dialogue of civilizations" was one of its themes) and to involve people active as change agents — especially inputs from members of oppressed groups (notably women) whose visions are not reflected in most futures studies, and whose experience of processes of (and obstacles to) change could be invaluable. Much of the discussion did indeed revolve around questions of the conditions for and outcomes of various types of change, and it rarely became an abstract confrontation between idealized futures. Of course, the presenta-

---

[1]Although not all of the papers of the 1979 meeting have been included, Ian Miles's summary has been left intact in order that the development of the meeting may be traced.

tions and discussions were not free of controversy and disagreement. While the liberation of the oppressed might have been shared as a stimulus and basis for developing visions, there was by no means agreement on what liberation can be and how it could be achieved.

This report deals with these issues, setting the main themes of the meeting. There is no attempt to summarize whole papers (which can be consulted in their printed form) nor is the account chronological. The specific work of the two working groups is omitted, too. Three broad areas of discussion will be outlined, each overlapping with the others (just as the subjects discussed interpenetrate). The first involves questions around the origin, development and use of visions. The second considers ways in which our contemporary situation conditions the creation of visions and their relations to action. And finally, problems associated with the transition from the world of the present to a more desirable future are taken up. Features of the desirable societies should be made sufficiently clear in the course of these three sections for a special section of this summary to delineate visions *per se* to be unnecessary.

2. Histories and visions

Visions of the future are constructed by real human beings using existing cultural material. Even impressions of immediate tendencies in the world of action and experience are themselves constructed. Far from being mere perceptual imprints on innocent minds, they also draw upon cultural themes. Is it possible, then, to identify the cultural sources used in existing visions of the future? To what extent, and when, do they present constraints on our visionary capacity? Do they also offer opportunities to infuse and activate visions with popular actions of social change? What is the role of individuals' skills and creativity in bringing visions to life?

Johan Galtung argued that two main sources of visionary material exist: the religious and escatological imagery of national cultures, and the goals and strategies developed in the liberation struggles of social classes. The discussion qualified both points. Religious imagery is not, of course, organized neatly within national borders (which are themselves by no means static), and it is itself shaped and reshaped as the social practices in which it is grounded change. Social classes are not the only sources of liberation struggles; while the role of classes is decisive, oppressed groups of various kinds may formulated distinctive visions complementing their distinctive struggles, while dominant classes (especially when first achieving power) may project their own utopias with limited relevance for the liberation of the masses. The extent to which the "national" source of material for visions is a product of the hegemony of dominant classes is a significant problem.

The main thrust of Galtung's presentation, however, was to attempt an assessment of the degree to which different religious systems in their portrayal of the afterlife and the implications for action in this world held to follow from their cosmologies. Very broadly speaking, he concluded that Occidental religions — the dominant forms of Christianity, Judaism, Islam — were less well suited than their Oriental counterparts — such as Hinduism, Buddhism, Confucianism, Taoism — to provide elements of liberatory images of the future. The hells and paradises of Western religions, in contrast with the more fluid afterlife images of Oriental systems, emphasize a static, completed future world rather than a dynamic process. This traditional Occidental view is of a static future process, exhaustive of alternative possibilities rather than co-existing with them, in which all contradictions have been removed supernaturally (e.g. by isolating heaven from hell). Being liable to inhibit thought about dynamic, unfolding futures with diverse societies co-existing, this provides a very limited source of visions of desirable futures. Galtung suggested that this matrix persists in secular Western thought about social change.

Taghi Farvar's presentation, however, indicated that Islam, at least, could be a source of visions radically different from those generally derived from the Koran. The strategy of the people's Mujhadeen in Iran, in particular, has been to relate their concept of what an Islamic Republic should be, to a reading of the Koran (and other sacred texts) that they claim to be *the* correct one, holding other readings to be class-biased. From the five basic principles of Shi'ite Islam, a system of laws supposed to apply to the whole universe is constructed. From these laws, assessments of the state of existing societies and the changes needed to achieve a society which would operate according to Allah's design can be outlined. In most respects the programmes of the Mujhadeen parallels those of Marxist–Leninist groups. Furthermore, their totalizing philosophy resembles the orthodox dialectical materialism of the 1930s — but this Islamic dialectic is one which takes complementarity, not contradiction, as primary.

In this world view, societies are seen as being, like other dynamic systems, composed of different parts which are related in mutuality (and not contradiction) and which tend to combine and integrate. Iranian intellectuals have been interested in systems theory, although in the First and Second worlds this typically lacks any revolutionary flavour. In the Mujhadeen view, class domination is a deviation superimposed upon this mutuality, and it can and should be expelled. Class struggle (and resistance to national dependency) is the attempt to restore a vital state whose mutual complementarity is restored, where "brotherhood" is restored. This is a holy striving for unity and wholeness, a dynamic force (expressed through the leadership of Imans). What is outlined here is by no means the predominant interpretation of Islam in Iran. While such ideas have not yet been actively suppressed — for their originators still exist as part of the power basis of the new régime — their impact is limited. For example, the Mujhadeen statement of the ideal characteristics of an Islamic republic in terms of freedom of religion, of ideas, democratic competition among Imans, equal access of all to productive forces, and other political and economic liberties is far from current state-building activities.

Whether Galtung's and Farvar's contributions are in contradiction remained an open question — Galtung, for example, regarded Shi'ism as a case of the penetration of "Eastern" orientations into a "Western" tradition (Sufiism would be another case of "Eastern" Islam). On the other hand, it seemed clear enough that, given the potential for reinterpreting religious documents and practices, we cannot be content with discussing "belief systems" in isolation from the specific social forces and relationships in which beliefs are articulated and reworked. The two papers dealing most explicitly with religion as a source of visions, then, need to be related to analyses of these factors.

The question was also raised as to whether any approach to political action holding up its programme as based on divinely revealed truth and all others as distortions of this truth really provides a basis for the demystification of ideologies (religious or otherwise). The parallel between general systems theory and religious totalisation — both starting from the idea as the source of truth — was raised again. Could an approach that shows that value-commitment — not divine or value-free reason — underpins social analysis have provided the Iranian people with intellectual tools adequate to appraise the emerging hegemony of the national bourgeoisie? If so, why was it not developed? Are there particular difficulties in developing such an approach, over and above those deriving from peoples being forced to express their needs through religious meetings and leaders in the face of massive repression of other forms of political action? Related to this, doubts were raised by *Ossorio Tafall* about the wisdom of abolishing the separation of religious and political power. He pointed out that this separation that has historically had emancipatory functions for the masses as well as for religious minorities, and the separation of power was cited by others as one of the positive — if partial — achievements of Western society.

Cora Shaw provided a panoramic view of some "non-occidental utopias", of visions deriving from ancient China (Confucianism, Taoism), Amazonia, (Tupi Indian mythology) and modern India (Gandhism) seeing these as presenting different models of future relationships between order and freedom. Confucianism suggested that virtuous societies would be constructed hierarchically around systems of rules, with rulers exercising power by virtue of intellectual capacity, while sharing their wealth and acting in the popular interest. Taoism seems to stress balance, avoiding gross action, and its classical thinkers emphasized the virtues of small-scale, isolated communities. The Gandhian vision, derived from Hinduism to a considerable extent, was likewise one of self-sufficient villages, united in a republic; elaborate technologies, which historically have been related to the centralization of socio-economic power, would be avoided. And the Topi people actually went on migrations in search of their ideal "land without evil" where a society of abundance and free of all coercive social relations was supposed to lie. Perhaps their magical quest is not so dissimilar from other attempts to discover utopias without identifying potential agents who might construct them!

It is apparent that the ways in which beliefs are produced from, and applied to, shaping the social world are complex ones. The role of existing character structures and social relations in conditioning the effects of new approaches (including new approaches to traditional material) needs investigation in concrete instances. For instance, *Corrine Kumar de Souza* found in her study of Gandhian projects in Gujarat that certain symbols from Gandhi's vision were practically all that continued to possess vitality. Running against the main course of Indian economic development, Gandhi's programme has been largely reduced to dogmatic vestiges. Thus, the particular tools he emphasised as component parts of a self-reliant strategy are proudly displayed; but their production and use is now actually embedded in a wider web of economic relations, increasing the dependency of villagers on powerful external organisations. *Juan Somavia* pointed, in turn, to the complexities of the relations between catholicism and antidemocratic forces in Latin America: drawing up a balance-sheet of the progressive and reactionary contributions of a given ideology is no substitute for understanding the particular roles of its different agents in changing circumstances.

Ashis Nandy led a discussion which followed on from his presentation at the first conference concerning the elements of a Third World Utopia. Two points in particular aroused comment. The first concerns the importance of developing "ideologies" (the term was in some dispute) which would not blind their adherents to what was being done in their name. Change agents should be able to apportion responsibility for the consequences of their actions and when necessary further develop their theoretical understanding rather than dismissing practical failures or bad consequences as aberrations or abuses of their "ideology". Citing the Vedas — "knowledge is that which frees" — Nandy raised the question of what would be necessary for a belief system to remain open, in the sense that its adherents could free themselves from irrational attachment to it. He also stressed again that a theory and practice of liberation must have a place in it for the "salvation" of the oppressor as well as the oppressed.

Controversy arose around Nandy's claim that he wished to abandon history as a way of diachronous thought, and use alternative systems — myths, epics — to deal with past times. He saw the idea of "history" as implying progress and justifying ethnocentric stances *vis à vis* destroyed or dominated cultures. Other speakers suggested that this involved ejecting one idea of history, a linear, deterministic one, but that other ideas might be useful. *Leopoldo Zea* suggested that different cultural areas might need to create their own histories as part of their struggle against domination. *Mihailo Markovic* quoted the aphorism that "we must wrest freedom from history", but argued that some notion of history was necessary to distinguish human production from natural processes: human history is qualitatively different from that of, for example, astronomical processes. This related to *Herb Addo*'s point: without some such concept of history, how are the values and visions of desirable societies to be forged?

3. Visions and the present

A number of presentations dealt with the conditions in which visions may now be created and used, with discussions ranging from the capacity of individuals to conceive of desirable futures in the present world to the structure of the world-system as prompting and inhibiting various visions. In general, the contributors showed an interest in identifying obstacles to our visionary capacities, and in suggesting ways of overcoming them.

Oscar Nudler set out to examine the relationships between a society's relation with the natural world, the typical state of human needs within such a society, and the prevalent consciousness of time corresponding to these. The model he derived has both implications for what would constitute a desirable future, and for what present factors inhibit visions of the same. On an individual, as well as on a societal level, needs constitute a system, not a bundle of fragmented drives; but this system need not be in equilibrium. Nudler suggested that in relatively undeveloped societies, where human life is dominated by natural forces, that particular types of needs (mainly subsistence needs) are emphasized and the development and expression of other needs impaired. Contemporary industrial societies, however, display a more depradatory orientation to nature and fragment daily life into separated spheres of activities (and age groups). They take this uneven development of needs even further constantly arousing and oversatisfying some needs while displacing other needs which are blocked. More desirable high-technology societies would establish a harmonious relationship with nature, and allow a fuller expression of human needs through a reintegration of the different spheres of social life.

Danilo Dolci's highly poetic presentation is hard to capture in this summary. It engaged with the questions taken up above in several ways. Dolci emphasized that creation depends upon desire, and that processes of growth involve the development of desires. By understanding that our desires are not necessarily bound within particular organs or bodies, but are communicable and transpersonal, we may move towards less hierarchical, less depradatory relationships with ourselves and with nature. This involves a new look at our assumptions about hierarchy in nature as in society and social thought. Typically, criticisms of the status quo are important in its own terms: the challenge is to transcend the hierarchical presuppositions of so many of our conceptual tools. *Eleonora Masini* related these contributions to visions: the need to create visions originates in the experience of suffering. In human development the freedom to be creative, and perhaps to let desires take shape beyond the linguistic constraints of everyday rationality, and to apply analytical and rational modes of thinking to matters of individual and collective needs, are both vital.

Nisar Aziz Butt, in contrast, discussing artists visions of the future as seen from Pakistan, brought to attention the ways in which suffering and the failure of ideals can inhibit visions. The creation of new alternatives in much of the Third World is hampered by the overwhelming examples of material production and consumption set by industrial societies, and by the ideological positions imported from the First and Second Worlds. Since artists from the industrial countries often wallow in their disillusion with the achievements of the Western idea of progress, it is difficult for Third World intellectuals to ignore these warning signals, even as they are battered by the wave of technological change from outside. *Magda Cordell McHale* was among those who felt that Western art and literature are not currently devoid of positive visions. Although she and her late husband had given up painting as a profession in order to focus on futures studies and other sorts of initiatives, she was optimistic about the possibilities of re-engagement in art and mass culture, and only too sorry that the possible futures of these areas of life had so far been rarely considered.

Other speakers took up the question of the ways in which the present world limited and restricted people's visions. *Leopoldo Zea* placed current interest in desirable futures in the context of the present world crisis, and the associated fears that existing patterns of growth were leading to disaster. Unlike earlier periods where there were upsurges in Utopian thinking, the present crisis is worldwide, and the Western-dominated world order was now facing the consequences of having paid for its successes at the expense of the Third World. The challenge was to formulate models of socialism corresponding to the societies of the Third World. *Juan Somavia* argued that an indispensable prerequisite for Latin American countries to move toward realising such models of social organisation was the re-establishment of democratic norms in the region. The insertion of these countries within a capitalist world system had earlier involved the transplanting of Western models of political organization to the Third World, but with recent increases in the rate of exploitation, more authoritarian régimes had been necessitated. The struggle for new visions in Latin America would involve conflict with the existing world order, in its cultural and ideological aspects as well as its economic organization. This was the significance of the slogan of collective self-reliance. *Carlos Moneta* pointed out that these problems were reflected in the social sciences in Latin America, which have found great difficulties in extricating themselves from the limitations which conventional (Western) social theory has placed upon visions.

From an Afro-Caribbean perspective, *Herb Addo* took up similar themes. The world is characterized as a single system, dominated by the motif of capital accumulation, resting fundamentally upon exploitation. While not every person or regional group is equally exploited or equally well placed to take action, there is nowhere the possibility of ignoring the barriers to progress placed by this world-system. What is required is that visions, then, imply means of linking alternative historical motifs — enhancement of humanity, social equality in a plural world — to this reality. This involves producing visions of transformation, not of reform, and of using the experiences of past civilizations to establish a new order of compatible cultures, rather than a return to precapitalist forms of society.

The discussion around these presentations was always lively, although the limitations of time meant that serious intellectual engagement tended to be cut short. Many of the problems that were raised in these discussions — about how higher forms of democracy could be realized, about the sorts of alliance that would be necessary to bring about change, about the relations of society and nature — were also the focus of the next and last groups of papers to be reviewed here.

4. Visions and change

The remaining presentations focused particularly on the realization of visions, both in terms of possibilities and of historical stumbling-blocks. Two presentations paid particular attention to technological change in this context, while concentrating on different types of society. *Deonatus Mbilima* discussed the role of technology in the reshaping of the poor sub-Saharan countries, with special attention to Tanzania. Perhaps the first task is to increase people's awareness of science, especially through education of children, so that skills appropriate to making technological decisions relevant to the needs of integrated rural development, industrialisation and basic social services can be created and more widely shared among the population. Such an increased awareness of science and technology is necessary for the technological revolution of our time to take a form which enables a reduction of the economic and technological dependency, and increase in the quality of life of the peoples of the poorer countries. The expansion of local skills should not simply mimic the educational practices of other countries: care has to be taken both to give indigenous technologies their due (they may often be improved with scientific methods rather than improved upon by imported technologies) and to prevent the monopolization of knowledge by minorities.

Ian Miles discussed some of the implications of new technologies, especially microelectronics, for the future of Western societies. These new technologies, radically reducing the costs of information processing, are already beginning to be used in restructuring the labour processes in manufacturing and services, in introducing a new range of consumer products, in "rationalizing" parts of the economic infrastructure, in promoting advanced communications networks, and in political administration and control. Without falling into the trap of technological determinism, it is possible to imagine various scenarios in which these potentials are developed in different ways — these range from participatory, decentralized socialist societies to highly repressive corporate states. The current crisis made such extreme alternatives acutely relevant for contemporary action. Miles attempted to spell out some of the political steps that were necessary to secure the more desirable paths of development that would constitute socialist democracy.

This latter task was the subject of several other contributions. *Marcos Kaplan,* for example, took up the possibilities for socialist democracy within Latin America in a future world order. Among the preconditions for achieving this, apart, of course, from replacing the logic of capital accumulation with social planning, would be steps to increase the access of the masses to the means of social regulation. For example, this would involve reducing the division between mental and manual labour, increasing free time, development of "institutional pedagogy" that would decentralize decision-making and prevent a bureaucratic caste establishing itself. Given the conditions of the world order, a state apparatus would need to be strong enough to counter economic and political dependency. But to preserve and extend direct organization and participation, mass action — involving peasants and middle classes as well as proletarians — must not be subordinated to the intellectual and political practice of elites. Kaplan identified three main ideological currents as antagonistic to such a desirable future for Latin American countries: modernizing conservatism, national population and dogmatic "Marxism". Despite their differences in respect of the goals of economic growth, the role of the nation, and the place of theory in politics, they share in common causalist, finalist thinking: for them, the future is already written in the present, is known already to a privileged group, and simply has to be communicated to the masses. The moulding of political organizations around such ideas is an immediate obtacle to progress in Latin America.

Mihailo Markovic also considered obstacles to socialist democracy, but in his case the focus was on the historical constraints that have shaped the repressive features of "real socialism" in Eastern Europe. It is just not adequate to condemn the revolutionary leaders for possessing a vision which seems as far as possible from present-day reality, nor to seek to identify a final cause for these failures as inherent within Marxism. Instead, socialist perspectives should be brought to bear on the objective conditions involved with the goal of changing them. The development of authoritarian socialist régimes has taken place in societies which were at relatively low levels of technological development, with communism being given the role in economic development elsewhere undertaken by the industrial bourgeoisie;

but explanations are required concerning why this should involve reproducing the everyday practices of possessive individualism. Among the factors that can be cited is the formation of political organizations in conditions of clandestinity, and the corresponding lack of a democratic experience for the masses. (Many of these masses, too, were peasants with little experience of class organization or of resistance to alienated labour and power). Other factors include the authoritarian family structure, whose patriarchy went largely unchallenged in the political revolution, and the persistence of nationalism as incorporated into the rivalry of the bureaucratic leaderships of each country.

In terms of the political practices and institutional forms which can make higher types of democracy possible, the preceding presentations and much of the discussion showed considerable convergence. For example, the idea of a single ruling party as a necessary instrument in social transformation was brought under question, and *a fortiori* the separation of means of communication and of cultural, social welfare and administrative agencies from party organizations was seen as helping to forestall the appropriation of political power. Likewise, despite the use of the term by imperialism, the defence of civil liberties is vital for democratic evolution. While the political movements in all spheres of life need to be brought out so as to challenge oppression in all its multifold aspects, social life cannot be *reduced* to politics, and in this respect there is much to learn from psychological exploration and from the ecological practices of non-Western societies, and from experiments in alternative family relationships.

One of the central questions in effecting social transformation, discussed in all these papers, is the relation of class-based organizations to the political interests of groups that may cut across class boundaries: groups such as oppressed national and ethnic groups, old and very young people, women, homosexuals, etc. *Corrine Kumar de Souza* and *Marie Angelique Savane* both provided insights concerning the role of women's needs, and women's visions, in the creation of a desirable society. On the basis of Indian and African experience both emphasized the distance of women's liberation movements in the Third World from the bourgeois feminism that has been such a strong current in many Western Women's movements. de Souza stressed that the struggle against women's oppression is a matter of changing social relations constitutive of class societies, not a matter of supplanting or suppressing men. In India this struggle takes the form of mobilizing women into pressing for equal minimum wages, and pay in general, for men and women (in contrast with the practice of many unions and socialist groups); into opposing the torture of women in prison and rape in the society at large; and into joining campaigns for childcare and other facilities. Savane argued that it was important to understand how women's oppression related to their roles, not only in sexual reproduction and household production, but also those in reproducing the capitalist mode of production through patriarchal socialist formations. In countries where capitalist relationships in production have been overthrown, these patriarchal relations persist as in need of dissolution in the continued class struggle through which a better society must be born.

5. Looking back, looking ahead

At the end of the meeting it was clear that we had succeeded in raising many more questions than had been answered. Yet it was felt by many of those who had participated in both meetings on *Visions of Desirable Societies* that considerable advance had been made over the first meeting, particularly in terms of relating the futures being discussed to present reality and its potentials for change. The difference contributions by no means presented a monolithic uniformity, but it seemed likely that much would be gained from exploring their interconnections. This suggests what may be an important point for future discussions to take up: that is, the implications of change in one part of the world, or among one group in a society, for others. In this conference, for example, it would have been useful to consider the consequences of the new technologies being developed in the West for Third World countries and their options. Likewise, the degree to which political changes in one area could help or hinder those in another area is an important issue for analysis, even if self-reliance is taken to be an appropriate goal.

Related to these points is the matter of change agents. There was little attempt to discuss the actual actors who are seen as being able to bring about particular sorts of social transformation, and this was largely taken up in relation to the integration of women's liberation into workers movements. The question of the role of the peasantry was mixed, but needs further attention (and different types of peasant experiences would need to be considered); likewise the place of middle classes and issue-oriented movements, and the contributions of intellectuals to creating and realizing visions could be taken as areas for contributions. In such cases it would probably make sense to relate the discussion less to general overviews and much more to concrete examples — for example, it could have been useful in this meeting to have taken issue more thoroughly with an actual attempt to relate cultural and artistic production to visions of the future. This would have also provided us with an example around which the linkage of traditional belief systems to newly constructed visions of the future could have been discussed rather more in terms of the relationships between people and rather less in terms of those between their ideas. It would have been useful, too, to have spent rather more time on considering the challenges posed by movements of the oppressed, and movements around specific concerns, to class-based organizations — to discussing what the obstacles are to revising organizational practices and priorities in the light of these movements, and how these may hinder the creation of visions.

This need to relate our discussions much more to the analysis of specific examples addressed in detail is one of the points which has emerged most strongly for the rapporteur in preparing these notes. I am struck by the way in which talking about individual cases observed at first hand — such as the Iranian revolution, contemporary Gandhian practice, the despair of Pakistani intellectuals, the limitations of "real socialism" — infused our discussions with a seriousness quite different from the axe-grinding of much academic confrontation. Such contributions suggest directions for further work — around matters of organizational forms and practice, about the embodiment and shaping of ideologies and beliefs about future possibilities in everyday life, about the transmutation of visions in practice, and so on — which would considerably deepen our efforts to tie desirable futures to present realities and potentials. Such work may be laborious, and clearly requires funding as well as inspiration; it cannot be wished into existence. I would suggest that we undertake to attempt to stimulate work along these lines, and to locate researchers/activists whose experience of these issues would enrich future meetings.

It testifies to the interest of the meeting that it continually generated such questions, and left the participants more aware of the blind spots of many of our visions. But we were also left feeling the need for visions, and for work on realizing visions, even more strongly. If the suffering and visions of different groups can be taken as a starting-point, then relating together their actions, as well as their ideas, may be made fractionally easier. A visionary effort is by no means sufficient to pull the world out of its crisis: but perhaps the visions of new civilization born of this crisis can help bring together and inform the thought of peoples on whose action hinges any desirable future.

12

Informing Visions of Desirable Future Societies Through Dialogue of Civilizations. A Peripheral View*

HERB ADDO
Institute of International Relations, University of the West Indies,
Trinidad, W.I.

I. Crucial properties in viable visions

Envisioning desirable future societies is an unavoidable activity for some among human beings. The more some individuals find the prevailing realities in particular societies undesirable, the more they are forced to indulge in the activity of envisioning desirable future societies. This activity can be fascinating, in that it can afford moments of bliss which compensate for the perceived and the felt undesirables which are experienced in the realities of particular societies. But the activity of envisioning desirable future societies comes with a cost. The cost is in the form of heightened frustration with the undesirable aspects of reality. This is due to the fact that, since life is real, the visioner of a desirable society must sooner or later come back to life to face the very undesirables which had led to the construction of the vision. These undesirables are made more painful to bear because of the sharp contrast between them and the desirables in the vision.

Visions of desirable societies also tend to be very personal. This is because visioners tend to approach their visions with sensitivities, choices and preferences which must spring from their individual experiences in the societies under scrutiny, and from their understanding of it. This personal nature of visions of desirable societies must not be decried; rather it must be encouraged, because it is by comparing different *personal* visions of desirable societies that their differences and similarities can be known; and it is by doing this that any *virtues* that different visions may possess can feed into each other in a cumulative manner.

---

*This paper has been revised to incorporate the comments and criticisms of the participants of the meeting.

Apart from coming with the cost of heightened frustration and being personal, or perhaps because of these same reasons, visions come in different kinds and forms. To begin with, we can divide visions into two broad kinds: (1) visions as laudable human activities and (2) visions as degenerate escapist human fantasies, which can only be imagined but not understood enough to be actualized. Visions as laudable human activities also come in two broad forms. They are: *acceptable* and *unacceptable* visions. It is true that nobody should be given the right to decree what is an acceptable vision and what is not. In this regard, the first impeachable principle is to "let a thousand flowers bloom". But then, because visions of desirable future societies are highly frustrating and highly personal, some visions can be considered unacceptable by some in that they would appear to accentuate what some will be right to consider among the undesirables in the existing reality. Assuming then that a vision is acceptable, it can fall in one or the other of the two broad categories of *reforming visions* and *transforming visions*. These two types of visions are considered acceptable because they seek to change the realities of a society for the "better".

Reforming visions, I would suggest, would be appropriate when the dissatisfaction with the existing order is not profound enough to warrant casting the envisioned new order in radical terms. In such cases, what is aimed at is no more than the pruning, at best the sanitizing, or, perhaps even merely, the whitewashing of the existing order. In the case of transforming visions, what is sought is a new and different order. Such visions are based on new basic principles; and, for the fact that the existing order may not be all bad, in fact, social orders are hardly ever all bad, the new order would incorporate some of the main features of the existing order. However, such features would acquire new importance and relevance in the new order of things envisioned. The departure of the new order from the existing one can be approached in terms of the quality/quantity contrast. And in these terms, we shall argue soon to the effect that the nature of the departure makes sense only when it is viewed in terms of the essentials of the nature of the *historic dominance* of the existing order.

I shall return to this in a moment, but let us proceed by saying further that an acceptable vision of either the transforming or the reforming type can be a *good* vision or a *bad* vision. The difference between the two is to be appreciated in terms of the presence, or the absence, of certain crucial properties in the nature of the visions. The supporting argument here is that, if the envisioning of desirable future societies are to be laudable human activities worth entertaining, that is, if visions are not to be mere escapes from reality, then they must possess certain crucial properties in their nature. There are many such properties,[1] but five of them strike me as being ex-

---

[1]The discussion at the meeting was most beneficial in clarifying these properties to me, due to the contextual re-call of Johan Galtung's paper "Eschatology, Cosmology and the Formation of Visions".

tremely important for a vision to be a good vision. They are the following: (1) that a good vision must possess *translational links* with the reality it seeks to reform or transform; (2) that a good vision must *not be too rigid;* (3) that a good vision must be *modest* in its claims and pretensions; (4) that a good vision must make it clear as to which *level of societal reality* it is dealing with, and, linking this with (1) above, it must explain why; and finally (5) that a good vision must show how its essence could be worked into the *political process* of the society concerned.

The above add up to the following description of a good vision of desirable future society. Such a vision must clearly establish its fundamental reasons for being different from the existing order by stating this difference in terms of specific and precise basic values, which must be seen as clearly different from the basic values of the existing order. In order not to be rigid, a good vision must not be unifocal, it must have the capacity to provoke criticisms within itself; that is, a good vision must be *autocritical.* To be modest, a good vision must not attempt to solve humankind's problems for all times. It is very easy to confuse the levels of society that a vision is concerned with. To avoid this, and to make a vision clear, a good vision of desirable society must make it clear what level of society it is dealing with and possibly where its visionary concerns link with, or touch on, other levels of society and their undesirables. And last, but far from being the least, a good vision must show how it can be implemented, that is, it must show how its translational links can be implemented, or actualized, through point(s) of entry into the political process of the existing society.

All these five properties, and more, must be present in the description of a good vision. To say this is not to suggest that a good vision is easy to contruct. It is, however, to suggest that, at the minimum, a good vision must have within it the five properties suggested above, because it is the ensemble of these five properties which would constitute the *virtue* of a vision. Every good vision must possess such a *virtue*; and it is this *virtue* which distinguishes one vision from another, and links one vision to others. Suffice it to say that I would consider all visions with these properties as *good* visions, even if, depending on other considerations, I would not consider a vision as an *acceptable* vision. To my mind, good visions, that is visions which embody these five properties, are not only *good,* they are also *viable* visions, and therefore laudable human activities.

My purpose in this present piece is not to provide a full vision of my vision of a desirable future society. That will be too ambitious for the moment. Toward that end, however, I undertake here to touch on the first and fifth properties of a good vision, namely *translational links* and the *level of vision.* I shall do this in a context which will make these elements of my vision of a desirable future society compatible with the present subject of informing visions of desirable future societies through a dialogue of civilizations. I treat these two properties at the moment, because I am inclined to think that, from both the methodological and the substantive points of view, these two properties are very crucial to the construction of a viable vision. To be precise, I choose to treat these particular properties because I would like to establish the existing basic principle of present reality and my visionary departure from it.

With respect to the first property of translational links, I should add that a good vision is one which leads from the statement of the translational links in terms of succinct and crispy set of values. It is even a better vision if the set of values can be resolved into an even simpler, or a more basic, principle, which requires no more to appreciate than just a modest use of intelligence as one looks at reality.[2] This is important because the translational links to which I refer are of interest in the construction of visions only in so far as their departure from the existing basic principle is clear. The argument is that a principled vision of a desirable society which is unrelated to the reigning principle of a real society is of little use.

On the matter of the level of a vision, one question in particular bothers me at this point. The question is whether, at this juncture in world-history, it is possible to treat a vision of any desirable future society without casting the translational links in the context of the world capitalist reality of the world-system? I am inclined to think that this is not possible. The reason for this is that for a vision of desirable future society to be both *good* and *viable* that vision will have to address itself to the *world-capitalist problematique,* which I understand in terms of the view that a systematic link exists between the network of world societal problems because of the capitalist nature of the world-system.

Let us recall the idea of *historic dominance;* and, in the light of this problematique, let us begin to approach the subject as I have tried to present it in this section.

II. The components of the historic category[3]

Human social history can be divided into specific and precise historic periods. The concept *historic* differs from the term historical, in that while the latter is nebulous and evasive of the precise contents of the categories and concepts constituting and describing a section of history, the former stresses the precise and specific contents of the categories and the concepts which constitute definite periods in human history, and distinguishes them one from the other in terms of real differences in the human-conditioning factors of the different periods. As it is often used, *historical* tends to stress

---

[2]I share Eugene McCarthy's feeling when he said "We are not asking for much really, just a modest use of intelligence as we look at the world to-day". *Globe and Mail,* 26 August 1968, p.3.

[3]This section borrows extensively from my "Toward a World-System Methodology" (mimeo, April 1979). The arguments that this view of history necessarily invoke have been omitted here.

the heroic wills and the poetics in history. The term *historic* is intended for viewing history in terms which are fundamental and precise in that they derive from, and relate, the distinguishing features of distinctly *different* periods in history. I would suggest that it would be extremely useful to view the historic identities of different periods in history in terms of the differences in their basic historic components, which I would suggest are the following: historic motives, historic forces, historic concomitants, and historic logical attendants. And when I refer to the *historic dominance* of a period in history of a society, I am only trying to refer to the complex which sums up reality, and which is composed by a precise *historic motive,* a *historic force,* precise *historic concomitants* and *historic logical attendants,* all of which are peculiar, if not unique, to a historic period of that society.

One would be right to ask what all these terms mean, and therefore it is time to attempt to define them. *Historic motive* stands for the dominant motive during a historical period; and it is best understood as a social order's *raison d'être.* This motive would tend to remain constant over the duration of an historic period. What tends to change are the means for attaining the motive and keeping it constant during the historic period. The *historic force* is the key element in the complex of varying means which keep the motive constant. It is the source of dynamism which must constantly "up-date" itself, if the historic period is to remain historic of a particular kind. The term *historic concomitant* refers to those aspects of social reality which are historical, in the sense of being trans-epochal, but which assume radically new relevance, or acquire new meanings, because of new circumstances brought about by the "up-datings" in the historic force. And the term *historic logical attendants* refers to the aspects of social reality which are historic in the sense of being peculiar to a historic period, because they are emergent of the changes in the historic force. Within the complex of means in pursuit of the historic motive, the concomitants and the logical attendants play supporting roles to the historic force of a historic period. Therefore, when I refer to the historic dominance of a historic period, I refer essentially to *the complex emulsion of an historic force suspending and unfolding in the intimate solution of precise historic concomitants and historic logical attendants, all operating in mutually supporting roles in pursuit of a precise historic motive.*

Because means can vary, indeed because they need to vary to keep the motive constant, the deception to look for is mistaking changing means for changing motive. What we should guard against is the false conclusion that social orders have changed just because the flamboyance of changing means has obscured the bland constancy of motive. Means have the uncanny ability to masquerade as motive; and motives have the misfortune of being easily ignored, once the appropriate means-machinery is set in motion to assure the automatic realization of the motive.

This method derives from the world-system perspective, and my understanding of it suggests to me that it addresses itself to a cardinal contradiction in social reality. The contradiction, as can be seen from the contrast between the "flamboyance of means" and the "blandness of the constancy motive", is the contradiction that, in social orders, things can very easily *appear* to have changed, while, in fact, from the *historic point* of view, they remain essentially the same, because the historic motive remains the same.

The relevance of all this must be made clear. The envisioning of desirable future society cannot be divorced from a critical approach to social change; and a critical approach to social change must be aware of, and sensitive to, the cardinal contradiction that things can easily appear to have changed while in fact they remain the same for historic purposes. The immediate relevance of the above for us is that it enables us to make the vital distinction between reforming visions and transforming visions.

A large part of the concerns of a reforming vision has to do with the complex of means which reflect the motion toward the motive of a social order. The difficulty with a transforming vision is that it first seeks to cut through the tough veneer of means to get to the motive; and, having done this, it then comes to realize that it is even tougher to deal transformationally with the motive, for, in this matter, one has to understand the motive in terms of the historic force of a particular clearly defined history, and one has to dislike it enough to want to change it entirely. Should it turn out that one does not find the historic force ugly enough, one can only return to deal in terms of means — modify them here and there, enough to look "acceptable", until the dominance of the historic motive reasserts itself to corrupt the means again.

The above is not meant to suggest that reforming visions are necessarily not implied by, or are not contributory to, transforming visions. In the final analysis they are. But since "the final analysis" is precisely what it is, it is important to make, and to note, the distinction between the two forms of acceptable visions of desirable future societies. The point is that, reforming visions deal with reforming historic concomitants and logical attendants without necessarily aiming to transform the historic motive, while transforming visions aim at radical transformation of this motive with the belief that the complex of means will logically change.

Let me explain further. It should not take much to appreciate that an absolutely thorough transforming vision can very easily become a fantasy, because it will have no meaningful *translation links* with existing reality. Such a vision will be unnecessarily, unrealistically, and perhaps even dangerously rejective of the irreversibles, or the reversible but good and rational parts, of history's contributions as they are embodied in the present. For these reasons, I warn myself that: total and nihilistic rejection of history is impertinent, and must not be entertained; but at the same time, I believe that critical views of history to inform the present, so as to transform tomorrow, are laudable. Transforming visions, no matter how radical they are, must therefore always embody some elements of reforming visions.

With these caveats firmly in mind, I proceed toward a very brief statement of the essence of my vision for a world society. But before I can do this parsimoniously, I must express precisely what I would like to see changed in the present world to make it compatible with my envisioned new order. I need also to call attention to some necessities which must inform such a vision by virtue of the fact that the present world has peculiarities which, for the better, are uniquely its own, and which must be respected if any futuristic order is to be viable. The problem, then, is two-fold: (1) how to transform the present world without rejecting it altogether; (2) how *not* to keep the capitalist world intact, by envisioning only the refurbishing of its concomitants and logical attendant, and by doing that, pretend to have envisioned a transformation of the system.

Reforming visions of the present order take the concomitant and logical attendant properties of capitalism as their starting-point, and they proceed to reform them, believing that their reformations amount to transformation. The causal connections between the historic motive and these concomitants are ignored. The historic motive is taken for granted, as some natural basis, and the worry is centred on the identified existence of the other properties as mere undesirables.

An example of such a vision for the world is Falk's *A Study of Future World*.[4] In this study, Falk does not mention, or touch, the historic motive of the capitalist world, which he seeks to change. He does not even see the world as having the capitalist identity. What he does is construct alternative structural forms of a future world concentrating more on the fear of future wars than on anything else. In the course, he blames the emergence of the nation-state, and in particular, the Treaty of Westphalia, as the source of the world's problems. Falk's constructions, as elegant as they may appear, lose their elegance, if they do not fall apart completely, as soon as one reasons that the nation-state and its formal source, the Treaty of Westphalia, are no more than mere concomitants of the world order, the direct products of the historic motive and the force of the capitalist world order.[5]

---

[4]Richard A. Falk, *A Study of Future Worlds,* New York: Free Press, 1975. Compare this conception of the world to Johan Galtung's conception of societies and the world in terms of his blue, red and green poles in his "On Alpha and Beta and Their Many Combinations", Proceedings of the WFSF Meeting on "Visions of Desirable Societies", Mexico City, 5-8 April 1978.

[5]See Herb Addo, "Some WOMP Values and Theories of Action: A Review Essay", *Peace Research,* IX, 3, 1977, 113-124; and for a contrasting review of Falk's book, see Francis A. Beer, "World Order and World Futures," *Journal of Conflict Resolution,* XXII, 1, 1979, 174: 192.

Transformation visions worry about the casual links between the historic motive, on the one hand, and the historic concomitants and the historic logical attendants, on the other. First these visions select which of the concomitants and the logical attendants they would like to retain, distinguishing them from those they reject; and second, having done this, they attempt to make it possible for what they retain to be compatible with the new historic motive in the envisioned order.

III. The problematique of the world capitalist reality and the principles of a vision

Every social order, that has ever been, has been part of a particular historic dominance. In the past, different historic dominance (even if similar in some respects) have existed in different parts of the world. Since the past 500 years or so, however, for the first time in the history of mankind, the whole world has steadily come under the dominance of one historic form: the *capitalist historic form*. In the world capitalist historic form, the *historic motive* is the accumulation of capital; the *historic force* is the rising level of efficiency of exploitation of both human and non-human resources; the *historic concomitants* and the *historic logical attendants* are those aspects of the capitalist social reality which must be present, and which must change as a result of the rising level of efficiency, in order to facilitate capital accumulation by legitimating and maintaining the historic motive of the capitalist order.[6]

The development of the world capitalist order has led to extreme dissatisfaction with the present. It is fashionable to describe the present world in such contradictory and paradoxical ways as: a global village, with cramped space-ship conditions; interdependent, yet largely dependent; wasteful in the midst of want; overproductive without regard for scarcity; unjust because of poor record of distribution; war-loving in a world of highly dangerous weapons; alienating for many reasons; and ecologically desecrating to the very detriment of nature and life.

Dissatisfaction with the current stage of world-system runs deep. Herbert Macuse, for example, commenting on the ideology of industrial society, says that a new mode of thought (total empiricism) has emerged in philosophy, psychology, sociology and other fields. "Many of the most seriously troublesome concepts are being 'eliminated' by showing that no adequate account of them in terms of operations of behaviour can be given. . . ."[7] Still on the ideology of industrial societies, John Galbraith has stated that the goals and values of the modern industrial system are that "technology is always good; that economic growth is always good; that

---

[6]The fuller description of these terms and capitalist referents are provided in my reference in note 3 above.

[7]Herbert Marcuse, *One Dimensional Man: The Ideology of Industrial Society,* p. 122.

firms must always expand; that consumption of goods is the principal source of happiness; that idleness is wicked; and that nothing should interfere with the priority we accord to technology; growth, and increased consumption".[8]

While all these things are going on in the industrial societies, the "gap" between them and the non-industrial societies is widening. And the wealth gap between the privileged and the underprivileged groups within the non-industrial societies widens more and more, as these societies plan their various ways toward emulating the industrial societies. Non-industrial societies focus attention on their plight in the world, demanding all kinds of short-term measures to correct injustices at the international level. While they do this collectively, they do all they can to divert attention from the peripheral capitalist formations of their individual nations, claiming that these conditions are their "internal" preserves.[9] These claims are correct so far as international law and other world capitalist considerations go. But from the point of view of envisioning a future world, is it true that internal conditions are unrelated to the world-condition? Of course not. The world is too interdependent and functions too much as a unit for this convenient excuse to stand.

At no place is it explicitly suggested that the ugly descriptions of the world given above are not related; but very few places attempt to treat the relatedness intimately in terms of the components of the historic dominance of the age.[10] The problem is that, even if all shades of opinion agree with the contradictions and the paradoxes presented above as true characteristics of the modern world, opinions will differ regarding the whys and the wherefores, which brought about these characteristics.

I shall not debate the differences in opinions. I shall simply state that the above characteristics have developed with the development of the historic dominance of the world capitalist formation. If the motive in this historic identity is the accumulation of capital, then what distinguishes it from other possible future economic forms is not so much the difference between private and public ownership of production as both ownership forms hold as their goal the accumulation of capital through increasing efficiency of production. In this mode of production the emphasis is on the *efficient* production of *things,* and *not* on the production of *things,* efficiently or otherwise, to enhance and dignify human existence in both its individual and societal senses. It is because of this motive, and the way its logical means

---

[8]John K. Galbraith, "Capitalism, Socialism, and the Industrial State", *Atlantic,* June 1976.

[9]For a slightly lengthy discussion of this issue, see Herb Addo, "Two Views on Interdependence and Self-reliance: Politics of De-orientation and Politics of Re-creation" (mimeo May 1979).

[10]This way of approaching the world reality is the major contribution of those writers employing the world-system perspective. See the major works of Oliver Cox, Andre Gunder Frank, Immanuel Wallerstein and Samir Amin.

and concomitants have developed, that in the past few hundreds of years the previously "unrelated relations" of the different parts of the world have dramatically given way to a single world-history; and it is for this reason that we have a world of political societies within one dominant capitalist world-economy.[11]

I have put down the above in order to be able to say that the world has, over the past 500 years, become *one,* a unit whole with its ethos, embracing all other units and affecting all else in this whole. This whole is the capitalist world-system, and it is so all-pervading that it is impossible to envision any viable desirable future society outside this whole. In other words, it is impossible to envision a desirable society without taking-off from the undesirables of the capitalist world reality.

My visions of a desirable future society differs from the present capitalist reality in the sense that its historic identity will be cast in terms of production for use for the singular purpose of enhancing human existence for all, and not in terms of production for the sake of accumulating capital. The historic capitalist fetish of capital accumulation has thrived logically, and historico-factually, on *exploitation.*

A few among human groups have always managed to exploit the many. The few have managed to exploit the many in such ways that the many have been dehumanized by not having been allowed to realize their full human potential. It is this dehumanizing exploitation that my vision of a desirable future society seeks to affect.

But before I turn to discuss exploitation and how I understand it, let me insert the translational link in my vision by saying that my vision of desirable future society is one in which dehumanizing exploitation does not exist. So that if it could, my vision would institute a kind of collective amnesia toward exploitation of the dehumanizing kind. But because the impossibility of such an institution is matched only by its potential dangers, I prefer to envision a future society where the historic motive of production for use to enhance human dignity exists with, and rides on, the firmly held conviction expressed by the paradoxical principle that: *an individual's strength is his or her weakness and his or her weakness is his or her strength.*

This principle will be explained by the reasoning that the motive which the society pursues is the evening out of human inequalities. The weak and the strong will not be put in the ring of social struggle with the loaded expectation that the "better person may win"; and the better person having won, is then free to use others in any ways he or she chooses. In this vision of desirable society, society will not take care of its weaker ones in benign and paternalistic ways. It will ensure that the weak participate and that the weak are made strong because they live with the strong in their society. All this will be rational in my envisioned society because the unimpeachable every-

---

[11]In particular see the major works of Andre Gunder Frank and Immanuel Wallerstein.

day rule in that society will be that all human beings are equal not because they are *born equal,* but because they are *equal by virtue of being human.*

Any society which decides to transform itself along these lines in the present capitalist world will face strong pressures from the capitalist world to return to the capitalist fold. The capitalist system does not allow departures which interfere with its expansionist and exploitative imperatives. It should be clear that capitalism is a world-wide system and that for this system to survive, i.e. for it to continue to pursue its historic motive of capital accumulation through exploitation, it must consistently invade all parts of the world. All parts of the world must either be capitalist, or those parts that are not (or claim not to be) must operate in the capitalist world if they were capitalist. This is as much true for the socialist countries of the world as it is for the peripheral capitalist formations.[12] Because the capitalist world system has become well entrenched, and it is a condition of its development that it affects and involves all societies within it, it has become almost impossible for any society in the present system to *transform* itself along non-capitalist paths.

It is much easier to *reform* the internal order of societies within the capitalist world order. Such reforms, of course, will deal only with the concomitants and the logical attendants of the historic motive of capital accumulation. But the problem with such reforms is that because the motive still remains capitalist and because the societies involved must operate, in the capitalist world order, as if they were capitalist, sooner or later the reforms themselves get corrupted, because the capitalist motive of using human beings to create things to accumulate capital reasserts itself. This is what I will call the *capitalist problematique.*

The discussion of the problematique is not meant to suggest that the capitalist world system is impossible to *transform.* It is meant first to indicate the enormity of the transformational problem in the sense that transformational visions must take the whole world into account; and second, that such visions must transcend the sterile expectation that only a section of humanity is charged with the transformation of the world capitalist system. The reasoning here is that if the cardinal objection against the capitalist world order is *dehumanizing exploitation* and if what our vision of desirable future society seeks is *humanizing exploitation,* then the plea should be that we begin to see the transformational problem as a human problem.

Once we begin to see the problem this way, I believe, we begin to transcend the restrictive call for a section, a comparatively privileged section in

---

[12]See the brief comment on this matter in Marlene Dixon, "Limitations Imposed by the Capitalist World-System on Socialist Construction", *Synthesis,* III, I, Fall 1979, 26-27; and see also A. G. Frank, "Long Live Transideological Enterprise! The Socialist Economies in the Capitalist International Division of Labour", *Review* 1(1), 91-140.

most instances, to be the sole carriers of transformation potential inherent in our capitalist world. I believe that if we intend to affect history enough to transform the world, then we need to raise our consciousness. I shall not, however, call it *class-consciousness* in the sense that this term is often used. My objection here is that if we are to wait till we all become workers, the proletariat in the class sense, we shall have to wait too long. I tend to see the problem more in its human, and not class, terms. As Wallerstein has put it, "it is only then . . . that we can begin to be 'scientific' about a central natural phenomenon, the human group, and 'humane' in opting for the possible choices that will in face enable us, all of us, to reach our potentials and create our worlds within our limits".[13] Further, if we mean and "hope to affect history and not merely to suffer it", as Wallerstein puts it elsewhere,[14] then, to my mind, the human consciousness factor, as the transforming agent, must refer to the irrationality of the dehumanizing exploitative foundations of world capitalism.

It is true that world capitalism will slowly fatigue itself through the natural contradictions in its historic motive, concomitants, and logical attendants. Put to my mind these contradictions and their significance must be seen as irrationalities in the *human* and in the *humane* senses if we are to aid the transformation of history, and not merely suffer history. And it is because we see dehumanizing exploitation as our main objection to the capitalist world that we now proceed to discuss exploitation as a key concept in the transformation problem.

IV. Exploitation as the cardinal contradiction[15]

Since my vision of a desirable future society is based on the negation of dehumanizing exploitation, it is in order to ask how I conceive exploitation and what the dehumanizing variant of it is. The concept exploitation har-

---

[13]Immanuel Wallerstein, "A World-System Perspective on the Social Sciences", *British Journal of Sociology,* XXVII, 3, 1976, 352.

[14]Immanuel Wallerstein, "Imperialism and Development", forthcoming in Albert Bergeson, ed., *Studies of the Modern World-System,* New York: Academic Press, 1980.

[15]In what follows in this section, I am playing the devil's advocate. My aim is to call attention to the presence and the persistence of exploitation in all large civilizations. I am not to be understood as saying that *exploitation* is good, but that *exploitation* is persistent. The plea underlying this section is that social critics should not rush to banish exploitation with the flippancy of a fiat, rather they should begin to appreciate its persistence in changing social organizations. This section stirred some interesting discussion at the Mexico meeting and it has been benefited immensely from comments from the Max-Planck-Institut group of social scientists, especially from Jurgen Heinrichs and Johannes Hengstenberg. The position adopted here is to be seen in close relation to the role allotted to the proleteriat in the transformation of capitalism, by Marxist theory. The general argument is that exploitation is not necessarily removed by public ownership of the means of production and the institution of the dictatorship of proletariat. This fact is becoming more and more recognized. See Alvin W. Gouldner, *The Future of Intellectuals and the Rise of the New Class,* New York: Seabury Press, as it is reviewed by Lewis Coser in "Marxism the New Class" *Dialogue* 12(4), 1979, 17-19.

bours a semantic ambiguity which must be clarified.[16] Exploitation can refer to the human relationships based on structured inequality and dependent relations; and it can also refer to the use which human beings make of the natural environments in which they find themselves. In both instances what is involved is that when human beings find themselves in stronger positions they tend to exploit other human beings and nature.[17] Both types of exploitation have been part of the human story. Our concern at the moment, however, is the exploitation of man by man, the cardinal contradiction which has persisted all through human history, in one form or the other, even though the modes of social organization have undergone many and far-reaching changes.

The Marxist conception of exploitation as a scientific concept which deals with the appropriation of surplus value for further production and further appropriation in rising terms is well known. In the Marxist scheme, exploitation exists only in a situation where commodity production exists and workers are paid by capital. While every society which has persisted must have produced *surplus,* in the Marxist terms exploitation exists only when capital utilizes labour to produce *surplus value,* which the capitalists then appropriate. Thus, it is only the worker who is exploited. This way of viewing exploitation is too specific and too tied to the European condition of capitalist development. It accords, however, with the acknowledged Eurocentricity that is so much a characteristic of the Marxist scheme.[18]

I would prefer to view the conception of exploitation as the capitalist appropriation of surplus value as only a special case of a general conception of exploitation. This general conception views exploitation as mechanistically composed by inequality and dependence, and dynamically as the mutually reinforcing relationship between these two factors, leading to the appropriation of surplus of others' labour, be they workers in the capitalist sense or not. Viewed this way, and from the world capitalist perspective, it is implied that in its world-wide quest of accumulating capital, capitalism has, from the very beginning, appropriated both surplus of capitalist workers and non-capitalist workers.

The capitalist mode of production, defined strictly in terms of the state of the development of the forces of production and the precise social relations of production in terms of the relations between owners of capital and owners of free labour, deprives the development of capitalism at the world-level too much of its genius. If accumulation is the way we explain the expansion of capitalism all over the world, and if expansion is not merely

---

[16]This point was brought out forcefully at the Mexico meeting by Johan Galtung and many others.

[17]The ambiguity vanishes, though, if we do not make the distinction between the human being and the natural environment, as though they were different and apart.

[18]I have discussed this matter in "World-System Critique of Euro-centric conceptions of Imperialism" (mimeo, March 1979).

contributory to capitalist development but in fact its motive, then it becomes very difficult to deny that world capitalism, viewed as a unit whole, has exploited, and continues to exploit, both proletarian and non-proletarian surplus.

There is another conception of exploitation which one can gather from the literature on exploitation.[19] This conception is hinged principally on dependencies, and its prescriptive thrust is to remove dependencies of all kinds in order not to have exploitation. The hope is to develop independent individual, so as to make exploitation of one by another impossible. The formula appears to me to be that individuals are to confront, and to interact with, each other from positions of independencies.[20]

This is a laudable conception, but a fear attaches to it in my mind. The fear is that until we find a way of dealing with the human inequalities which lead to dependencies and to exploitation, individuals may pretend to be strong. Weakness will be frowned upon so much that most will pretend to be strong in situations where they are in fact not strong, or at least not as strong as they pretend. This will breed dangerous insecurities.

There is another way of viewing the sempiternal presence of exploitation in the human condition. It is, to my mind, to begin by accepting that to the extent that human beings are not all fully equal in their endowments and opportunities and/or fully and equally autonomous, and for these reasons must depend one on the other to some extent, to that extent opportunities will exist for exploitation, between and within human groups. Opportunities for exploitation, therefore, would appear to be part of the human condition, inevitable in human relations.[21]

The point then is that we should not frown on exploitation *per se* as a general category in human relations. The challenge lies in being able to use the inevitable exploitative opportunities in human relations not to dehumanize the human being but to enhance the human in the human being. This manner of confronting the sempiternal agony in human relations, to my mind, is more honest. It does now allow the indulgence in the impossible and dangerous dream of setting out to banish exploitation, through the sheer acts of changing certain historic concomitants and certain logical attendants, and by doing this come to believe sincerely that a new historic moment in the history of man's social relations without exploitation has dawned. This dream is an impossible dream because of the reasons

---

[19]Carlos Mallmann's works on "Synergy" lend themselves to such interpretation. See his "Needs-satisfaction-oriented Alternative Societies", Proceedings of the WFSF meeting on "Visions of Desirable Societies", Mexico City, 5-8 April 1978. Discussions with Mallmann have helped me to see his point of view, but the fears expressed here persist to some extent.

[20]If my reading of Mallmann's works is correct, then I will call this the "Mallmann formula".

[21]This point must not be understood to mean capitulation to exploitation. The argument is that all large civilizations have displayed one form of exploitation or the other.

given above; and it is dangerous because, as I have indicated above, we can very easily come to believe that things have changed while in fact, essentially, they remain the same.

What I am groping to explain here is not meant to give comfort in any way to the fascist and some liberal thinking that just because exploitation appears to have always existed in human relations, there is very little that can be done about it and must therefore be left alone. Nothing could be further from my argument. If an analogy will help in clarifying my argument, it is that my vision of a desirable future society approaches exploitation, the fulcrum of the vision, with the studied recognition that a good boxer, or a good soccer player, approaches an opponent and uses the strength of the opponent against the opponent himself.[22] In constructing visions of desirable future societies, I believe we should endeavour to transcend the flippant and get to the essence of the inherent challenge. This is the way I honestly see the persistence of human exploitation.[23]

Frankly, I ask, what are human beings worth to one another, if not to exploit other human beings and be exploited in return? If this question has the least bit of sense in the context of what we have been saying, then I would suggest that what should concern us with respect to exploitation, and in the context of the vision, are the following questions: Toward what end is this mutual exploitation?; to even-out human inequalities or to worsen these inequalities? Are all individuals, or groups of individuals, as much open to exploitation as they are able to exploit? In other words, is mutual exploitation fair, in that it leads to the enhancing of the collective and the individual human lives and dignities? The acceptability, or the unacceptability, of exploitation, as it has contributed to and shaped the modern world-system, is to be judged by the answers to these questions. Exploitation is bad to the extent that its role in the motion toward the attainment of the different historic motives, in the context of the different historic dominance, has tended to dehumanize the *human in the being* of the human being. Exploitation is irrational to the extent that its dehumanizing excesses may not even be necessary for the attainment of the historic motive at this stage of world capitalism.

The argument is that exploitation is not to be hated by itself, and for itself, since it is futile to do so because of its omnipresence in human group life. What is to be hated are the *bad* and the *irrational* uses of exploitation in the senses indicated above. If we are to reach our full human potentials by re-creating our world(s) within our limits, and if we are not to pretend to do so for all time, then we must admit that we have not yet learnt how to tame the wild fires of exploitation. Perhaps the first step in the direction of taming the wild fires of exploitation is to admit this much, especially in an age

---

[22]Wrestling is perhaps a better example, but I am more familiar with boxing and soccer.

[23]I wish it were otherwise.

where the world has become so very complex, and as a result the roots of exploitation have become so obscure.

To conclude this section, let us reason this way: even if we all agree that the present historic motive of capital accumulation is dehumanizing, because of its particular brand of exploitation, the question still remains as to what we mean exactly by "enhancing human dignity". It is a beautiful formula, we must admit, but in this age when very few human beings worth their body temperatures will admit to exploiting other human beings in a dehumanizing manner, we must admit also that this beautiful formula can be employed in many different and conflicting ways.[24] To avoid the wrong usage, we must fill in the contents of the category of *human dignity*. This is precisely where the services of the dialogue of civilizations is called for. To fill in this category we must learn from other civilizations. No civilization should be allowed in this dialogue to pretend it has the answer, certainly not all the answers, for the dialogue also means criticisms of civilization. The Western civilization, in particular, because of its dominance in the present world civilization, must be held in check, for it might seek to lead in this as it leads in most other things in the capitalist world.

V. Dialogue of civilizations toward human dignity

The substantive matter on the agenda of the dialogue of civilizations, of course, will be how to organize societies so that the exploitation of man by man enhances human beings rather than dehumanizes them. This matter will entail many issues. For example, it will entail the consideration of whether, in order to avoid dehumanizing exploitation, human groups must not be organized into "critical sizes";[25] and whether production and production relations should not be organized in such ways as to meet only "basic needs" and no more — the fear being, that once we aim to produce for any other reason, dehumanizing exploitation might set in.

Such a dialogue will have to take many forms, and it will have to occur on many levels. The form that interests me at the moment is the dialogue between the peripheral civilizations within the capitalist world-system. The intention of this dialogue is to enable the peripheral civilizations to confront the dominant capitalist world civilization. The purpose is to bring influences and ideas from the peripheral civilizations to bear on the transformation potential inherent in the capitalist world civilization. To do this, however, a few basic truths must be appreciated.

The first deals with what we mean by civilization. In such a dialogue, it will be useful if we do not understand civilizations to mean atavistic and

---

[24]Oscar Nudler raised this point in Mexico.

[25]Yona Friedman's papers on critical size, Johan Galtung's papers on alpha and beta social organizations and the Ghandian conception of small societies are examples of social organizations which can minimize exploitation.

antedeluvian hand-downs from generations to generations. It will be better if we understood civilizations to mean the critical uses of the lessons of histories and cultural lives to inform the present so as to help transform the future. Civilizations are not to be revered and maintained simply because they are old, but because they bear some useful lessons for explaining the present and for making the future better.

The second basic truth, which must be appreciated, is precisely what it is that we mean when we refer to the capitalist world-system as a unit whole, and as having a civilization. By a unit whole, we are not referring to a solid monolith with a homogeneous consistency.[26] We are not saying that all parts of this whole are capitalist in the same sense and to the same degree. What we mean is that in the course of its development, the capitalist system has gone a long way toward creating a world in which the capitalist ethos, in its various guises, increasingly dominates. This domination, seen in its world-wide relational terms, rather than just in its structural terms, is what makes other civilizations in the world behave as though they were capitalist, even when they may not be thoroughly capitalist.

The capitalist processes go on between units of the world and within them, creating deformed capitalisms in the periphery of the world-system, for the purpose of accumulating capital in the centre, which the world system itself develops, in complexity and intricacy, from one "high stage" to a "higher stage". These processes have meant that other civilizations in the world have been subordinated to the capitalist civilization. It appears that for security, and as a condition of its development, the capitalist civilization has affected all other civilizations, leaving in its wake a motley collection of insecure civilizations. A hierarchy of civilization has thus been formed. At the top is the capitalist civilization, superintending the subordination and the rapid decay of other civilizations.

The third matter to consider is the very world-wide nature of the capitalist civilization. Any viable vision of a desirable future society, transforming or otherwise, has to take this fact of the capitalist life into account. The capitalist civilization is the first truly world-wide civilization that we *know* we have ever had. This civilization has affected the present world so much that it is unrealistic for even the most thorough transforming vision of any society to envisage its complete and total roll-back. Our envisioned new order has to benefit from the capitalist civilization without this new order being capitalist. The creative challenge in this regard lies in the quick realization that the capitalist civilization has used the inevitable exploitation relationships, which exist between objects and subjects of nature, to deify not man, not even a god, but things. In its terms, man has been made the means to the deification of things so that more capital, and the impersonal means of production, can be enhanced.

---

[26]Magda McHale stressed this point in the discussion in Mexico.

The argument is that we have known only one global world, and that the short period of its history has been so intense and so all-pervasive that we must admit to ourselves that, in one sense or the other, we are all its products. No part of the world can claim to have escaped capitalism entirely. In my vision, therefore, I do not seek to negate, even if I could, some of the *historic concomitants* and some of the *historic logical attendants* of the capitalist civilization. The future must gain in some respects from the past. The transformed present must carry with it, into the future, some good benefits from the past. The challenge is precisely how we maintain these benefits without them working against the human in the human being.

To do this, we must first admit the culpability of capitalism in the fundamental sense in which it has used exploitation in the course of its history to degrade man. Having acknowledged this, it will become clear that if we seek not merely to reform but to transform the capitalist civilization, then we must go outside its historic motive of capital accumulation to seek ideas for its transformation. Luckily, for this task, the capitalist civilization has not yet succeeded in completely destroying all the non-capitalist peripheral civilizations.

Some other civilizations exist, even if insecurely so and even if they are poorly judged by capitalist standards. What we should do then is to turn to these non-capitalist civilizations to find out whether they have anything to offer regarding the use of mutual exploitation to enhance human life.

This may appear obvious. But to admit that other civilizations may have the ability to humanize the capitalist civilization is to have gone a long way, when we consider that other civilizations have been degraded, and some even obliterated, in their unequal struggle with capitalism over the past 500 years or so.

At this stage of this unequal struggle between civilizations, we must turn our attention to a dialogue between the various civilizations with the intention of transforming capitalism. What should be aimed at in this dialogue is a vision of a society which seeks to use mutual exploitation to produce for human use and no more. One need not be any more precise about the purpose of the dialogue than this, except to add that controlled production must coincide with equity in distribution. The main point here is that I believe that a society with such goals will begin with the human being degraded, and end with the human being enhanced.

There is neither the dearth of explicit writings on models of new orders for societies, nor is there a scarcity of sources, anchored in different civilizations, from which such models can be derived. The intimate relationship which capitalism has established between different civilizations and itself, necessitates that any serious piece on the visions of desirable societies, whether aimed at the world as a whole or any particular part of it, must somehow be a neat blend of dialogues between the many civilizations. But because the capitalist civilization has positioned itself at the top of the hierarchy of civilizations, and, because of this, communication between other civilizations takes place through the medium of the capitalist civilization, in short because the world is one, but not at one, a few words are in order.

The capitalist civilization has made it such, that to understand another civilization, one has to understand it in terms of the extent to which that civilization is not like the capitalist civilization. And to compare two non-capitalist civilizations, one is almost compelled to do so in terms of the capitalist civilization. This creates a situation where in most cases the other civilizations are prejudged before they are even examined.

Beginning from this basis, I will prefer to approach the issue of dialogue between the different civilizations in the world by sailing close to the mode(s) of exploitation underpinning the non-capitalist civilization to see how it was that these other civilizations were not able to withstand the capitalist onslaught initially, and having fallen victim to its exploitation mechanisms, continue to support capitalism at this stage of its world-wide development. This is not as silly an undertaking as it might appear at the first encounter. By doing this, we could come to identify why some civilizations failed at, or did not attempt, world-wide conquest. And knowing this, we could perhaps come to understand what is similar, if not common, between the peripheral civilization of the world.[27]

The reason for doing this is not so that we can replace the capitalist civilization with a particular peripheral civilization, but so that we can then take a fresh look at the world capitalist civilization with the intention of transforming it in ways which will affect its historic motive for the better. Another reason for doing this will be so that we can avoid a "Babel" of civilizations; and, instead, go directly to the point of *confronting the world's historic dominance with its historic subordination*. Such a confrontation will lead to the crucial realization that what the present subordinate civilizations are about, is neither an Asian, African, or Latin American view of world reality, but the *peripheral view* of it; and that the extent to which this peripheral view can compel and aid the dominant civilization of the capitalist reality to transform itself, is all that the dialogue of civilizations should be about, in so far as it seeks to inform visions of better future societies.

VI. Conclusion

The process of transforming societies in the present world-capitalist system will undoubtedly be long. Some will even say that it will be futile because the human race will probably blow itself up long before the transforming exercise of rescuing human dignity has advanced enough to be

---

[27]The potency of eschatology to the understanding of non-capitalist civilization can be seen in Johan Galtung, "Is There a Chinese Strategy of Development?" (mimeo, 1979).

recognized. I am not oppressed by the morbid fear that the human race will blow itself up in time to make the transformation exercises useless. I reason that the process of transforming societies in the present world capitalist system includes the vital process of ensuring that the human race does not blow itself up. In any case, assuming that the human race survives much longer than some expect, then it is at present that we should begin to raise our eyes from the levels of stale formulae bred by utter pessimism and unwarranted optimism, to see the transformation problem as both a world and a human problem, and therefore, necessarily difficult but not necessarily impossible.

The tension in this regard lies in distinguishing between the platitudinous and the self-inevident proposition that "all humans are created equal", irrespective of the objective circumstances in which their humaneness is situated. It is dangerous to take the equality of humaneness as an initial "given". It is an end for which we must strive, if this equality as an idea is not to be instrumental in enhancing and perpetuating human inequality. The empty category of the idea of enhancing human dignity is to be filled, in part, by the further idea that the desired society is one in which all humans exist in circumstances which make them socially equal, and where all individuals advance their circumstances together at even pace.

In conclusion, if the idea in this vision is the enhancing of human dignity, then the organization of the idea is based on the mutual exploitation of man by man to produce things for humans in ways which enhance their dignity. The general frame, for the organization of the idea, deals with the transformation of the complex — of "the whys and the wherefores" — which maintain the existing system — the historic motive, the historic force, the historic concomitants and the historic logical attendants. The gap between the idea and the organization of it is very wide and deep. A lot can very easily fall, and get lost, in between the sublimity of the idea and the ugly realization of it. The dialogue of civilization intervenes between the idea and the organization of it, only to ensure that the gulf between the two is not only narrowed but also shallowed. The subordinate civilizations of the world should confront the capitalist world civilization and its centre precisely for what they can contribute toward the narrowing and the shallowing of this gap.

13

Towards a Third World Utopia

ASHIS NANDY

Centre for the Study of Developing Societies, Delhi, India

"Alas, having defeated the enemy, we have ourselves been defeated. . . . The . . . defeated have become victorious. . . . Misery appears like prosperity, and prosperity looks like misery. This our victory is twined into defeat."

— *The Mahabharata*[1]

I

Theories of salvation do not save. At best, they promise some restructuring of human consciousness. Utopias too, being secular theories of salvation, promise a sharper awareness and criticism of contemporary cultures, particularly of institutional suffering — the unnecessary suffering which is born, not of the human condition, but of faulty social institutions and goals.

In this sense, all utopias whether drawn in majestic architechtonics or in tame mundanity or in vindictive ferocity, are a language. They are an attempt to communicate with the present in terms of the myths and allegories of the future. Like history, which exists ultimately in the mind of the historian and his believing readers and is thus a means of communication, utopianism is another aspect of — and a comment upon — the here-and-the-now, another means of making peace with or challenging institutional suffering in the present, another ethics apportioning responsibility for this suffering and guiding our fight against it on the plane of contemporary social consciousness.[2]

---

[1] *The Mahabharata,* Sauptik Parva: *10:* Slokas 9, 12, 13. Translated by Manmatha Nath Dutt, Calcutta: Elysium, 1962, p. 20.

[2] Such a utopianism is, of course, very different from the ones Karl Popper ("Utopia and Violence", in *Conjectures and Refutations, The Growth of Scientific Knowledge,* London: Routledge & Kegan Paul, 1978, pp. 355-363) or Robert Nozick (*Anarchy, State and Utopia,* Oxford: Basil Blackwell, 1974, Part III) have in mind.

No utopia can, thus, be without an implicit or explicit theory of suffering. Particularly so in the peripheries of the world, euphemistically called the Third World. The concept of the Third World is not a cultural category; it is a political and economic category born of poverty, exploitation, oppression, indignity and self-contempt. The concept is inextricably linked with the efforts of a large number of people trying to survive, over generations, "quasiextreme" situations.[3] A Third World utopia — the South's concept of a "decent society", as Barrington Moore might call it — must recognize this basic reality.[4] To have a meaningful life in the minds of men, such a utopia must start with the issue of man-made suffering which has given the Third World both its name and its uniqueness. This essay is an intercivilizational perspective on oppression, with a less articulate psychology of survival and salvation as its appendage. It is guided by the belief that the only way the Third World can transcend the sloganeering of its well-wishers is (i) by becoming a collective representation of the oppressed everywhere in the world and in all past times (ii) by internalizing or owning up the outside forces of oppression and, then, coping with them as inner vectors, and (iii) by recognizing the oppressed selves of the First and the Second Worlds as civilizational allies in the battle against institutionalized suffering.[5]

The perspective is based on three assumptions. First, that as far as the core values are concerned, goodness and right ethics are not the monopoly of any civilization. All civilizations share certain basic values and such cultural traditions as derive from man's biological self and social experience. The distinctiveness of a complex civilization lies, not in the uniqueness of its values but in the *gestalt* which it imposes on these values and in the weights it assigns to its different values and subtraditions. So, certain traditions or cultural strains may, at a certain point of time, be recessive or dominant in a civilization, but they are never uniquely absent or exclusively present. What looks like a human potentiality which ought to be actualized in some distant future is often only a cornered cultural strain waiting to be renewed or rediscovered.

Second, that human civilization is constantly trying to alter or expand its awareness of exploitation and oppression. Oppressions which were once outside the span of awareness are no longer so, and it is quite likely that the present awareness of suffering, too, would be found wanting and would change in the future. Who, before the socialists, had thought of class as a

---

[3]I have in mind the extremes Bruno Bettelheim describes in his "Individual and Mass Behaviour in Extreme Situations" (1943), in *Surviving and Other Essays,* New York: Alfred A. Knopf, 1979, pp. 48-83.

[4]"The Society Nobody Wants: A Look Beyond Marxism and Liberalism", in Kurt H. Wolff and Barrington Moore (Eds.), *The Critical Spirit: Essays in Honour of Herbert Marcuse,* Boston: Beacon, 1967, pp. 401-418.

[5]Though this is not relevant to the issues I discuss in this essay, the three processes seem to hint at the cultural-anthropological, the depth-psychological and the Christian-theological concerns with oppression respectively.

unit of repression? How many, before Freud, has sensed that children needed to be protected against their own parents? How many believed, before Gandhi's rebirth after the environmental crisis in the West, that modern technology, the supposed liberator of man, had become his most powerful oppressor? Our limited ethical sensitivity is not a proof of human hypocrisy; it is mostly a product of our limited cognition of the human situation. Oppression is ultimately a matter of definition, and its perception is the product of a world-view. Change the world-view, and what once seemed natural and legitimate becomes an instance of cruelty and sadism.

Third, that imperfect societies produce imperfect remedies of their imperfections. Theories of salvation are not uncontaminated by the spatial and temporal location of the theorists. Since the solutions are products of the same social experiences that produce the problems, they cannot but be informed by the same consciousness or, if you allow a psychologism, unconsciousness. Marx wrote about the process of declassing oneself and about breaking the barriers of one's false consciousness; Freud, about the possibility of working through one's personal history or, rather, the defences against such history. I like to believe that both were reflecting an analytic attitude that allows a human organism to work through its own history, and to critically accept, reject or, if necessary, use it as a part of its living tradition. It is perhaps in human nature to try to design — even if with only limited success — a future unfettered by the past and yet, paradoxically, informed with the past.

II

What resistance does a culture face in working through its remembered past and through the limits that past sets on its cognition? What are the psychological techniques through which the future is controlled or pre-empted by an oppressive or unjust system or by the experience of oppression and injustice? What are the "inner" checks that a society or civilization erects against minimizing institutionalized suffering? What can liberation from oppression in the most utopian sense mean?

We cannot even begin to answer these questions without explicitly recognizing three processes which give structured oppression its resilience.

The first of these processes is a certain antipsychologism which oppression supports and from which it seeks legitimacy. Many years ago Theodor Adorno and his associates had found a link between authoritarian predisposition and anti-psychologism (which they, following Henry Murray, called anti-intraceptiveness).[6] Implicit in that early empirical study of authoritarianism was the recognition that one of the ways an oppressive social system can be given some permanence is by promoting a tough-mindedness which considers all attempts to look within to the sources of

---

[6]*The Authoritarian Personality,* New York: Harper: 1950.

one's consciousness, and all attempts to examine one's authenticity, as something compromising, soft-headed and emasculating. Twenty-five years afterwards Adorno recast that argument in broader cultural terms:

"Among the motifs of cultural criticism one of the most long-established and central is that of the lie: that culture creates the illusion of a society worthy of man which does not exist; that it concedes the material conditions upon which all human works rise, and that, comforting and lulling, it serves to keep alive the bad economic determination of existence. This is the notion of culture as ideology. . . . But precisely this notion, like all expostulation about lies, has a suspicious tendency to become itself ideology. . . . Inexorably, the thought of money and all its attendant conflicts extend into the most tender erotic, the most sublime spiritual relationships. With the logic of coherence and the pathos of truth, cultural criticism could therefore demand that relationships be entirely reduced to their material origin. . . . But to act radically in accordance with this principle would be to extirpate, with the false, all that was true also, all that however impotently strives to escape the confines of universal practice, every chimerical anticipation of a nobler condition, and so to bring about directly the barbarism that culture is reproached for furthering indirectly . . . apart from this, emphasis on the material element, as against the spirit as a lie, has given rise to a kind of dubious affinity with that political economy which is subjected to an immanent criticism, comparable with the complicity between police and underworld. Since Utopia was set aside and the unity of theory and practice demanded, we have become all too practical . . . today there is growing resemblence between the business mentality and sober critical judgement."[7]

Thus, in a peculiar reversal of roles, the vulgar materialism Adorno describes is now an ally of the global structure of oppression. It colludes with ethnocide because culture to it is only an epiphenomenon. In the name of shifting the debate to the real world, it reduces all choice to those available within a single culture, the one affiliated to the present global system. In such a world, ruled by a structure that has co-opted its manifest critics, the struggle for liberation might have to begin in the minds of men, with a defiance of the cultural themes which endorse oppression. Oppression to be oppressive must be felt to be so, if not by the oppressors and the oppressed, at least by some social analyst somewhere.

There is a second issue involved here. Theories of liberation built on ultra-materialism invariably inherit a certain extraversion. The various

---

[7]*Minima Moralia*, translated by E. F. N. Jephcott, London: NLB, 1977, pp. 43-44.

perspectives upon the future emerging from the women's liberation movement, from the ongoing debates on the heritability of IQ and from the
North–South differences, all provide instances of how certain forms of
antipsychologism are used to avoid the analysis of deeper and long-term
results of cruelty, exploitation and authoritarianism. The idea that the problem is exclusively with the political position of women and not with the
politics of femininity as a cultural trait, the idea that racial discrimination
begins and ends with the racial differences in IQ and does not involve the
definition of intelligence as only productive intelligence as a substitute for
intellect, the belief that North–South differences involve only unequal
exchange of material goods and not unequal exchange in theories of salvation themselves — these are all significant tributes to a global culture which
is constantly seeking new and more legitimate means of short-changing the
peripheries of the world. Yet, most debates around these issues assume that
the impact of political and economic inequality are skin-deep and short
term. Remove the inequality and oppression, they say in
effect, and you will have healthy individuals and healthy societies all
around.

This anti-psychologism, partly a reaction to the over-psychologization of
the age of the psychological man, is another means of underplaying the
long-term cultural and psychological consequences of exploitation, poverty
and injustice — consequences which live on even when what is conven-
tionally called political and economic oppression is removed. Continuous
suffering inflicted by fellow human beings, centuries of inequity and
deprivation of basic human dignity, many generations of poverty, long
experience of authoritarian political rule or imperialism, these distort the
cultures and minds, specially the values and the self-concepts, of the suf-
ferers and those involved in the manufacturing of suffering. Long-term suffering also generally means the establishment of powerful justifications for
the suffering in the minds of both the oppressors and the oppressed. All the
useful modes of social adaptation, creative dissent, techniques of survival,
and conceptions of the future transmitted from generation to generation are
deeply influenced by the way in which large groups of human beings have
lived and died, and have been forced to live and forced to die. It is thus that
institutionalized suffering acquires its self-perpetuating quality.

In sum, no vision of the future can ignore that institutional suffering —
''structural violence'' is the most important special case of it — touches the
deepest core of human beings, and that societies must work through the
culture and psychology of such suffering, in addition to its politics and
economics. This awareness comes painfully, and each society in each period
of history builds powerful inner defences against it. It is in the nature of
human consciousness to try to vest responsibility for inexplicable suffering
in outside forces — in fate, in history or, for that matter, in an objective
science of nature or society. When successful, such an effort concretizes and

exteriorizes evil and thus makes it psychologically more manageable. When unsuccessful, it at least keeps questions open. Predictably, every other decade we have a new controversy on nature versus nurture, a new incarnation of what is presently being called sociobiology and a new biological interpretation of schizophrenia. Biology and genetics exteriorize; psychology owns up.

The second process is a certain continuity between the oppressors and their victims. Though some awareness of this continuity has been a part of our social consciousness for many centuries, it is in this century — thanks primarily to the political technology developed by Gandhi and the cultural criticisms ventured by at least some followers of Marx and Freud — that this awareness has become something more than a pious slogan. Though all religions stress the cultural and moral degradation of the oppressor and the dangers of privilege and dominance, it is on the basis of these three eponymic strands of consciousness that a major part of our awareness of the subtler and more invidious forms of oppression (which make the victim willing participants and supporters of an oppressive system) has been built. The most elaborate development of the theme can be found in Freudian metapsychology. It presumes a faulty society which perpetuates its repression through a repressive system of socialization at an early age. Its prototypical victim is one who, while trying to live an ordinary "normal" life, gives meaning and value to his victimhood in terms of the norms of an unjust culture. Almost unwillingly Freud develops a philosophy of the person which sees the victim as willingly carrying within him his oppressors.

In other words, Freud took repression seriously. He did not consider the human nature a fully open system which could easily wipe out the scars of oppression and could, thus, effortlessly transcend its history. Like all history, the history of oppression has to be worked through. This piercing of collective defences is necessary, Freud suggests, because human groups can develop exploitative systems within which the psychologically deformed oppressors and their psychologically deformed victims find a meaningful life style and mutually potentiating cross-motivations. Such cross-motivations explain the frequent human inability to be free even when unfettered, a tendency which Erich Fromm, as early as the 1940s, called the fear of freedom.

That is the warning contained in Bruno Bettelheim's and Victor Frankl's chilling accounts of the Nazi extermination camps based on their personal experiences.[8] Both these gifted and courageous psychoanalysts describe how some of the victims internalized the norms of the camps and became

---

[8]Bettelheim, "Individual and Mass Behaviour in Extreme Situations". *op. cit.,* and Victor E. Frankl, *Man's Search for Meaning,* New York: Pocket Book, 1959. See also the excellent summary of related studies by Barrington Moore, Jr., *Injustice: The Social Bases of Obedience and Revolt,* New York: Macmillan, 1978, pp. 64-77. Moore also covers the Untouchables of India from this point of view; see pp. 55-64.

the exaggerated, pathetic, but dangerous, versions of their oppressors. Losing touch with reality out of the fear of inescapable death and trying to hold together a collapsing world, they internalized the norms and the worldview of the SS and willingly collaborated with their oppressors, thus giving some semblance of meaning to their meaningless victimhood, suffering and death, and to the degradation and monstrosity of their tormentors. (Elsewhere Bettelheim affirms that this was, everything said, an instance of the death drive wiping out the victim's will to live.[9] It is possible to view it also as a part of a dialectic which offsets the ego defence called "identification with the aggressor" against the moral majesty of the human spirit which, when faced with the very worst in organized oppression, would rather give up the last vestiges of self-esteem and see itself as an object of deserved suffering than believe that another social group could deliberately inflict suffering without any perceivable concern for injustice.[10]) The oppressors in this case, of course, skilfully built upon this resilience of the victim's social self, particularly the persistence of his moral universe, and used it as a vital element in their industry of suffering.[11] The Nazis, one is constrained to admit, knew a thing or two about oppression.

The third process which limits man's vision of the future is his refusal to take full measure of the violence which an oppressive system does to the humanity and to the quality of life of the oppressors. Aimé Césaire says about colonialism that it "works to *decivilize* the colonizer, to *brutalize* him in the true sense of the word . . .".[12] And, that decivilization and that brutalization one day come home to roost: ". . . no one colonizes innocently, . . . no one colonizes with impunity either."[13] If this sounds like the voice of a black Cassandra speaking of a form of oppression which takes place only outside civilization, there is the final lesson Bettelheim derives from his study of the holocaust — "So it happened as it must: those beholden to the death drive destroy also themselves."[14] Admittedly we are close to the palliatives promoted by organized religions, but even in their vulgarized forms religions do maintain a certain touch with the eternal varieties of human nature. At least some of the major faiths of the world

---

[9]"The Holocaust — One Generation Later", *op. cit.,* pp. 84-104.

[10]That this is not merely wishful thinking is partly evidenced by Helen Fein, *Accounting for Genocide: National Responses and Jewish Victimization During the Holocaust,* New York: Free Press, 1979, Chapter 12. As Gerda Klein says so movingly, "Why? Why did we walk like meek sheep to the slaughter house? Why did we not fight back? . . . I know why. Because we had faith in humanity. Because we did not really think that human beings were capable of committing such crimes." *All But My Life,* New York: Hill & Wang, 1957, p. 89, quoted in Terence Des Pres, *The Survivor,* New York: Oxford University Press, 1976, p. 83.

[11] *Minima Moralia, op. cit.,* p. 108.

[12]*Discourse on Colonialism,* translated by Joan Pinkham, New York and London: Monthly Review Press, 1972, p. 11. Italics in the original.

[13]*Ibid.,* p. 170.

[14]"The Holocaust — One Generation Later", *op. cit.,* p. 101.

have not failed to affirm that oppressors are the ultimate victims of their own systems of oppression; that they are the ones whose dehumanization goes farthest, even by the conventional standards of everyday religion. We have probably come here a full circle in post-modern, post-evolutionary, social consciousness. It now again seems obvious that no theory of liberation can be morally acceptable unless it admits that, in addition to the violence done to the obvious victims, there is the exploitation by imperfect societies of their instruments of oppression.

This general continuity between the slaves and the master apart, theirs is the more easily identifiable penumbra of the oppressed in any organized system of oppression. In addition to the millions of direct victims, there are also millions of secondary victims of the oppressive systems. Their brutalization is planned and institutionalized,[15] so is the hostility these "legitimately" violent groups often attract to protect those more central to the oppressive system. The ranks of the army and the police in all countries come from the relatively poor, powerless or low-status sectors of society. Almost invariably, imperfect societies arrive at a system of mobility under which the centres in the lower rungs of the army and the police are some of the few channels of mobility open to the plebians. That is, the prize of a better life is dangled before the socio-economically deprived groups to encourage them to willingly socialize themselves into a violent empty lifestyle. In the process, a machine of oppression is built; it has not only its open targets but also is dehumanized cogs. These cogs only seemingly opt for, what Herbert Marcuse calls, "voluntary servitude"; actually they have no escape.

Though I belong to a society which was once colonized and ruled with the help of its indigenous population, and where the number of white men rarely exceeded 50,000 in a population of about 400 million. I shall give an example of this other oppression from another society in more recent times. The American experience with the Vietnam war shows that even anti-militarism, in the form of draft dodging or avoidance of military service, can become a matter of social discrimination. Pacifism can be classy. The better placed dodge better and avoid the dirty world of military violence more skilfully. In the case of Vietnam, this doubly ensured that most of those who went to fight were the socially underprivileged, men who were already hurt, bitter and cynical. As is well known, a disproportionately large number of them were Blacks, who neither had any respite from the system nor from the "progressive" and privileged fellow citizens protesting the war and feeling self-righteous. They were people who had seen and known violence and discrimination — manifest as well at latent, direct as well as institutional, pseudo-legitimate as well as openly illegitimate. Small

---

[15]See, for example, Chaim F. Shatan, "Bogus Manhood, Bogus Honor: Surrender and Transfiguration in the United States Marine Corps", *Psychoanalytic Review,* 1977, 66, pp. 585-610.

wonder, then, that in Vietnam many of them tried to give meaning to possible death and mutilation by developing a pathological overconcern with avenging the suffering of their compatriots of "buddies", by stereotyping the Vietnamese and the communists, or by being aggressive nationalists. The Vietnam war was, in the ultimate analysis, a story of one set of victims setting upon another set of victims on behalf of a reified, impersonal system.[16]

III

An insight into such processes helps us visualize a utopia of the Third World different from the one which a straight interpretation of some of the major civilizations can be made to yield. This does not mean that cultural themes or cosmologies are unimportant. It means that the experience of exploitation and suffering is a great teacher. Those who maintain, or try to maintain, their humanity in the face of such experience perhaps develop the skill to give special meaning to the fundamental contradictions and schisms in the human condition — such as the sanctity of life in the presence of omnipresent death; the legitimate biological differences (between the male and the female, and between the adult, the child and the elderly) which become stratificatory principles through the pseudolegitimate emphases on productivity, performance and "substance"; and the search for spirituality and religious sentiment, for human values in general, in a world where such a search is almost always a new sanctification of unnecessary suffering and status quo. Like Marx's "hideous heathen god who refused to drink nectar except from the skulls of murdered men", human consciousness has sometimes used oppression to sharpen its sensitivities and see meanings that would have been otherwise lost in the limbo of oversocialized thinking.

One important element in their vision which many major civilizations in the Third World have protected with care is a certain refusal to think in terms of opposed, exclusive, clear, Cartesian dichotomies. For long, this refusal has been seen as an intellectual stigmata, the final proof of the cognitive inferiority of the non-white races. Today, it triggers debates on race and IQ and on the metaphors of primitivism and infantility. Arguments against such accounts of the non-West have ranged all the way from the empirical-statistical to the philosophical. (Césaire, for example, has mentioned the barbaric repudiation by Europe of Descartes' charter of universalism "reason . . . is found whole and entire in each man".[17]) Perhaps the time has come to work through this sordid memory of intellectual racism, to admit that Descartes is not the last word on the intellec-

---

[16]This issue has been approached from a slightly different perspective in Maurice Zeitlin, Kenneth Lutterman and James Russell, "Death in Vietnam: Class, Poverty and Risks of War", in Ira Katznelson, Gordon Adams, Philip Brenner and Alan Wolfe (Eds.), *The Politics and Society Reader*, New York: David McKay, 1974, pp. 53-68.

[17]*Op. cit.*, pp. 35, 51-52.

tual potentials of humankind, and to acknowledge that what was once an embarrassment may some day become a hope.

Many have lamented the "genetic" gap between man's intellectual and moral development. Arther Koestler is only the last in a long line of thinkers to feel that, in this matter, nature, particularly human evolution, has "let us down".[18] Perhaps, what looks like a failure of nature is after all one civilization's death wish, restricted in time as well as in space. Let us not forget that Freud had a purely psychological — and, big implication, time-and-space-bound — account and a name for this Cartesian pathology; he called it the ego defence of isolation, a process which isolated reason from feelings.[19] And there is also an implied cultural context when Adorno quotes Holderlin: "If you have understanding and a heart, show only one. Both they will damn, if both you show together."[20] In such a world, it is remarkable that in spite of all the indignities and exploitation they have suffered, many of the Eastern civilizations have not drawn a clear line between the victor and the defeated, the oppressor and the oppressed, and the rulers and the ruled.[21] Unwillingly they have recognized that the gap between cognition and effect tend to get bridged outside the Cartesian world, whether the gap be conceptualized as an evolutionary trap or as a battle between two halves of the human brain. Often drawing inspiration from the monistic traditions of their religions, from the myths and folkways which have set some vague half-effective limits on intergroup violence and on the objectification of living beings, the civilizations of the Third World have carefully protected the faith that the concept of evil can never be clearly defined, that there is always a continuity between the aggressor and his victim, and that liberation from oppression is not merely the freedom from an oppressive agency outside, but also ultimately a liberation from a part of one's own self.[22] This can be seen as wishy-washy collaboration with oppression; it can be also seen as a more humane strain in political and social awareness.

---

[18]*The Ghost in the Machine,* London: Picador, 1976, Chapter 18.

[19]See a fuller discussion of this subject in "Science, Authoritarianism and Culture" in this volume.

[20]Adorno, *Minima Moralia, op. cit.,* p. 197.

[21]The post-Renaissance Western preoccupation with clean divisions or oppositions of this kind is, of course, a part of the central dichotomy between the subject and the object, what Ludvig Binswanger reportedly calls "the cancer of all psychology up to now". Charles Hampden-Turner, *Radical Man,* New York: Doubleday Anchor, 1971, p. 33. For "psychology" in the Binswanger quote, one must of course read "modern Western psychology".

[22]See, for example, an interesting cultural criticism of Hinduism by even a person as humane and sensitive as Albert Schweitzer (*Hindu Thought and Its Development,* New York: Beacon, 1959) for not having a hard, concrete concept of evil. For discussions of the debate around this issue, see W. F. Goodwin, "Mysticism and Ethics: An Examination of Radhakrishna's Reply to Schweitzer's critique of Indian Thought", *Ethics,* 1957, 67, pp. 25-41; and T. M. P. Mahadevan, "Indian Ethics and Social Practice", in C. A. Moore (Ed.), *Philosophy and Culture: East and West,* Honolulu: University of Hawaii, pp. 479-493.

Frantz Fanon's concept of the cleansing role of violence — and the implicit ideology of the drive to "annihilate class enemies" in some Third World societies — sounds so alien and so Western to many sensitive Afro-Asians mainly because of this awareness.[23] Fanon admits the presence of the oppressor within the oppressed, but calls for an exorcism, where the ghost outside has to be finally confronted in violence and annihilated because it carries the burden of the ghost inside. The outer violence, Fanon suggests, is only an attempt to make a painful break with a part of one's own self. He fails to sense that such a vision ties the oppressed more deeply to the oppressor and to the culture of oppression than any collaboration can. Continuous use of the major technique on which an oppressive system is based, namely, the cultural acceptance of violence, gradually socializes the oppressed fighting oppression to some of the basic values of the system. Violence converts the battle between two visions of the human society into a fight between two groups sharing some of the same values, for spoils within a permanently power-scarce and resource-scarce system. The groupings may change; the system does not. If Fanon had lived longer, he might have come to admit that in this process of internalization lies a partial answer to two vital questions about the search for liberation in our times, namely, why dictatorships of the proletariat never end and why revolutions always devour their children. Hatred, as Alan Watts reminds us at the cost of being trite, is a form of bondage, too.

In contemporary times, no one understood better than Gandhi this stranglehold of the history of oppression on the future of man. That is why his theory of conflict resolution is something more than a simple-minded emphasis on non-violence. It recognizes that the meek are blessed only if they are, in Rollo May's terms,[24] authentically innocent and not pseudo-innocents accepting the values of an oppressive system for secondary psychological gains. Gandhi acted as if he was aware that non-synergic systems, driven by zero-sum competition and search for power, control and masculinity, force the victims of oppression to internalize the norms of the system, so that when they displace their exploiters, they build a system in which the older norms covertly prevail. So his concept of "non-cooperation" set a different goal for the victims; he stressed that the aim of the oppressed should be, not to become a first-class citizen in the world of oppression instead of a second- or third-class one, but to become the citizen of an alternative world where he can hope to win back his human authenticity. He thus becomes a non-player for the oppressors — one who plays a different game, refusing to be either a player or a counter-player. Perhaps

---

[23] *The Wretched of the Earth,* Harmondsworth: Penguin, 1967; and *Black Skin, White Masks,* New York: Grove Press, 1967.

[24] Rollo May, *Power and Innocence: A Search for the Sources of Violence,* New York: Delta, 1972.

this is what a Western biographer of Gandhi means when he suggests that Gandhi's theory of conflict resolution imputes an irreducible minimum humanity to the oppressors and militantly promotes the belief that this humanity could be actualized.[25]

The basic assumption here is that the oppressor in his state of dehumanization is as much a victim of the exploitative system as the oppressed; he has to be liberated, too. The Gandhian stress on austerity and pacifism does not spring as much from the traditional Indian principles of renunciation and monism as from a deep-seated belief in the superiority of the culture of the victims of oppression and from an effort to identify with the more humane cultural strain within an oppressive system. All his life, Gandhi sought to free the British as much as the Indians from the clutches of imperialism and the Brahmins as much as the untouchables from the caste system. Such a position bears some similarity with certain readings of Marx. Father G. Gutierrez, for instance, says: "one loves the oppressors by liberating them from their inhuman condition as oppressors, by liberating them from themselves. But this cannot be achieved except by resolutely opting for the oppressed, i.e. by combating the oppressive classes. It must be real and effective combat, not hate."[26]

This other identification, which Gandhi so successfully made, is something even those apparently identifying with the victims find difficult to make. The temptation is to use a psychological mechanism more congruent with the basic principles of the exploitative system which gives a better scope to express one's aggressive drives. As a result, identification with the oppressed has often meant identification with his world-view, in turn cruelly distorted by his experience of oppression. Through this two-step identification, even the interpreters of oppression internalize to some extent the norms of one exploitative system or another. Consequently, the fantasy of the superiority of the oppressor lies deeply imbedded in contemporary consciousness. We may be manifestly contemptuous of the exploiters of the world, we may even speak of their decadence, mental illness or dehumanization, but we are unable to feel pity or sympathy for them — as if one corner of our mind continued to believe that the privileged were superior to the underdogs with whom we sympathized; that they were more powerful economically, politically or socially and, as powerful counterplayers, at least deserved to invite jealousy or hatred.[27]

---

[25]Erik H. Erikson, *Gandhi's Truth: On the Origins of Militant Nonviolence,* New York: Norton, 1969.

[26]*A Theology of Liberation,* New York: Orbis Books, Maryknoll, 1973, p. 276. Quoted in P. Masani, "The Common Ground of Marxism and Religion", mimeographed, p. 8.

[27]The obverse of this is, of course, the oppressors' search for the "proper" worthy opponent among the oppressed. For an analysis of such a set of categories in an oppressive culture, see "The Psychology of Colonialism: Sex, Age and Ideology in British India", *The Intimate Enemy: Colonialism as an Encounter of Cultures,* forthcoming.

I have made an attempt to convey some idea of how Gandhi's future began in the present, why he constantly tried to convert the struggle against oppression from an intergroup conflict to a within-person conflict, and why his utopia was, to use Abraham Maslow's word, an eupsychia.[28] For better or for worse, this is the age of false consciousness; it is the awareness of the predicament of self-awareness which has shaped much of this century's social thinking and contributed to the emergence of the psychological man. In this sense, Gandhi's concept of self-realization is the ultimate product of an age which has been striving for the means of locating *within the individual* and *in action* the subject–object dichotomy (man as the maker of history versus man as the product of history; man as a product of biological "evolution" versus man as a self-aware aspect of nature; the ego or reality principle versus the id or pleasure principle; praxis versus dialectic or process).[29] The concept is also probably a "primitive" corrective to the post-Enlightenment split in the vision of the liberated man. During the last two and a half centuries — starting probably with Giovanni Vico — the Western sciences of man have worked with a basic contradiction. They have sought to make man the maker of his own fate — or history, if you like — by making him an object of the modern incarnations of fate — of natural and social history, evolutionary stages and cumulative reason. I am convinced that this overcorrection can only be remedied by world-views which re-emphasize man's stature as a subject, seeking a more humble participation in nature and society, who is a subject by virtue of being a master of nature and society *within.* This can only be done by acknowledging the continuities between the suffering outside and the suffering within and by defining the self as consisting of both the sufferings of the self and that of the nonself.[30]

Here lies the significance of someone like Gandhi who, probably more than anyone else in this century, tried to actualize in practice what the more sensitive social scientists and litterateurs had already made a part of our awareness, namely, that any oppressive system is only overtly a triad of the oppressor, the victim and the interpreter. Covertly the three roles cannot be

---

[28]As it happened, he was clearly influenced by important strands of Indian traditions which did stress such interiorization and working through. Being a critical traditionalist, he therefore had to do the reverse too, namely, exteriorize the inner attempts to cope with evil as only an internal state. His work as a political activist came from that.

[29]I have derived this formulation from a set of somewhat casual comments made by Neil Warren in his "Freudians and Laingians", *Encounter,* March 1978, pp. 56-63. See also Philip Reiff, *The Triumph of the Therapeutic,* New York: Harper, 1966.

[30]Though some Western scholars like Alan Watts would like to see such location of others in the self as a typically Eastern enterprise (see his *psychotherapy East and West,* New York: Ballantine, 1961) this has been occasionally a part of Western philosophical concerns, too. See, for instance, Jose Ortega Y Gasset, *Meditations on Quixote,* New York: Norton, 1967. Within the Marxist tradition Georg Lukacs has argued that in the area of cognition and in the case of the protetariat at least, the subject–object dichotomy is eliminated to the extent self-knowledge includes molar knowledge of the entire society. *History and Class-Consciousness,* London: Merlin, 1971.

separated. A complicated set of identifications and cross-identifications makes each actor in the triad represent and incorporate the other two. This view — probably expressed in its grandest form in the ancient Indian epic on greed, violence and self-realization, Mahabharata — is the flip side of Marx who believed that even the cultural products thrown up by the struggle against capitalism and created by the victim and enemies of capitalism were flawed by their historical roots in an imperfect society.[31] In fact, one may say that Gandhian praxis is the natural and logical development of radical social criticism, because it insists that the continuity between the victim, the oppressor and the observer must be realized *in action,* and one must refuse to act *as if* some constituents in an oppressive system were morally pure or uncontaminated.

To summarize, a violent and oppressive society produces its own special brands of victimhood and privilege and ensures a certain continuity between the victor and the defeated, the instrument and the target, and the interpreter and the interpreted. As a result, none of these categories remain pure. So even when such a culture collapses, the psychology of victimhood and privilege continues and produces a second culture which is only manifestly not violent or oppressive. Not to recognize this is to collaborate with violence and oppression in their subtler forms, which is, in effect, what much of social activism as well as social analysis begin to do once the intellectual climate becomes hostile to manifest cruelty and exploitation.

IV

A second example of this consciousness of non-duality can well be the refusal of many cultures to translate the principles of biopsychological continuities, such as sex and age, into principles of social stratification. Many of the major Eastern civilizations, in spite of all their patriarchal elements, have continued to see a certain continuity between the masculine and the feminine, and between infancy, adulthood and old age. Perhaps this is not all a matter of traditional wisdoms. At least in some cases it is a reaction to the colonial experience which assumed a clear break between the male and the female, and the adult and the child, and then used these biological differences as the homologues of the colonial political stratification. In the colonial ideology, the colonizer became the tough, courageous, openly aggressive, hyper-masculine ruler and the colonized became the sly, cowardly, passive-aggressive, womanly subject. Or, alternatively, the colonizer became the prototype of a mature, complete, adult civilization while the colonized became the mirror of a more simple, primitive, childlike state of civilization.

---

[31]It is one of the minor tragedies of our age that many of Marx's disciples sought to place Marx outside history and culture. He himself knew better. In the following essay ("Evaluating Utopias") I have briefly discussed how far any theory of salvation, secular or otherwise, can shirk the responsibility for whatever is done in its name.

Once again, I shall invoke Gandhi, who built an articulate model of political action to counter the models of manhood and womanhood implicit in the colonial situation in India.

It is an indication of how systems of oppression draw their strength from certain aspects of the "mother culture" that British colonialism in India made an explicit order out of what they felt was the major strength of the Western civilization *vis-à-vis* the Indian. It went:

$$\text{Masculinity} > \text{Femininity} > \text{Femininity in man}$$

In other words, masculinity is superior to femininity which, in turn, is superior to effeminacy. (One major pillar of this cultural strategy was the British emphasis on the differences between the so-called martial and non-martial races of India. The other was — and this I venture as another instance of the continuity between the oppressors and the oppressed — the belief in a similar strategy in some Indian sub-traditions which acquired a new cultural ascendency in British India.) As against this, Gandhi posited two alternative sets of relationships. In one, masculinity was seen to be at par with femininity and the two had to be transcended or synthesized for attaining a higher level of public functioning. Such "bisexuality" or "transsexuality" was seen as not merely spiritually superior both to masculinity and to femininity, as it was in traditional Hinduism, but also politically so. Gandhi's second model saw masculinity as inferior to femininity which, in turn, was seen as inferior to femininity in man. The following is a crude representation of the relationships:

$$\text{androgyny} > (\text{masculinity} \simeq \text{femininity})$$
$$\text{androgyny} > \text{femininity} > \text{masculinity}$$

I have discussed the psychological and cultural contexts of these concepts in some detail elsewhere.[32] All I want to add is that the formal equality which is often sought by the various movements fighting for the cause of woman is qualitatively different from the synergy Gandhi sought. In the first case, power, achievement, productivity, work, control over social and natural resources are seen as fixed quantities on which men have held a near-monopoly and which they must now share equally with women. In the Gandhian model, these values are seen as the indicators of a system dominated by the masculinity principle, and the system and its values must both be jettisoned for the sake of building a new world, unfettered by its history of sexual oppression. To fight for mechanical equality, Gandhi

---

[32]"Woman Versus Womanliness: An Essay in Social and Political Psychology", *At the Edge of Psychology: Essays in Politics and Culture,* New Delhi: Oxford University, 1980, pp. 32-46, and "The Psychology of Colonialism", *op. cit.*

seems to suggest, is to accept or internalize the norms of the existing system, and pay homage to the masculine values under the guise of pseudo-equality.

Similarly with age. While societies which have built upon the traditions of hyper-masculinity have conceived of adulthood as the ultimate in human life cycle because of its productive possibilities, many of the older civilizations of the world, left out of the experience of the industrial and technological revolutions, have refused to see childhood as merely a preparation for, or an inferior version of, adulthood. Nor have they seen old age as a decline from full manhood or womanhood. On the contrary, each stage of life in these societies is seen as valuable and meaningful in itself. No stage is required to derive its legitimacy from some other stage of life, nor need it be evaluated in terms of categories extraneous to it. It has been said in recent times that alternative visions of the human future must derive their ideas of spontaneity and play from the child.[33] Implied in this very proposal is the tragedy of Western adulthood which has banished spontaneity and play to a small reservation called childhood, thus protecting the adult world from contamination. Spontaneity, play, directness of experience, and tolerance of disorder are for the children or their homologues, the primitives in their own world.[34] Power, productive work and even revolutions are for the mature adults and their homologues, the advanced historical societies with their ripened revolutionary consciousness and experience with modern urban-industrialism.

On the other hand, the dominance of the productivity principle in Western modernity does not allow age to be seen as giving a touch of wisdom to social consciousness or transmitting to the next generation valued elements of culture, elements which cannot be precisely articulated or transmitted in the form of packaged products but must be transmitted in the form of shared experiences. Old age is seen primarily as creating a problem of management of less productive or non-productive human lives. With the decline in physical prowess in men and sexual attractiveness in women, the self-image of the Western man or woman becomes something less than that of a complete human being. The pathetic worship of youth and the even more pathetic attempts to defend oneself against the inner fears of losing youthfulness and social utility — with the help of pseudo-

---

[33]It's of course complementary to the ideas of "graceful playfulness" in Ivan Illich; see his *Tools for Conviviality,* Glasgow: Fontana/Collins, 1973. For the same awareness within "proper" Marxism see Evgeny Bogat, "The Great Lesson of Childhood", *Eternal Man: Reflections, Dialogues, Portraits,* Moscow: Progress Publishers, 1976, pp. 288-293. The somewhat prim psychoanalytic idea of "regression at the service of the ego" can also be viewed as an indirect plea for the acceptance of the same principle. It is possible to hazard the guess that these are all influenced in different ways by the association Christ made between childhood and the Kingdom of God. That association survives within Christianity in spite of what Lloyd deMause ("The Evolution of Childhood" in *History of Childhood*, New York: Harper Torchbook, 1975, pp. 1-74) considers to be the faith's overall thrust.

[34]See "Reconstructing Childhood" in this volume.

respectful expressions such as "senior citizens" — is not merely the creation of rampant consumerism and unfettered industrialism; it is also a product of the world-view required to run and legitimize complex systems of oppression. Gerontocracy may be a non-creative alternative to such a world-view, but it nevertheless provides a better baseline for envisioning an alternative civilization where age and sex do not serve as principles of social stratification, and where it is recognized that an appreciation of the qualities of old age gives completeness to youth and young adulthood, too.

V

This brings me to my third example of a non-dual vision of freedom from oppression, namely, the cultural refusal in many parts of the savage world to see work and play as clearly demarcated modalities of human life. Once again I shall refer to modern colonialism not solely because it is a shared legacy of the Third World but because it did much better than many other exploitative formations of the modern world in terms of having an articulate ideology, a culturally embedded legitimacy and, sometimes, a tendency to avoid counter-productive violence. That colonialism is, for this very reason, a more dangerous prototype of human violence is part of the same argument. It is not accidental that the British empire lasted two centuries, the Third Reich for twelve paltry years. Successful institutionalization of a large-scale oppressive system is not an easy attainment. It needs something more than martial skills and nihilistic passions; it needs some awareness of human limits.

One of the first things the colonial cultures invariably did was to promote the belief that the subject communities had a contempt for honest work, that they consisted of indolent shirkers who could not match the hard work or single-minded pursuit of productive labour of the colonizers. This was a belief sincerely held by the rulers. But sincerity in such matters, one knows, is only a defence against recognizing one's deeper need to justify a political economy which expects the subject community to work without human dignity, without adequate economic incentives, and without a meaningful concept or goal of work.

The victim of oppression, I have already argued, is not always a pure victim. One part of him collaborates, compromises and kowtows; another part defies and "non-cooperates" or subverts and destroys, often in the name of collaboration and under the garb of obsequiousness. (The modern tradition of social criticism is unidirectional. It has no place for the demystification of collaboration or for the discovery of secret defiance. This is because critical analysis is equated with debunking and all it can do is to reveal the base of evil under the superstructure of the "good".) The colonized subjects, too, soon learnt, through that subtle communication which goes on between the rulers and the ruled, to react to and cope with the obsessive, driven concept of productive work brought into the colonies by the European and Christian subtraditions which dominated the colonial cultures and had already cornered other subtraditions within Western Christianity.[35] At a certain level of awareness, the subjects knew they could retaliate, tease and defy their oppressors — "fools attached to action", as the Bhagavad Gita might have called them — by refusing to share the imposed concepts of the sanctity of work and work-values such as productivity, control, predictability, manipulation, monitoring and utility. The differences between work and play, stressed by a repressive conscience which had to idealize colonialism in terms of a civilizational mission, could only be confronted by an unconscious non-cooperation which sought to resist through "malingering", "shrinking" and "indiscipline". This is the resistance the colonized offered. If this vaguely reminds the reader of the folk response of American Blacks to slavery[36] it only once again shows the shared experience of social suffering the world over. And it was not that folk after all. In India at least there was the ancient religious text of Gita, waiting to be "misused" by those on the wrong side of history:

> "who dares to see action in inaction,
> and inaction in action
> he is wise, he is yogi,
> he is the man who knows what is work."[37]

This may not be the scholar's idea of the true meaning of the *sloka,* but what are religious texts for, if they cannot occasionally provide folksy guides to survival?

If colonialism took away the human dignity of its subjects, the subjects unconsciously tried, in attempts to minimize suffering and protect self-esteem, to take away the dignity of their oppressors by forcing them to use ugly force to make their subjects work, produce and be useful. This is perhaps the way helpless victims are often forced into controlling and monitoring their tormentors. In their near-total impotency, they strip their masters of their pretences to civilized authority, humane governance and, ultimately, self-respect. This is the unnoticed magic of subjugation. It ensures that if the victims are sometimes pseudo-innocent part-victims, the victors too are all too often pseudo-profiteering part-victors.

In rejecting the principle of productivity and work, many subjugated Third World societies have also rejected the concept of workability. They have preserved with some care the banished consciousness of the First and

---

[35]On activity and work as the first postulate of a Faustian civilization, see a brief statement in Roger Garaudy, "Christian Faith and Liberation", in Masini and Galtung, *op. cit.*

[36]Cf. E.D. Genovese, *Roll, Jordan Roll: The World the Slaves Made,* New York: Pantheon, 1974. See also Moore, *op. cit.,* pp. 465-466.

[37]*The Bhagavad Gita,* IV: 18, transcreated by P. Lal, New Delhi: Oreint Paperback, 1965, p. 33.

Second Worlds that knowledge and ideas are valuble, not only in terms of applicability, usefulness or testability, but also in terms of aesthetics, relatedness to man and nature, self-transcendence and self-realization, and in terms of forms which are not subservient to so-called substances. Certain intuitive and speculative modes of perception have come naturally to them, giving rise, on the one hand, to an institutionalized dependence on music, literature, fine arts and other creative media for the expression of social thought and scientific analysis: and, on the other hand, to a dependence upon highly speculative, deductive, mathematical and, even, quantitative-empirical modes of thinking as vehicles of normative passions and as expressions of religious or mystical sentiments. I have in mind here not the feeling man which Leopold Senghor offsets against the Cartesian man of the West, but a culture which refuses to partition cognition and affect, both as a matter of conviction and as a technique of survival.[38]

This blurring of the boundaries between science, religion and arts is also of course a defiance of the modern concept of classification of knowledge and education.[39] At one plane it represents an obstreperous refusal to be converted to the modern world-view which is seen, from before such perceptions became fashionable among the social scientists, as legitimation of structural as well as cultural imperialism. At another plane, it is a recognition that the megamachines of the technocratic societies — as Lewis Mumford would describe them — have coopted mainstream science to their purpose and, since about the seventeenth century, have consistently con-tributed to the blurring of the difference between science and technology. It is a recognition that technology now legitimates science in these societies and it is not the spirit of scientific inquiry but the spirit of technological dependency which is the dominant consciousness of the modern world. You need technological marvels not only for acquiring a sense of personal potency and self-esteem but also acquiring a sense of national power, self-esteem and self-fulfilment. It is also a recognition that as techniques have grown in power, they have begun to confer status, to perform a pace-setting role within science, and to use scientific knowledge for increasing produc-tivity and control. As opposed to this culture of instrumental science, which works with a concept of a universal, perfectly objective, modern science and admits, at best, only the existence of peripheral folk-sciences from which modern science may occasionally pick up scraps of information, the sub-jugated and marginalized sections of the world — the third-class citizens in-habiting the Third World — have sought to maintain their dignity by con-ceptualizing the world of science as an area of a number of competing or co-existing universal ethnosciences, one of which has become dominant and

---

[38]For a fuller treatment of the psychology of partitioning cognition and affect, see "Science, Authoritarianism and Culture" in this volume.

[39]See on this subject J. P. S. Uberoi, *Science and Culture,* New Delhi: Oxford University, 1979.

usurped the status of the *only* universal and modern science.[40] Various traditional systems of medicine, artisan skills which retain the individuality of the producers and refuse to draw a line between art and craft, certain agricultural practices which have resisted modern agronomy — these are not only aspects of a resilient cultural self-affirmation; these are indicators of a spirit which defies the power of a way of life which seeks to cannibalize all other ways of life. The Third World has a vested interest in refusing to grant sanctity to a science which sees human beings and nature as the raw material for technological and scientific growth. What seems an irrational resistance to the products of modern science and technology in the peripheries of the world is often a deeply rooted and perfectly legitimate suspicion of sectors which live off these peripheries and a desperate attempt to preserve an alternative concept of knowledge and technique in the interstices of the "uncivilized" world.

VI

Fourthly, the experience of suffering of some Third World societies has contributed a new theme to utopianism by sensing and resisting the oppression which comes as "history". By this I mean not only the limits which our past always seems to impose on our visions of the future, but also the use of a linear, progressive, cumulative, deterministic concept of history — often carved out of humanistic ideologies — to suppress alternative world-views, alternative utopias and, even alternative self-concepts. The oppressed of the world often feel that they are constrained not merely by partial, biased or ethnocentric history, but by the idea of history itself.

One can give a heavily clinical interpretation of such scepticism towards history, often inextricably linked with painful fearsome memories of man-made suffering. Defiance of history may look like a primitive denial of history and, to the extent the present is fully shaped by history in the modern eyes, denial of contemporary realities. But, even from a strict clinical point of view, there can be reasons for and creative uses of a historicity. What Alexander and Margarete Mitscherlich say about those with a history of inflicting suffering also applies to those who have been their victims:

> "A very considerable expenditure of psychic energy is necessary to maintain this separation of acceptable and unacceptable memories; and what is used in the defence of a self anxious to protect itself against bitter qualms of conscience and doubts about its worth is unavailable for mastering the present."[41]

---

[40]See "The Traditions of Technology", in this volume.

[41]"The Inability to Mourn", in Robert J. Lifton and Eric Olson (Eds.), *Explorations in Psychohistory, The Wellfleet Papers,* New York: Simon and Schuster, 1974, pp. 257-270, quote on p. 262.

The burden of history is the burden of such memories and anti-memories. Some cultures prefer to live with it and painfully excavate the anti-memories and integrate them as a part of the present consciousness. Some cultures prefer to handle the same problem at the mythopoeic level. Instead of excavating for the real past, they excavate for the other meaning of the present, as revealed in traditions and myths about an ever-present past.

What seems an ahistorical and, even, anti-historical attitude in many non-Western cultures is often only an attempt, on the part of these cultures, to incorporate their historical experiences into their shared traditions as categories of thinking, rather than as objective chronicles of the past.[42] In these cultures, the mystical and consciousness-expanding modes are alternative pathways to experiences which in other societies are sought through a linear concept of a "real" history. In the modern context these modes can sometimes become what Robert J. Lifton calls "romantic totalism" — a post-Cartesian absolutism which seeks to replace history with experience.[43] But that is not a fate which is written into the origins of these modes. If the problematique is the totalism and not the romance, the *history* of civilizations after Christopher Columbus and Vasco da Gama also shows that that totalism can also come from a history which seeks to replace experience. Specially so when, after the advent of the idea of scientific history, history has begun to share in the near-monopoly science has already established in the area of human certitude. Albert Camus, it seems, once drew a line between the makers of history and the victims of history. The job of the writer, he reportedly said, was to write about the victims. For the silent majority of the world, the makers of history also live in history and the defiance of history begins not so much with an alternative history as with the denial of history as an acreage of human certitude.

In their scepticism towards history, the oppressed cultures have an ally in certain recessive orientations to history in the Western culture, manifested in the ways of thinking that have been formalized in recent decades by structural anthropology and psychoanalysis, which see history either as a language, with its own semiotics, or as "screen memory", with its own rules of psychological defences. Both these disciplines see the construction of history as an important clue to the principles of the human mind, on the one hand, and the experiences of the here-and-the-now, on the other. The dynamics of history, according to such a point of view, is not in an unalterable past moving towards an inexorable future; it is in the ways of thinking and in the choices of present times.[44]

---

[42]See a fuller discussion of these theme in the context of Gandhi's world-view in "The Psychology of Colonialism", *op. cit.*

[43]*Boundaries: Psychological Man in Revolution,* New York, Simon & Schuster, 1969, pp. 105-106.

[44]I need hardly add that within the modern idea of history too, this view has survived as a strain. From Karl Marx to Benedetto Croce and from R. G. Collingwood to Michael Oakshott, students of philosophy of history have moved close to an approach to history which is compatible with traditional orientations to past times.

There is a fit between this hostility to history and the need to protect self-esteem and ensure survival in many Third World societies. History, as it is commonly defined, has never been fair to them. Nor could it be otherwise, given the structure of cognition it presumes. The more scientific a history, the more dangerous a kitbag of ideas it is for the inhabitants of the experimental laboratory called the Third World. It is history which has frequently allowed ideas of social intervention to be swallowed up by concepts of social engineering in modern times. In the dominant cultures of the West, history has always been the unfolding of a theory of progress, a serialized expression of a *telos* which, by definition, cannot be shared by the communities, placed on the lower rungs of the ladder of history or outside the scope of history. Even the histories of oppression and the historical theories of liberation include stages of growth which, instead of widening the options of the victims, reduce them. In fact, one of the main functions of these theories is to ensure the centrality of cultural and intellectual paradigms within which not only the experiences of a few societies dominate, but within which even the models of dissent from these experiences can be accommodated. As an old Bengali saying goes, such paradigms first bite in the incarnation of snakes and then offer a cure in the incarnation of witch doctors.

The ethnocentrism of the anthropologist is corrigible, because he is segregated from his subject only spatially and because, ultimately, his subjects can some day talk back. The ethnocentrism towards the past often goes unchallenged. The dead do not rebel, nor can they speak out. In this sense, the subjecthood of the subjects of history is total and absolute, and to admit the existence of a real or scientific history is to admit a continuity between subjecthood in history and subjection in the present.

The refusal to acknowledge the primacy of history, thus, is also the refusal to fetter the future in terms of the past. This itself is a special attitude to human potentialities, an alternative form of utopianism that has survived till now as a language alien to, and subversive of, every theory which, in the name of liberation, circumscribes and makes predictable the spirit of human rebelliousness.

VII

As my final example, I shall briefly discuss the controversial dependency syndrome in some Third World culture. When offset against the occidental's search for autonomy or independence, it is this syndrome which allegedly explains the origin, meaning and resiliences of colonial rule as well as subjugation.

Such explanations have been savagely attacked, by both Césaire and Fanon, as parts of a racist psychoanalysis. Césaire quotes the following words of Manoni as virtually the final proof of the Western psychologist's prejudice against the oppressed cultures:

"It is the destiny of the Occidental to face the obligation laid down by the commandment *Thou shalt leave thy father and thy mother*. This obligation is incomprehensible to the Madagascan. At a given time in his development, every European discovers in himself the desire . . . to break the bonds of dependency, to become the equal of his father. The Madagascan, never! He does not experience rivalry with the paternal authority, 'manly protest', or Adlarian inferiority — ordeals through which the European must pass and which are civilized forms . . . of the initiation rites by which one achieves manhood. . . ."[45]

I have not been able to locate this passage in Manoni's *Prospero and Caliban* and do not know in which context it occurs.[46] Nor do I know Manoni's politics which presumably can provide the other context of these lines. Thus, I have to accept at face value Césaire's and Fanon's plaint that Manoni vends "down-at-heel clichés" to justify "absurd prejudices" and "dresses up" the old stereotype of the Negro as an overgrown child.

However, there cannot but be a nagging suspicion that a third view on the subject is possible. That view would recognize that the modern West has not only institutionalized a concept of childhood which legitimizes oppression in terms of an ideology of masculine non-dependent adulthood, it has also popularized a devastatingly sterile concept of autonomy and individualism which has now totally atomized the individual. Many non-Western observers of the culture of modern West — its lifestyle, literature, arts and its social sciences — have been struck by the extent to which contractual, competititive individualism — and the utter loneliness which flows from it — dominates the Western consciousness. From Frederich Nietzsche to Sigmund Freud and from Karl Marx to Franz Kafka much of Western social analysis, too, has stood witness to this cultural pathology. And what once looked like independence from one's parental authorities, and defiance of the larger aggregates they represented, now increasingly look like aspects of a Hobbesian world-view gone rabid. They have manifestly reduced the Western individual to a consumption unit to which impersonal "machines" sell consumables and from which other machines get work in order to produce more consumables. To the extent Manoni imputes to the Madagascan some degree of anti-individualism, he unconsciously underscores the point that the Western version of individualism — and the insane search for unlimited autonomy it has unleashed — cannot be truly separated from the thirst for colonies and for dominance over one's fellow humans. In an inter-related world, total autonomy means reducing everyone else's autonomy.

---

[45]Cesaire, *op. cit.*, p. 40.

[46]*Prospero and Caliban, The Psychology of Colonization,* translated by Pamela Powesland, 2nd Ed., New York: Frederick A. Praeger, 1964.

Thus, while the much-maligned dependency complex may not be the best possible cultural arrangement when facing the juggernaut of a modern system of oppression, it could be seen as a more promising baseline for mounting a search for a genuine social relatedness and, for that matter, for a maturer form of individualism than the individuality that now dominates the modern world. It may not meet the standards of the Westernized critics of the West in the Third World, it may be even intended as a slander of the non-West, but those who have lived for centuries with only the extremes of relatedness and dependency will probably never know that, in a world taken over by the autonomy principle and by the extremes of individualism, dependency and fears of abandonment represent a hope and a potentiality. The pathology of relatedness has already become less dangerous than the pathology of unrelatedness. What looks like an ego "wanting in strength" in the Malagasy or a straightforward instance of a weak ego in the Indian can be viewed as another class of ego strength; what looks like insufficient independence training in the non-achieving societies and "willing subservience" and "self-castrations" in the Hindu may be read also as an affirmation of basic relatedness and of the need for some degree of reverence.[47] Elsewhere in his *Discourse on Colonialism,* Césaire relates Nazism to Europe's blood-stained history in the colonies.[48] He is unaware that some scholars have already indirectly traced the first kind of satanism to the unrestrained spread in Europe, over the previous century, of the doctrines of amoral realpolitik and *sacro egoismo* and of the "morals of a struggle that no longer allows for respect".[49] One must now take this argument to its logical end, too, and relate the second kind of satanism to the same set of values. One must also, as a part of the same exercise, refuse even indirect sanction to the search for total autonomy and total individualism, even when they are a part of a post-colonial ideology.

VIII

I have chosen these examples to illustrate what I have described in the beginning as the indissoluble bond between the future of the subjugated peripheries of the world and the apparently powerful, prosperous, imperial cultures. The reader must have noticed that each of the examples I have given also happen to be a live problem in exactly those parts of the world which are traditionally considered privileged. The various forms of neo-

---

[47]'Manoni, *op. cit.,* p. 41; Sudhir Kakar quoted by V. S. Naipaul, *India, A Wounded Civilization,* London: Deutsch, 1977; David C. McClelland and David G. Winter, *Motivating Economic Achievement,* New York: Basic Books, 1969; G. Morris Carstairs, *The Twice-Born: A Study of a Community of High-Caste Hindus,* Bombay: Allied, 1971, p. 160.

[48]Cesaire, *op. cit.*

[49]Frederick Meinecke and Gerherd Ritter, quoted in Renzo de Felice, *Interpretations of Fascism,* translated by Brenda H. Everett, Cambridge, Mass.: Harvard University, 1977, pp. 17-18.

Marxism, the various versions of the women's liberation movement, the numerous attempts to build alternative philosophies of science and technology by giving up the insane search for total power, control and predictability are but a recognition that the differences between the so-called privileged and underprivileged parts of the world are only notional. As the peripheries of the world have been subjected to economic degradation and political impotency and robbed of their human dignity with the help of dionysian theorems of progress, the First and the Second Worlds too have sunk deeper into intellectual provincialism, cultural decadence and moral degradation. If you grant me the right to my own cliché, no victor can be a victor without being a victim. In the case of nation-states as much as in the case of two-person situations, there is an indivisibility of ethical choices. If the Third World's vision of the future is handicapped and enriched by its history of suffering, the First World's future, too, is shaped by the same experience.

The reader may have also noticed that I have tried to give moral and cultural content to some of the common ways in which the savage world has tried to cope with modern oppression and then projected these common ways as possibilities or opportunities. How far is this justified? After all, as one popular argument goes, history is made through the dirty process of political economy and it has no place to accommodate the dubious moralism which springs from motivated readings of human frailty under conditions of stress! My response to the query is as naïve as my formulation of it. I would like to argue that the so-called ultimate realities of political economy too could be further demystified to obtain clues to a new vision of human future. The frailties of human nature produced by a given social arrangement can begin to look like the baseline of a new society, once another social arrangement is envisioned. A brain researcher has recently said, summarizing comparative zoological work on evolution, that there is a "survival of weak", too, and the weak do inherit the world.[50] The present context is different, but the principle probably holds.

For instance, what looks like an inability to build proper nation-states in large parts of the world can surely be read as a political or cultural failure to enter the modern world. If nothing, such failures seem to further underwrite the rule of a few chosen nation-states in the global arena. However, by only slightly straining one's primitive credulity, it could be also read as a refusal in some cultures to believe that when the reasons of state under a nation-state system do not coincide with the needs of personal or collective morality, it is the former which should get priority. The second reading is not negated by the blood-drenched history and the coups and counter-coups in the Third World — I am speaking of possibilities and opportunities, not

---

[50]Paul D. MacLean, "The Imitative–Creative Interplay of our Three Mentalities", in Harold Harris (Ed.), *Astride the Two Cultures: Arther Koestler at 70,* New York: Random House, 1976, pp. 187-213.

offering a prognosis of the future based on a trend analysis. Likewise, what looks like superstitious pantheism or crass anthropomorphism may be celebrated as a defiance of totalist monotheism and modern anthropocentrism and their arrogant ecocidal world-conception. Once again, the second interpretation is not disproved by the poor-conservationist record of much of the Third World. I am speaking of what could be, in the future, a new cultural self-expression of an ancient man–nature symbiosis; I am not projecting statistically the past or the present into the future.

I hope all this will not be seen as an elaborate attempt to project the sensitivities of the Third World as the future consciousness of the globe or a plea to the First World to wallow in a comforting sense of guilt. Nor does it, I hope, sound like the standard doomsday "propheteering" which often preface fiery calls to a millennial revolution. All I am trying to do is to affirm that ultimately it is not a matter of synthesizing or aggregating different civilizational visions of the future. Rather, it is a matter of admitting that while each civilization must find its own authentic vision of the future and its own authenticity in future, neither is conceivable without admitting the *experience of cosuffering* which has now brought some of the major civilizations of the world close to each other. It is this cosuffering which make the idea of cultural closeness something more than the chilling concept of One World which nineteenth-century European optimism popularized and promoted to the status of a dogma.[51]

The intercultural communion I am speaking about is defined by two intellectual coordinates. The first of them is the recognition that the "real" values of different civilizations are not in need of synthesis. They are, in terms of man's biological needs, already in reasonable harmony and capable of transcending the barriers of social consciousness. In other words, the principle of cultural relativism — that I write on the possibilities of a distinct eupsychia for the Third World is a partial admission of such relativism — is acceptable only to the extent it accepts the universalism of some core values of humankind. Anthropologism is no cure for ethnocentrism; it merely pluralizes the latter. Absolute relativism can also become an absolute justification of oppression in the name of scholarly commitment, as it often becomes in the apolitical treatise called the anthropologist's field report.

The second coordinate is the acknowledgement that the search for authenticity of a civilization is always a search for the "other face" of the

---

[51]As Fouad Ajami recognizes, "The faith of those in the core in global solutions came up against the suspicions of those located elsewhere that in schemes of this kind the mighty would prevail, that they would blow away the cobwebs behind which weak societies lived. . . . in a world where cultural boundaries are dismantled, we suspect we know who would come out on the top". See Ajami's "The Dialectics of Local and Global Culture: Islam and Other Cases", *Alternatives*, 1981, 7, in press. Ajami rightly advises us to walk an intellectual and political tight rope, avoiding both the "pit of cultural hegemony" and "undiluted cultural relativism".

civilization, either as a hope or as a warning. The search for a civilization's utopia, too, is part of this larger quest. It needs not merely the ability to interpret and reinterpret one's own traditions, but also the ability to involve the dominant or recessive aspects of other civilizations as allies in one's struggle for cultural self-discovery, the willingness to become allies to other civilizations trying to discover their other faces, and the skills to give more centrality to these new readings of civilizations and civilizational concerns. This is the only form of a dialogue of cultures which can transcend the flourishing intercultural barters of our times.

14

New Technologies, Old Orders

IAN MILES[1]
Science Policy Research Unit, University of Sussex, UK

1. Introduction

This paper sets out to discuss alternative possibilities for the development of Western societies, putting these into the focus provided by an account of current economic and technological changes. The discussion is in some ways at quite a high level of abstraction: it is concerned very much with tendencies within advanced industrial capitalist countries, and puts on one side questions concerning developments within the wider world-system, except when these demand to be considered. There is no doubt that global developments may play a major role in altering the opportunities and constraints relevant to the scenarios to be outlined below. A further abstraction means that most of the discussion will concern an idealized "Western society": only occasionally will difference between countries of this type be alluded to, and likewise their international economic and political relations will only be touched upon.

The aim is to deal with the ways in which the next few decades may be shaped by tendencies and counter-tendencies being evoked in and conditioned by the current economic restructuring in Western societies, taking up the possibilities suggested by changing technology in particular. Again a limitation of the analysis should be pointed out. The technological change which this paper will focus on is that concerning the new information technologies. Other technological innovations on our horizon may also drastically condition the directions of social development, and it is easy to be dazzled by the vast range of possibilities which they suggest.[2] But the

---

[1]This is a second draft of the paper presented at the conference. The comments of participants at the conference were helpful in suggesting revisions, as were those of other members of the Science Policy Research Unit, University of Sussex, where I am presently based. Chris Freeman, in particular, took the trouble of providing detailed critical comments. This paper is thus the better for the contributions of several people, and if it does not adequately reflect their valuable points, this is the author's responsibility.

[2]Among these new technologies should be mentioned the possibility of major developments in: biotechnology (biologically based industrial processes, genetic engineering); psychotechnology (electronic and pharmaceutical means of mood and behaviour control, systematic programming of childrearing, education and penal activities); space technology

"microelectronics revolution" is already well under way, and will clearly affect a vast range of social activities in very direct ways, so a focus on information technology seems justified.

Microelectronics are important less because they perform completely novel functions — while new applications have been developed, in general the operations involved are well-established ones — than because they represent a dramatic reduction of costs. Now that computing devices can be manufactured with far less in the way of labour and materials inputs — and these costs are continuing to decline rapidly — it has become economically practical to apply them very extensively. As this has been recognized in recent years, there has arisen on the one hand an intense and often poorly informed debate about immediate impacts on employment and industrial competitiveness in the medium-term future (the next decade or so), and on the other hand, rather fanciful predictions of the efficient glories of a future "information-based society".

This paper draws on these literatures, among others, but seeks to take a very different approach. It begins with an assessment of current tendencies and counter-tendencies underpinning social and technological change in Western societies. On this basis, it is possible to move on to discussing possible futures. Different possible resolutions of the social forces whose conflict underpins current developments are considered, and these provide very different visions of future societies. The aim of this paper, however, is not to present a menu of different images of the future from which readers may select their favourites. It is intended to point to some of the conditions and practices which may determine the course of future development. Rather than taking the form of options which can be put into effect by, say, different shadings of government policy, these are among the possible outcomes of present and future struggles. The only way in which one can choose a future is to decide in what way one is to relate to and participate in these struggles.

2. Futures in the present[3]

The striking developments currently occurring in microelectronics technology are inseparable from broader processes of social change that have been evident for some years. The period of the "post-war boom" is clearly over: since the late 1960s the structures and institutions which had permitted fairly smooth and rapid economic growth in Western societies following the Second World War have one by one shown signs of buckling under the pressure of their own products. In the sphere of international

---

(space colonies, military activity in deep space); oceanic technology (aquaculture, seabed mining); weaponry (modernized non-nuclear armaments, environmental and biological warfare); nuclear power (fast-breeder reactors, fusion power) and many more.

[3]This title is a modification of that of a selection of C. R. James's work, *The Future in the Present* (London: Allison & Busby 1977).

relations alone, this has been manifold. International trade and currency organizations have lost their direction, with the negotiations they foster suddenly faltering and facing stalemates. Revolutionary movements and governments in the Third World (sometimes, even revolutionary movements have become the governments) have challenged the political and economic domination of their countries by Western interests, and there have been results as diverse as the "oil crisis" and new waves of armed struggle. Even East–West *détente* is by no means as certain as it seemed a few years ago.

Within Western societies the international flux, especially its recurrent threats of world economic recession, has increased the strains upon structures which had already gone considerable distance towards undermining themselves. The "fiscal crisis of the state", as O'Connor terms it, has meant that the improved living standards associated with the "welfare state" are now put into question again, and, indeed, the whole balance of private and public production and consumption seems to be changing. At the same time as disquiet has been growing about the social and environmental consequences of such major programmes as those around nuclear power, the scope of many decisions that need to be taken and the powerful organization of certain of the interests affected (notably industrialists, financiers and unionists) have been such as to provide a displacement of crucial areas of policy out of the public or parliamentary sphere and into the closed-door realms of corporate decision-making. Social polarization has grown in other ways too. On the one hand, there has been growing unionization and militancy among previously unorganized workers (e.g. among groups such as women, youth, immigrant and minority group workers, and in public sector employment, white-collar and technical jobs and the like), as well as the emergence of new political and cultural movements (e.g. the women's movement, environmentalism). And on the other hand, in many countries racist and fascist groups and ideologies have reappeared, sometimes in influential portions of the state apparatus; and repressive state practices involved with the maintenance of particular forms of domestic order have multiplied.

These are all indicators of a major restructuring of social relations that is under way in the present world. Conflicts have in many cases become more acute simply because a restructuring of a situation is likely to imply a new distribution of costs and benefits, and those affected seek to see their interests advanced. The reasons for the current significance of such restructuring — after all, many social forms are continually being changed — is that the varied developments mentioned above, along with others too numerous to mention, are related together through an unfolding crisis in the sphere of economic production. Rather than representing an accidental interruption of natural economic stability, this crisis stems from the contradictory dynamics of capital accumulation. Whether it will manifest itself in the form of a full-fledged world crisis along the lines of the Great Depression of the 1930s may be resolved within the next few years. These are obvious differences between the 1930s and the 1980s: for one thing, the state is now deeply involved in economic affairs. The state now takes a major role in restructuring the accumulation process to cope with its contradictions and thus proceed.[4]

These differences between current and past economic restructurings are not necessarily incompatible with the argument that the recessions and instabilities of the 1970s mark the beginning of a downturn in a "long-wave", "Kondratiev cycle".[5] There have been a number of attempts to account for what appear to be about 40-year-long cycles in industrial capitalist economies, with technological change occupying a significant place in most recent discussions; explanations tend to revolve around the reproduction and disintegration of proportionality between capital goods industries and infrastructure construction on the one hand, and consumer goods industries on the other. But even if these arguments that future decades may well be filled with continuing recession and instability are flawed, it would seem that the present global restructuring is likely to be protracted and painful.

This paper will not take up the problems of restructuring international relations in the wake of the decline in the economic power of the USA relative to that of other Western countries, and the challenges from the Third World. The basic concern here is the restructuring of social relations within Western societies, and the role of new technologies in this. Without lapsing into economic determinism, it is possible to argue that the restructuring of productive capital, as the means of overcoming economic crisis, is fundamental here. Technological change in production is a vital part of this restructuring, but before turning to the issue of the new technologies it is worth making a few general points.

The restructuring of productive capital means changing the positions occupied by its two elements, labour-power and constant capital (new materials and means of production), in the production process. Broadly following Fine and Harris (1979), this can be said to directly promote conflict between capital and labour in the production process — for example, over speed-ups of work and over the displacement of workers and changing work conditions involved in technological innovation. And it indirectly

---

[4]This is not the place to launch into an exposition of crisis theory and detailed studies of the current global restructuring. The arguments here draw upon Amin (1974), Fine and Harris (1979), Gambarotta (1978), Mandel (1973, 1978), U.R.P.E. Economics Education Project (1978), Walton and Gamble (1977) and Wright (1978).

[5]This argument has been made by numerous authorities, among them the Marxist Mandel (1975) and various consultants to the conservative Trilateral Commission, the computer modeller Forrester (1978), the critic of doomsters Freeman (1978), and the prophets of microelectronics Barron and Curnow (1979). Despite the wide spectrum of support, however, the idea of long waves is at present very controversial.

affects conflict in the sphere of exchange: that between capital and labour over wages, and that between different fractions of capital over the distribution of surplus value. The state is involved in such conflicts; and despite the "freedom" rhetoric of monetarists and conservatives in general,[6] the tendency over successive crises has been for the state to move increasingly into the forefront of restructuring. As always, the capitalist state maintains its coercive potential, here applying it to limit the expression of opposition to restructuring. "Social contracts" and wages policies are used to limit wages, trades unions are regulated so as to contain workers' dissent and to secure cooperation with industrial change. Welfare services are squeezed in order to release funds for private enterprise. Ideological systems are brought into play to portray restructuring as socially neutral "modernization". And as well as providing incentives and infrastructure to stimulate coordinated development toward more productive corporations, the state may be directly responsible for the restructuring of nationalized industries.

Microelectronics technology is certain to play important roles in the unfolding of these tendencies, although in no way are these roles completely predetermined. The microprocessors makes it economically attractive to fit many machines and instruments with control devices: this allows for much greater automation of the workplace as well as the sophistication of many consumer durables and other products.

Taking first the development and introduction of the new electronics technologies within the sphere of production, two broad issues may be addressed: changes in the labour process itself and changes in employment. In the case of the labour process, the aim of introducing new technologies is to increase profitability via increasing worker productivity. In many respects microelectronics promises to improve working conditions, reducing physical effort and mental strain. On the other hand, there are indications that it may often lead to dehumanization and new hazards at work. It is difficult to assess the balance of different tendencies here, in part because these tendencies are affected by work-place conflict. Capital accumulation, rather than fulfilling work or socially beneficial products, sets the logic of industry in Western societies: whether these outcomes converge or contradict each other is not a matter of inherent properties of technologies so much as the product of the clash of social forces mobilized behind each goal.

Clearly there are circumstances in which new technologies have been used to improve work and work conditions. Microelectronics offer the possibility of making many manual jobs easier and safer. In principle devices like word processors can eliminate much drudgery and repetition in clerical work.

---

[6]Thus *The Minimum State* (1979), proposed by Brian Crozier, guru of the National Freedom Association and the Institute for the Study of Conflict, is minimal only in its lack of concern for public welfare and for those who are submitted to its far-from-minimal repressive apparatus.

(Raw material and energy savings can also be achieved with more sophisticated information-processing devices.) When repetitive tasks are automated, the worker is "freed" to attend to more complex and perhaps creative tasks: but this can also mean that decisions about the pacing and variety of work may be removed from workers and their established skills and practices, and regulated instead by machine characteristics. For example, Harman (1978) cites a word-processor operator as reporting that "the natural breaks you get by using a typewriter . . . disappear since the word processor does all these things (e.g. moving from one line, one page, one job to another) for you at very high speed. . . . The mental effort is more repetitive and more continuous".

Related to this, "deskilling" could be a possible consequence of change which simplifies and standardizes tasks, thereby reducing workers' control over tasks. This deskilling of many workers is by no means incompatible with the need for new skills on the part of a fraction of the workforce who need to be able to adapt and maintain new technologies.[7] Further, some observers and activists (e.g. Cooley, 1976) have noted a "proletarianization" of groups of intellectual and technical workers: many white-collar workers may come to face the speed-ups, shift work and deskilling previously reserved for blue-collar workers as the use of such techniques as computer-aided design.

As control is removed from workers' hands, there are also moves towards introducing more surveillance of workers by management, and to making this surveillance more comprehensive by the use of impersonal record-keeping (and even, perhaps, warning-issuing) machines. One such computerized system (Brighton Labour Process Group, 1977, described this) keeps tracks of telephone calls, absences from work zones (e.g. visits to toilets) and can monitor employees' whereabouts in the building at any point in time — and it can also be used to restrict access to parts of the building. Finally, it should be noted that health hazards may be associated with the current round of technological innovation: problems have been noted with job speed-up, with the intensive use of TV screens (leading to eyestrain), with new printing techniques (possibly dangerous chemicals), etc.

To these rather heterogenous implications of the new technologies for the labour process, questions of employment should be noted. After all, if the restructuring of productive capital demands technological innovation, then conventional industrial conflict (and legislative reforms) may be an appropriate strategy for preventing worsened working conditions; but if some predictions of the employment effects of microelectronics are borne out, then this strategy would seem to be quite inappropriate.

---

[7]Elger (1979) provides a detailed, if preliminary, account of the complex issues surrounding skill-formation and deskilling. Discussion of these matters owes a great amount to the pioneering work of Braverman (1974).

While predictions of an extremely automated production system are rather premature, a wide range of tasks involving information processing may well be removed from direct human operation. There is enormous potential for work processors and office computers to reduce secretarial work. Automated tellers and electronic fund transfers can eliminate many clerical functions in banking and finance. In wholesale and retail distribution, accounting may be extensively automated; telecommunications technology is likewise offering considerable labour savings. Blue-collar jobs are threatened both through workplace automation (e.g. in assembly of electrical components) and product changes (e.g. electronic watches and cash registers displacing mechanical ones).

Against this unemployment-generation, some tendencies may be cited which would demand new jobs. Manufacture of the new workplace technologies themselves, and of new consumer products (such as those electronic products to be discussed below), clearly involves human labour. But these processes are highly capital-intensive, and with fierce international competition emerging around the new products, it is unlikely that these tendencies will have a short or medium-term impact anywhere comparable with tendencies toward increasing unemployment.[8] A commonplace argument is that increased automation of manufacturing poses no problem of mass unemployment, for as the West develops into a "service economy" jobs in service work will mushroom, is no comfort here. Gershuny (1978) has demonstrated that many services are tending to be provided by consumers themselves with the aid of commodities they have purchased, rather than the labour involved in the service being subject to a market transaction — for example, consumers buy washing machines instead of laundry services. And microelectronics has considerable potential for displacing white-collar and service workers (including many employed by the state). Along with the likely increased unemployment among unskilled workers, then, there is likely to be pressure upon white-collar jobs — especially those of young women in office work.

The fact that many people, through lack of work, possess much reduced income, does not imply that new luxury goods will swarm onto the market. Among the implications of new technologies are the marketing of many new consumer products. Some of these have become familiar in the last few years: digital wrist watches, pocket calculators, TV games, chess-playing machines, electronic notebooks and foreign language dictionaries, etc. A number of characteristics of information-processing systems can lead to

---

[8]Thus numerous commentators (e.g. Hines, 1978) have postulated levels of unemployment soaring in the 1980s, perhaps to Great Depression levels. (For one of the few attempts to empirically assess employment prospects in different industries see McLean and Rush, 1978.) The divergent tendencies working themselves out over the cycle of accumulation as a result of major technological innovations are central to some theorizations of Kondratiev waves — see, for example, Freeman (1978).

modifications of existing commodities. For example, there have been developments towards "personalization" of operation (e.g. controls to reprocess recordings to taste and room characteristics), programmability (e.g. complex routines for cookers and washing machines), and energy conservation (e.g. regulatory devices in automobile engines). Novel commodities, too, are being produced and, in some cases, diffused. Television-linked services are being introduced for domestic and business uses (in Britain viewers with special equipment can call up vast quantities of computerized information on such things as current affairs, weather and traffic conditions, financial trends). Many extensions of such services have been postulated: video-telephones, electronic access to libraries (including libraries of films and music), to shops (for price comparisons and placing orders), automation of health and welfare services; and electronic transmission of mail and newspapers. Small household computers can be used to regulate household finances and such functions as heat, lighting, music, reception (or barring of visitors) and even decoration (electronic replacements for paint and paper).

New consumer products often imply new infrastructure: the motor car surely affected the road systems of the West, and the possibilities for automated guidance of vehicles on appropriate roadways may do so too. But changing equipment for electronic communications may be the prime area of impact of the current new technologies. New communications systems may thus be a corollary of the diffusion of domestic, business and other computers, especially if they are to be linked into wider networks. Increased data flows may require new infrastructure: thus optical fibres are widely touted to replace conventional wire transmission lines, and digital encoders/decoders may compress signals while reducing noise. Large-scale change in communications systems may also involve the growth of specialized electronic links among businesses and state agencies. The argument has been made that state encouragement of new communications systems is essential for increasing economic competitiveness, and in addition will provide work for some of the unemployed.

Microelectronics can be used to restructure many economic activities. In retailing and distribution electronic scales and cash registers have been joined in the USA by sales terminals which permit rapid accounting of stock flows. Organizational difficulties seem to have delayed moves that have been afoot to introduce automated checkouts that directly deduct bills from customers' banks. If an anachronistic urge for money is cultivated, one is likely enough to use cash machines as a 24-hour means of withdrawing money, inspecting the balance, and so on. In the transport system computer monitoring of traffic flows may be the first step toward automation of much driving itself.

Current developments make it apparent that the state may make use of microelectronics to regulate more than traffic flows. Not all individual data banks are controversial — they are fairly standard in both central and local government welfare and planning agencies — but when arguments to link these together into national networks are made (e.g. Avebury *et al.,* 1972), questions of possible dangers to privacy and political liberties should be raised. These are given new force by recent revelations concerning pilot work going on around machine-readable passports and identity cards. Already political police agencies in many Western countries have set up computerized data banks to store information and intelligence on vast numbers of citizens: when linked to officers on patrol by radio, this can mean that technologies advocated as increasing efficiency in dealing with crime can be used fairly directly for purposes of political surveillance and control.[9] Not only security agencies of the state are involved here: private police forces have been booming, and it takes no great imagination to see these taking to computers, just as credit assessment firms have begun to develop electronic data banks. And other government agencies can make use of political information. For example, the domestic Information Display System gives the President of the USA access to large quantities of data from national to urban levels (Paulden, 1979). Market research firms could also find such systems useful for their purposes.

The preceding paragraphs have attempted to give a panoramic overview of issues of new technology in the current restructuring of social relations. Time will show if too much stress has been placed on transitional factors; the case can hardly be otherwise, but even so the underlying tendencies and counter-tendencies will surely play an important part in framing the future. Hopefully, the next sections of this paper will stimulate more of the empirical and theoretical work needed to sharpen analyses of possible futures.

3. Alternative futures for Western societies

So far the discussion has outlined certain tendencies without really considering how different social groups are seeking, and may in future seek, to facilitate or restrict their unfolding. The primary polarity in capitalist social formations, even those as affluent and technologically advanced as the Western industrial societies, is that between capital and labour, and its expression in class terms between the bourgeoisie and proletariat. Its primacy

---

[9]On identity cards, see Anning (1979). For technology of political control in the UK see Ackroyd *et al.* (1977) and the *State Research Bulletin* (annually collected into the "Review of Security and the State"). Among the information they provide (in addition to the official distinction between "information" and "intelligence") is that half of the population of Northern Ireland is covered by British Army data banks; the Special Branch computer has information on over a million individuals completely lacking in criminal records; about one-fifth of Britain's population is included in police files of one kind or another; several specialized data banks focus upon immigrants, associates of suspected and known drug users, etc. Recently the practice of secretly "vetting" juries in the light of these data has been embarrassingly exposed: for reasons of their own, the police and legal systems have been amassing data on political and sexual orientations of large numbers of ordinary people.

derives from the centrality of economic production in determining the reproduction of the whole social formation. Other classes do, of course, exist in even the most capitalist social formations (viz. Wright, 1978) and classes are also divided into fractions around different locations in the social division of labour. Capitalist development also gives rise to conflicts cutting across class boundaries, such as environmental problems, or the conflicts resulting from the specific forms that patriarchy and ethnic oppression take in industrial capitalism.

The heterogeneity of Western societies means that complex and shifting patterns of coalition and opposition may occur among social groups. In different countries local conditions have promoted quite distinct national political development: in one country regionalism is a burning issue, in another nuclear power, in a third women's rights, and so on. As pressures for restructuring mount, then, even quite elemental and wide-reaching conflicts of forces are likely to be mediated through chains of political action so as to take — initially at least — quite different forms. What does seem likely, however, is that polarization of interests will often emerge: and that restructuring also has potential for disturbing existing "balances" of forces.

Out of the infinitude of possible outcomes, four possible scenarios for the future of the West are taken up here. These are abstract images of the future, based on a rather undialectical identification of the projects for which major social groups are likely to strive. An attempt will be made to go beyond the self-images promoted for these groups by their ideologists. To some extent the result still is rather more like a set of caricatures without the contradictory shading of most concrete situations: but at least broad alternatives will be shown up in stark relief to the extent that the scenarios are based on real tendencies.

(i) *Corporate society*

The restructuring of capital to resolve its economic problems is represented by industrialists, many government leaders and economists, dominant groups in the mass media, and the like, in terms of the need to introduce new technologies, to reduce unproductive expenditure, and to restore a "responsible" work ethic. This being accomplished, inflation will be curtailed, international competitiveness maintained, economic growth secured; so that conflicts between countries can be more easily kept in check, social policies to provide welfare services extended and full employment achieved through market equilibration. After a period of some stress and discomfort, then, the future will be pretty much like the recent past of the post-war boom. As long as people can be persuaded to accept an equitable distribution of temporary costs — some of which are in reality disguised benefits, for too much welfare has been making them overdependent on the "nanny state" — then a future of increasing living standards, reduced working hours, more automated work and more exciting consumer products can be anticipated.[10]

The massive promotion of variants of such views through leading institutions, such as the mass media, political bodies and even education and religion, is by no means the only reason for these to be the ruling ideas in Western countries at the beginning of the 1980s.[11] In many cases independent action by workers has involved direct costs for large portions of the population dependent upon the devices they provide, whereas government cuts in social services typically only affect the particularly needy. Economic crises can seem to be more a function of overseas threats (e.g. oil sheikhs) and autonomous technological change than of the very structure of private capital accumulation. It is little wonder that most of the population of the West fail to see class relations as fundamental to the present restructuring, and believe instead that equitable measures can be pursued in the "national interest" to relieve familiar ways of life from external pressures. Many leaders of labour movements reflect and reinforce these attitudes by their own obeisance to the need for technological changes oriented to increasing profitability.

Thus there are powerful forces making for a capitalist trajectory of development for the West, based upon intensified exploitation of labour-power as the logic of restructuring. Whether or not this trajectory eventuates in a successful restoration in the long-term of economic growth and stable international relations, a number of conditions must be fulfilled in the short term for it to be realized. Political and cultural action is required to sustain restructuring of relations in the economic sphere — "Purely economic" mechanisms such as increased unemployment are not sufficient to enforce labour discipline and reduced living standards in a time of flux.

Putting it very crudely, the role of capital will be strengthened to the extent that ruling classes are internally cohesive while opposition movements and subordinate classes are divided. Certain threats have marvellous power to close the ranks of business groups and their immediate entourage — for example, shows of militancy by sections of social democratic parties, terrorist attacks on society figures, or pressure upon their foreign holdings. Popular movements may be fragmental along ethnic, national and regional lines, with racist and sexist currents gaining ground in them; mutual distrust and lack of solidarity for groups facing repression can inhibit the realization of effective action by movements threatening to dominant interests. Here,

---

[10]See, for example, the recent report of the Henley Forecasting Centre (Bellini *et al.,* 1977). There are few political speculations to be found here, but it is accepted that the rocky road to recovery for Britain may evoke considerable discontent. Social and military service are mooted as means of coping with unemployment (and indiscipline?).

[11]And even if it were, it is too simplistic to view these institutions as conspiring to pump out propaganda: ideology and ideological institutions operate in a much more complicated way than this — and their contradictions permit of significant interactions to be made.

too, the monopolization of cultural production by procapitalist groups can maintain a hegemony of ideas, which may be reinforced by the linking of socialist groups with repressive Eastern régimes, and by "demonstrations" of failed oppositional initiatives (e.g. collapsed worker cooperatives, failed strikes, exhausted cultural movements, etc.). Key groups and leaders in trades unions and social movements may be co-opted and/or compromised.

The fragmentation of working-class action and the privatization of individuals are the daily results of largely unplanned operations in the West. In a time of major restructuring a more systematic effort to contain popular opposition to the reorganization of and expulsion of labour from the production system and the changes in social welfare and living standards may be necessary. Political interventions are required from the state, and, following Ackroyd *et al.* (1977), the three probable modes of state response can be identified as fascism, military rule and the "strong state". It is the latter that seems most probably in the emergent Western conditions, involving a steady increase in the repressive and ideological activity of the state as mobilizer and defender of capitalist interests. Fascism and military takeovers are not out of the question, but tend to reflect reaction to only partially successful and insecure attempts to create socialist or populist solutions to political and economic crises. The "strong state", in contrast, requires less discontinuous restructuring of the state apparatus, and, being carried out in a series of small stages, can retain a fairly high degree of public legitimacy.

Then political developments are advanced as positive goals by some right-wing theorists — notably the band of 'counter-insurgency experts' — and these find ready allegiance among sections of the military and police. But they are less the product of a few strong wills than of the results of the existing state apparatus transforming itself in the process of trying to "muddle through" a major restructuring. Each step toward the strong state would be (and is) represented as a temporary and unfortunately necessary response to immediate crises such as the particularly damaging consequences of specific strikes, terrorist activities and the like. Many state officials will accept such representations and be as trapped in the escalation of repression and curtailment of civil liberties as the general public.

The new technologies have a role to play in the political surveillance and coercive activities of the state. Already in the 1970s television cameras have been installed in a network in London so that major thoroughfares can be observed, and there have been numerous cases of spying devices planted by both state and private agencies — and not only in public places. Public activities such as telephone calls may be more readily and extensively monitored with automated information-processing, and data concerning individuals' activities can be transmitted almost instantaneously to a wide range of officials. Machine-readable identity cards are likely to be introduced to monitor movements across frontiers: their use might be extended to cover various domestic activities. Criminology's boundaries from counter-insurgency studies and political science more broadly could become blurred: data banks could cover increasing ranges of information, so that current ways of identifying militants and social networks could be sophisticated.

This sort of repressive activity — along with the more general restrictions that can be expected for political activities beyond narrow limits within educational institutions, public services, and society at large, for trades unions operations and structure, for less well-disciplined media and cultural workers — could require quite complex legitimation. The new technologies could also be used so as to monitor the extent to which justifications of restricted liberty, in the name of the defence of civil society, are accepted. Referenda (along well-planned lines) seem already to be moving into favour as a means for displacing the perceived origin of political initiatives in the direction of the general public (for example, Marsh, 1979). State and private (market research) agencies may use communications equipment to monitor public opinion more thoroughly (a prerequisite for planning referenda as well as for the timing and portrayal of policy measures more generally): electronic referenda are a favourite speculation of futurologists, and a revival of the techniques of "Mass Observation" is conceivable.

The strong state must be characterized not only by its repressive agencies, but also by its corporatist structure. Historically, the states of advanced capitalist societies have tended to adopt an active role in relation to successively broader areas of social life with each major economic crisis in the world-system. Among extensions in the economic role of the Western state, the twentieth century has so far seen nationalizations of failing industries and (in some countries) national transport, communications and energy services. What seems plausible as a future tendency in state activity is the intervention of the state into growth sectors of the economy: many advanced capitalist states in the late 1970s have become deeply involved in trying to structure a rapid and effective development of national capital in microelectronics technologies — in the production of "chips" in some cases, more generally the design of products around the new technologies, and associated software (Evans and Sharp, 1979). At the same time, the boundaries of state and private enterprise are being redrawn: with the restructuring of the welfare state and telecommunications, to take two examples, some state activities are being passed over to private profit. This even includes police activities: private security agencies have mushroomed in Britain and are now employed by the state for some duties (e.g. immigration control).

What has this got to do with corporatism, which is usually defined in terms of a contrast with parliamentary democratic forms of capitalist state? Corporatism is the tendential outcome of the transfer of major politico-economic decisions from purely private or parliamentary hands, to bodies which represent the leadership of industry and organized labour, together with state officials. As these major decisions can be neither attributed to the spontaneous play of market forces or electoral will, a legitimation of the political economy in terms of corporate representation of interests becomes necessary — although this can provoke conflicts with existing *laissez-faire* and parliamentary ideologies. Beneath this lies the need to integrate the leadership of more powerful unions into the capitalist state, in order to achieve a disciplining of the labour force and its acceptance of state interventions. With a further step in such interventions, and the need to negotiate a restructuring of welfare activities, increased moves towards corporation may be anticipated.[12]

A corporate strong state, then, would seem to be, dialectically, a condition for and consequence of the realisation of tendencies for economic restructuring to be carried out in the interests of capital. The success of this political programme will depend upon numerous factors: the strength of working-class movements, existing political culture and so on. These factors vary considerably across Northern and Southern Europe, let alone when Europe and North America are contrasted. But assuming that it is more or less realized, what would the future be like? The answers must be speculative, but suggest some possibilities that may seem rather extreme.

The labour process, for example, would be carried out in conditions worsened in many respects: the new technologies would have been introduced with labour control the latent determinant of many of the "technical reorganizations" in pursuit of higher productivity (under intensified international competition). Some physical strain in some manual jobs may have been lessened by automation; union leaders may have won some cheap and visible improvements in health and safety conditions in exchange for their involvement in corporate decision-making; and some particularly sensitive groups of workers might be motivated to work steadily through experiments with job rotation, group assembly, flexible working hours and the like. But in general the interplay between greater surveillance and less satisfaction at work is likely.

The image of work being sketched out here, then, is one in which both white-collar and manual jobs are more fragmented, with workers finding them meaningless, unrelated to intellectual and personal development, and privatizing (i.e. the co-operative basis of labour would be obscured by the intermediation of machines, and the tightening of authority relations between workers). Surveillance would be more automated; perhaps wages could be tied to individual productivity (some forms of piece work become more practicable again with advanced information-processing systems) or bonuses to group outputs. Individuals with "suboptimal" adaptation to

[12]On corporatism, see the April 1977 issue of *Comparative Political Studies* (ed. P. C. Schmitter), Gough (1979) on corporatism and welfare state, Jessop (1979) on UK and URPE (1978) on US tendencies; on legitimation issues see Habemas (1976), Lindberg *et al.* (1973); on the future role of the state see O'Connor (1973), Wright (1978).

new technologies — on health, constitutional, or attitudinal grounds — could be screened out. New hierarchies would be established within the workforce — as well as those around control, it may be that shortages of technical skills relevant for maintaining, installing or adapting new technologies would lead to high-wage strata of workers. The vulnerability of computer systems to disruption, and the potential for criminal use of political blackmail with material from data banks, may also mean a growth in security procedures and ideological training of workers with access to these systems.

The unemployment generated in this programme of restructuring is potentially vast, and various approaches to coping with associated problems may be adopted by the state. For while individuals might cope with hardship by their own devices, such as by providing cheap personal services (e.g. gardening, domestic work), there would be the likelihood of political responses, and repression alone might provoke increased public discontent. Dividing the working class along racist and sexist lines is practically inevitable, if unconscious strategy in the light of the strength of these ideologies in Western societies. Already, for example, various women's rights won in the post-war boom are threatened with reverse in Britain in the late 1970s: abortion and nursing facilities being reduced and the like, with the effect of forcing women from the labour market into the disguised unemployment and social isolation of the family. Forms of compulsory work may be introduced (military service expanded, and new types of social service introduced); "job creation" may keep young people working in pseudo-apprenticeships for low wages. Less grimly, trades union action currently seems to have some success in winning reduced working hours, although the liberal technocrats' prophecies of much reduced working weeks requires either drastic wage reductions or extraordinary international co-ordination if the competitiveness of national capital is not to be slashed.

It is the industrial and political responses to such developments, as well as those around the restructuring of welfare services, which are likely to be met with the strengthening of the state. It is likely that even the new consumer technologies would have political repercussions — for example, by new status symbols sharpening perceptions of inequality, or through competence with, and access to, new sources of information reinforcing existing patterns of social disadvantage. It is difficult to envisage such repercussions in very clear terms: what is probably more meaningful is a brief discussion of some of the characteristics of new technologies outside of the conventional industrial and political spheres.

While many people may be receiving only low incomes, cheapened electronics can propel many new consumer products into the market. Domestic computer systems, video equipment, new toys and games, electronic "wallpaper" and "muzak" are all possible means of filling increasing privatized leisure time. One probable tendency in the development of mass communications — whether entertainment or educational — would be depoliticization and immobilization of isolated households (viz. Enzenberger, 1976); another possibility is an electronic "bread and circuses" scenario (Darwin, 1979). Through the development of communications systems with the new technologies, some educational, welfare and medical services, taxation, financial transactions could be carried out electronically — leading to a cheapening of social services, an increased use of credit, and the like. It is possible to speculate that such communications systems would here take a hierarchical form, with some centralization of information flows and associated controls; this would be compatible with the reproduction of existing capacities to override public telecommunications facilities when military quarters wish so, and with surveillance and censorship functions. (There may be countertendencies, however, as private firms might provide more specialized communications networks and plug-in devices.).

With a growth in electronic funds transfers the circulation of capital may be speeded — a counter-crisis effect. Other effects might include rigidifying existing income inequalities: for example, wealthier people might be able to shop at highly automated outlets, while those too poor to afford credit cards would have to pay cash at more expensive traditional shops. Also. computer crime could blossom in conditions of expanded computer use: the prospects for fraud and blackmail are good. The extreme possibilities here would be the mafia-like machine based on manipulating cash and data to the advantage of a few "bosses" (electronic Watergate), and the ideologically sound, uncorruptible and highly rewarded elite of computer operators (electronic priesthood). Neither development would change the basic nature of the corporate society, but they suggest possible redistributions of its political and economic benefits among dominant groups.

(ii) *Another development?*

In some Western societies the corporate state is well under construction in its "strong" form; in other societies this seems far from everyday realities. Nevertheless, the malevolent unfolding of these tendencies has meant that the search for alternatives has preoccupied many liberals and social democrats. There are various ways of proposing the questions underlying this search, but one frequently heard may be summarized as: how can a great displacement of labour from manufacturing and service work be accommodated without risking either political turmoil from the masses or repression from the state? The solution of public works provided by New Deal and Keynesian philosophy carries little weight in a period where restructuring demands a reduction in state employment, and it might seem that the search for a new alternative is purely utopian. But this would be too facile, for there is a surprising convergence between different political currents, on the one hand, and on the other between the preliminary solutions that they have been formulating and certain empirical tendencies in Western economic systems.

In terms of political currents flowing together, there has been much shared recently between liberals concerned with the spectre of unemployment, and critics of Western ways of life who argue from ecological or cultural perspectives. These latter, for example, will point out that contemporary social relationships are wasteful and inhumane: that they fail to conserve resources and employ labour productively, that they lead to cultural barrenness and the diseases of civilization. And in terms of their normative prescriptions, they come very close to some rather more formal analyses of existing tendencies in the West. Gershuny (1978, 1979), for example, has described the development of a "dual economy" here, in which there is a trend for many activities producing services for sections of the public to be carried out "informally" (in households, in the "underground economy", etc.) with the aid of equipment and resources provided by the highly productive formal economy.

The argument that is being developed by many commentators, in Northern Europe especially, is that these tendencies should be encouraged. Policies should be devised to stimulate "another development" alongside the growth of the formal economy, to capitalize upon emerging initiatives in creating meaningful work in the informal economy and rewarding alternative ways of life. The vision is one of a future in which people divide their time between limited periods of work in the formal economy, and more fulfilling, needs-oriented, small-scale work in areas of manufacturing (e.g. construction, furniture, foodstuffs) and services (e.g. transport, health, leisure, education, and of course, housework) in a decentralized informal sector. (For a clear statement of this perspective, albeit one a little too optimistic for many liberals, see Robertson, 1978.)

The images of the future provided by proponents of "another development" are somewhat crisper than those yielded from the apologists for the emerging "corporate society" — perhaps because in seeking to reroute social development it is necessary to spell out how the future would differ from the present. Although it will be argued below that this image is not a reliable guide to the likely shape of "another development", it will be first useful to spell out some of the prescriptive forecasts associated with it. On this basis the attractions and the problems involved can be made clearer.

Current tendencies, it is argued, are promoting high productivity in the formal economy — particularly in manufacturing industry, but also for much of agriculture and for some public services. There is a threat that an underground economy of the formally unemployed and poor will grow as an impoverished, criminalized, uncoordinated, second-rate means of providing otherwise expensive services and otherwise inaccessible work (as in the "corporate society" scenario). The idea of "another development" would be to pursue policies which can consolidate and improve both formal and informal economies simultaneously.

Taking the formal economy first, little change is explicitly proposed in the pattern of ownership of manufacturing industry, but a high level of development of the new technologies is assumed, and in this context their resource-saving properties are often stressed. However, this formal high-technology production would not be devoted to an over increasing range of gimmicky consumer products. To a large extent, it would manufacture cheap goods for direct consumption, and intermediate goods (tools, accessories, etc.) with which people would make their own final products. Furthermore, patterns of work in this formal economy have been dramatically changed so that people would spend less of their time in formal employment. There would be shortened working hours and a great deal of job sharing, for example. Extensive studies would be designed to promote the redeployment of skills made obsolete by industrial restructuring so as to retain workers in new technologies or in production under informal auspices. A major reversal would be required in the role of the "welfare state". To change attitudes which portray employment as a measure of individual worth for example, it would be possible to provide incentives for only partial participation in formal employment, and to encourage reduced dependency on the formal economy in general.

What, then, is the supposed shape of the informal sector? A number of semi-formal institutions seem to be involved here — for example, small businesses, encouraged by state assistance in their earlier stages, if shown to be responsive to community needs. Redundant workers might be paid sufficient remuneration to enable them to set up their own small firms with necessary capital goods provided for them on favourable terms. But apart from this vision of a revival of non-monopolistic capitalist firms (or worker co-operatives operating under capitalist rules of the game, after an initial period of shelter by the state), there is the idea of a growth of non-monetary production. This is sometimes referred to as an extension of the "household economy", with many more households (or even communal or extended families) possessing basic tools with which to produce their own goods. Such tools — themselves efficiently manufactured in the formal economy — might be owned, not by individual households, but by neighbourhoods or community groups; each street, say, possesses a workshop, a lathe, some power tools, equipment for rebuilding houses, tailoring gear and so on. A system of incentives for consumer or local authority expenditure on such equipment would be needed, as well as initiatives designed to promote the necessary community organization and responsibility.

Most adult individuals, then, or some members of most households at least, would labour for a fraction of the week in the sorts of industry with which we are familiar now. But they would also spend at least an equivalent amount of time in the more satisfying production of goods or services for local needs. The state would facilitate these processes by measures mentioned above, and also by such means as: removing penalties which prevent recipients of welfare benefits from engaging in creative spare-time work; subsidies providing for job-creation in the initial phases of establishing community action and crafts; promoting more labour-intensive and ecologically sound (low energy, resource-conserving) technologies via R and D, tax relief and subsidies. And the state would be, if not withering away, at least pruning itself. There would be considerable decentralization in economic and urban affairs, with more emphasis on regional and neighbourhood self-reliance and diversity. Some state activities — like health and education services — would be increasingly self-managed, and here new communications technologies could provide access to accumulated resources and expertise.

It would be possible to expound these visions of the future in much more detail, distinguishing between several variants.[13] But rather than dwell on the attractive prospects offered by proponents of "another development", it is important to scrutinize the assumptions on which this model of the future is based. The limitations of the social analysis underlying "another development" mean that even if aspects of this programme were to be adopted, the outlook might be considerably different from that anticipated. The programme has been devised in abstraction from the class relations which produce the tendencies on which it hopes to be borne into being, and it is likely that the form in which parts of this programme are taken up and related together — while other parts are discarded — would be very different in futures where the logic of capital accumulation holds sway from that taken in futures involving an alternative structure of social needs.

The image of the future is one in which a formal economy is coordinated with and underpins a vastly expanded informal production system, and in which the state has consistently acted so as to facilitate this end. How is this compatible with capitalist industry and a capitalist state? The questions of power here cannot be elided: the high-technology formal economy is essential to the whole social order, and without extensive "restructuring" in its ownership and control, its interests would presumably diverge from those of the informal economy in numerous ways: and on numerous occasions choices would have to be made concerning whose interests to pursue. For example, the threat of investment strikes, or of relocating transnational capital elsewhere in the world, or more subtle forms of pressure on state officials, could be brought into play by the formal sector: the informal sector — unless its members effectively controlled formal political economy, a

---

[13]See Robertson (1978) for a fairly full statement of "Another Britain": in the late 1970s the IFDA Dossier (International Federation for Development Alternatives) has been carrying studies relevant to other Western countries. Robertson's Newsletter *Turning Point* is a useful source of information. The Society for International Development has stimulated discussion of these issues: see Jolly (1979) for a discussion of development strategies for Europe. The recent report of the OECD's Interfutures team (1979) also speculates (more timidly) in this direction.

socialism which is not proposed in "another development" — has no similar power. At most its workers could strike and withhold their labour from formal employment, and while it might be argued that longer and stronger strikes would be possible when many subsistence goods can be produced locally and informally, there is the likelihood of large firms already having developed ways of limiting the effectiveness of such action. This is far from the image of a contented future with which we began: what sorts of conflict of interest might arise to provoke such discord? The formal sector would identify these in terms of its profits being sloughed off to support community activities, and of its international competitiveness being reduced by the less intensive employment of equipment due to reduced working hours and by product ranges being narrowed to produce for community needs — so-called "household capital goods" — rather than for manipulated demand for changing status symbols and for profitable export.[14]

This does not mean that certain developments of the informal sector would not be welcomed by the high-technology monopoly sector: these will be discussed in a moment. First the role of the state should be discussed — after all, why should not the state promote "another development" over and above the opposition that may emerge from vested industrial interests; for example, to limit capital movements abroad and to prevent pressures to reduce wages? The point is, however, that the state is itself a crystallization of power relations in society. It is not a neutral instrument that can be applied readily to radically different ends, such as taking forthright steps to overturn this structure of power relations. While the state may well have interests in developing the informal sector — to ward off political unrest, to escape the contradictions of the welfare system — these interests are pursued with much the same logic that structures the behaviour of capitalist firms. Some proponents of "another development", admittedly, see the state as hopelessly bureaucratized, and look to a popular groundswell of enthusiasm and action for social change; but this is to place the problem on one side rather than to solve it.

Before going on to indicate the form that "another development" might take in the West without radical change of power relations in these societies, some other problems with which this programme might be faced should be briefly noted. For example, internal inequalities could well be stimulated in this scenario. Strategies stressing local self-reliance are likely to amplify existing divergences in access to skills, resources and money, thus promoting new regional, cultural or ethnic hierarchical divisions of labour. Women's oppression could be reinforced by a new emphasis on the family as a basic

---

[14]Of course, it is possible that the export structure of the West could change in a direction compatible with a local dual economy: whether this is feasible is doubtful, and whether it would benefit the Third World markets who would receive such commodities is unlikely. Another possibility would be a move toward protectionism and autarchy!

social unit which could simply make the reproduction of patriarchy easier. Further, the establishment of small businesses and worker-co-operatives would presumably bring the classical forms of petit-bourgeois ideologies into operation, giving rise to conflicts with other stated political objectives. And finally, the degree to which existing Western ways of life depend upon an imperialistic international system is not addressed in these schemes, which means that the forms of development of local resources and of trade necessary for a more equitable world order are missing from the analysis.

Such problems need to be squarely confronted if the dynamics of the informal sector are itself to be compatible with the decentralist, humanitarian thought of "another development". But the dynamics of the dual economy *in toto* are perhaps most vital in directing the way in which the informal sector will develop: and related to a capitalist mode of production there is little doubt as to what will be dominant. The suspicion with which many trades unionists have greeted these proposals testifies to such suspicions as well as to more short-term concerns with maintaining employment levels in existing occupations.

Elements of a "dual economy" are by no means incompatible with advanced capitalist society. Indeed, monopoly capital achieves some of its profitability by relinquishing some of the tasks of assembly, repair and maintenance to smaller firms in a competitive, low-wage sector (O'Connor, 1973; Hodson, 1978). The stimulation of new small businesses could further facilitate the new structures of monopoly production emerging from the capital restructuring around the new technologies. While the roles involved here are difficult to define in the present flux, one might be the provision of cheap, non-institutionalized R and D of new products; another might be the repair of the bodywork and motors of vehicles and machines whose crucial microelectronic controls would remain the preserve of the monopoly sector. The "small firms" policies of some Western governments — described as "new sweatshop" policies by radical critics (e.g. CDPPEC, 1979) — may be a signal of such developments.

Another function that dual economies may play for capital lies in the cheapening of labour-power. Already the work of housewives provides an unpaid contribution to the maintenance and reproduction of the workforce. How much more convenient, then, if workers did not require payment for all the household goods and other items of consumption they require, but could be paid just enough to enable them to buy the new materials and power needed! If the household economy is made more productive with modern technologies, all well and good — apart from the declining demand of certain commodities produced for consumers! While some markets would be lost in this way, there would, at any rate, be new demands for tools, for construction of infrastructure to suit the emerging social order — and the battle for foreign markets could go on as before. Perhaps industrial disputes could be lessened, too, by reducing working hours in the formal economy, and by presenting that which was available as a kind of service to society at large (although the contrast between different forms of production might actually prompt workers into asking difficult questions about the organization of the formal sector).

For the state, too, certain advantages may be postulated concerning the dual economy. In particular, though many of the proposals of "another development" involve increased state expenditure, others — like more voluntary work and community organization — suggest ways of reducing this expenditure, of relieving the fiscal crises of the state. By sloughing off many social welfare and health services to voluntary neighbourhood agencies, the state might be able to actually increase its efficiency as an agent of social control. For there would be little anarchy in this transfer of responsibilities: although undoubtedly political conflicts would emerge in some areas over community decision-making, it is obvious that the state would seek to impose a bourgeois form on the new institutions — in other words, they would be hierarchical, open to manipulation from the central agencies, effectively individualizing their "clients" while professionalizing and bureaucratizing their voluntary workers, involving privately codified administrative and quasi-legal rules, creating political passivity and so on.[15] Some marginal activities would be decriminalized, communities would "police" themselves. In all this could be cynically — or realistically — viewed as a convenient containment of the poor and unemployed, a means of forcing women back into the household economy, and a new basis for ideological explanations of social inequalities would be provided.

A thorough analysis of the economics of such a system would be needed to tell how far a programme along these lines would be economically feasible within modern capitalism. More importantly, it seems unlikely that it would be politically feasible for too much of "alternative development" to be incorporated in this way. For one thing, there would be class conflict around the new institutional structures, and trades unions would resist the undercutting of some established wage work by informal activities. Even if a corporate state was able to control popular objections to such a development, it is unlikely that it could readily cope with the conflicts between different capitalist firms in the course of a restructuring of consumption away from existing patterns.

Thus what may remain of the "dual economy" is something of a mixture of the three images of the future hinted at by Gershuny (1979). Within the context of a corporate society, with a perhaps less obtrusive "strong state" there would be (a) some spontaneous underground economy involving unemployed workers in low wages, labour-intensive, service work; (b) some repression of parts of this economy in order to gain more taxation, prevent

---

[15]For discussions of such issues around the local state see Cockburn (1977), Edinburgh CSE Group (1978); see also CDPPEC (1979) and booklets from the CSE State Group (1979).

competition for services provided corporately; and (c) some exploitation of the informal sector in the service of private profit and public order. In particular, social and welfare services, public transport, house and urban renovation, public works, and subsidized subcontracting for the monopoly sector, might be actively facilitated by the state. It is likely that this would benefit middle- and high-income areas disproportionately.

The image of the future has its attractive points compared to "corporate society", and may provide a more stable resolution of political and economic crisis tendencies than would otherwise be possible within a classical capitalist framework. Of course, it has many less desirable attributes, too. The extent to which these are developed will be a product of natural conditions; possibly "another development" will come closest to being a significant influence in political development in the Scandinavian countries.

(iii) *Bureaucratic collectivism*

The strongest by far of the interests opposed to the logic of capitalist development in the West is the organized working class, but its very organization tends to take the form of trades unions and social democratic movements rather than militant socialist parties, and its political perspectives tend to be reformist ones. The position of many union and social democratic activists is, to say the least, ambiguous. Some see improved working conditions and reduced inequality within capitalism as sufficient goals. Others see these as worthwhile reforms, but seek to relate them to a longer-term reorganization of power in Western societies. By far the majority of this latter group would tend to oppose tendencies which obviously lead to the sort of "corporate society" discussed above; so would members of the former group who would see the erosion of civil liberties as presenting difficulties in the way of pursuing even their restricted goals. Again, some support may be forthcoming from both groups for revolutionary socialist strategies, particularly under crisis conditions.

Accordingly, it is difficult to identify a coherent image of the future behind the talk about "common programmes" and "alternative strategies" which tends to dominate the organized Left in the West. It is, nevertheless, possible to identify a number of themes, spelled out most clearly in the Eurocommunist programme, from which such an image can be brought into focus. The theme is stressed that capitalism is in crisis because, dominated by large monopolies, it cannot rationally manage its own economy; accordingly, what is needed is for a state attuned to working-class interests to impose such rationality. A Left-wing majority in parliamentary institutions would mean that simultaneously modernization of national industry would be accompanied by a defence of working-class interest. This would require the nationalization of financial institutions and major monopolistic industries, increases in state expenditure to boost the economy (with cuts in such areas as military spending), much more interventionist economic planning, and worker participation in industrial management. (For a particularly detailed account of these strategies as they apply to Britain, see London CSE Group (1979); A. Freeman (1979) provides a critique of this.)

It is likely that such a strategy will be opposed from the Right and the Left, for it is by no means obvious that both working-class and capitalist interests can be met in the course of such a wholesale restructuring of industry. On the one hand, a likely economic response to such a strategy is capital flight, capital "strikes", political responses may even include the mobilization of military and other repressive forces, as well as the unelected civil service, against an elected left-wing government and its supporters — the shape that resistance to left-wing and populist programmes could take here may be prefigured in the Chilean tragedy. The image of the future in this case will be even more dire than that of the "corporate" society. On the other hand, given that such a "left" government does seek to strike a compromise with capital, workers may refuse to accept sacrifices in living standards which they would see as aimed at restoring capitalism to a healthy condition. Their activities might lead to the development of workers' plans and councils, and a future more like the image of "socialist democracy" discussed below.

Are there other possibilities which would be more in keeping with the programme outlined? For one thing, external forces could fend off threats from capital while not requiring the sort of working-class mobilization that would be likely to demand a programme of workers' control. One unlikely, but not completely impossible, course of events would give this role to the Soviet Union (or China in a future "radical" phase?) which might be prepared to give practical support to left-wing governments in Western countries in certain circumstances. (It must be said, however, that a rather different consequence of socialist upsurges in the West could be a severe destabilization of power relationships within Russia and Eastern Europe.) Eurocommunists certainly put a distance between themselves and the political leadership of "state socialist" societies, but history has shown that Third World revolutionary régimes have often been forced to align themselves increasingly with these societies. Other possibilities are conceivable, too: if other Western countries have earlier turned to socialist development paths, these might take such a role, possibly under the impact of conflicts within the West.

What about internal forces which might result in such strategies? Perhaps nations "broken up" by internal nationalist movements would require left-wing "bonapartist" action from the new state to secure necessary economic activity if both capital and labour were poorly organized by regions. Or an attempt at "socialist democracy" might have had its back broken by internal or external violence again giving opportunities for a "take-over" by a well-knit group — acting, of course, under the guise of having to impose order before establishing popular democracy. So, although it seems rather an unlikely prospect, it is perhaps worth considering briefly what sort of society might emerge from this scenario. The restricted internal democracy within Eurocommunist parties, their stress on improving economic efficiency (which they understand as a technical problem), and other aspects of the Stalinist legacy (including their ties to the Soviet Union), makes the term "bureaucratic collectivism" an apt one for the resulting image of the future.

What might this future be like? For once, there might be some virtue in conservative analyses of the Left as seeking, or inadvertently supporting, the imposition of Eastern European-type social structures upon the West. The lack of civil liberties in these societies (which actually may vary considerably even in these aspects) is seen as fundamentally retarding their economic dynamism and quality of life. The fact that it is in the West that microelectronic technology has been developed furthest, for example, is seen as proving the superiority of liberal capitalist political economy. As suggested above, however, there may be good reasons for suspecting that advanced capitalism produces tendencies which themselves threaten a wide range of political freedoms, so the appropriate response may be to consider those real possibilities which transcend both corporate/market and state/bureaucratic rule.

Furthermore, while the strategies outlined above are perhaps those most widely proposed among militant workers and major labour organizations, and while some sections of such organizations are doubtless compromised by their relationship with state socialist countries, both the levels of education and experience with political democracy (albeit of a liberal form), and the observation of the limitations of Stalinism for workers' self-organization, would be big obstacles to any attempts to impose bureaucratic roles upon a dynamic socialist movement. It might then prove that "bureaucratic collectivism" in the West would permit of more political freedom than in Eastern Europe; only if leading sections of the labour movement were effectively obliterated (in civil war?) would repressive "state socialism" be feasible and open to legitimation in terms of the necessity to impose discipline upon leaderless chaos. In either case, such a society would generate forces tending to move it back towards a market system or forward to a higher form of democracy — although as existing state socialization has demonstrated, such forces can be contained for lengthy periods.

What seems a possible form of bureaucratic collectivism, then, resembles the image of "corporate society" in many respects. The major decisions concerning social development would be made by planning agreements between different groups: but now the workers' representatives and state officials would be negotiating with state-appointed bureaucrats rather than capitalist managers as heads of industry, and the rules of the game would be determined less by the exigencies of capital accumulation than by the need of leading officials to retain political power. Thus in contrast with corporate society there might be a drive to reduce major social inequalities, to provide better public services to meet basic needs such as transport and housing, and to prevent workplace degradation. Instead of the pervasive electronic surveillance of civil society postulated for "corporate society", there might be a rather more obvious and extensive political control of cultural affairs, in a populist guise.

There would thus be some resemblances to the wealthier East European countries, and while there would probably be a degree of streamlining by the new technologies, the standard Western objections to "technical inefficiency" in Eastern Europe might apply. The attack upon unemployment is this society would probably take the form of overmanning and reduced working weeks, and perhaps by compulsory service of various kinds and extended public works. But these measures are a containment of workers within an alienated political sphere rather than part of a release of their energy. In these terms, there would be little alternative provided to the consumerist ideologies of advanced capitalism, and such a society might be forced to emulate its earlier path of development in terms of introducing (importing?) consumer goods based on the new technologies.[16]

As remarked, it is difficult to imagine such a future coming into being without the intervention of some outside force, or some catastrophic debilitation of both the coercive power of capital and the democratic power of labour. The "alternative strategies" do pose a tightrope walk — but with some sort of weakening and balancing of forces, a stable bureaucratic post-capitalist society could, in principle, be established. This would then have institutionalized its own methods of political coercion and legitimation — which would contain their own contradictions, yet might have a reasonable viability. Another route to such a future might be cited: that a degree of humanization of corporate society might be achieved by a fairly powerful movement in support of democratic rights and living standards, at the cost of reduced international competitiveness and increased emphasis on "state capitalism". This would imply a period of economic decline, presumably culminating in political and economic crises; nevertheless, it is not an outlandish scenario in the case of successful nationalist upsurges in some Western countries. One further possibility that might be considered is that some compatibility could be established between "bureaucratic collectivism" and elements of "another development": some of the practices of

---

[16]For interesting perspectives on State Socialist societies and the response they evoke in the Western Left, see the Il Manifesto (1979) report; other useful sources include, the *Motive* series by the London publishers Allison and Busby, and the journal *Critique*. The pioneering work of the East German Bahro (1978) should also be noted.

the Italian Communist Party might be useful guides to the feasibility of such an historic compurgation.

(iv) *Socialist democracy*

A final image of the future to be considered here is based upon the possible confluence between first, the historic aspirations of oppressed and exploited groups for the transformation of Western society in a direction compatible with the democratic articulation and satisfaction of social needs; second, the possibilities for providing a technical base for such a transformed society with judicious use and development of the new technologies; and third, the immediate actions and emerging forms of organization in the Western working class and social movements. These three levels interpenetrate at a number of points in the contemporary West, for example in the utopian thought of some writers[17] and in the practices of some political groups and cultural activists. But what may be the clearest expression of future possibilities here lies in those groups trying to generate alternative economic strategies based on workers' plans rather than on state reforms. Initiatives around workers' control and planning of industry and services involve various types of action: practical demonstrations, in the course of strikes, for example, that workers can manage operations successfully; demonstrations on paper or with small-scale experiments that, for example, alternative energy sources are compatible with full employment; that declining industries in the military sector are quite capable of producing products relevant to social needs; that workers' cooperation can be successful, and that they are compatible both with national planning and community control of local resources.[18]

The idea of workers' plans is nothing new, but it has been prominently revived as groups of highly skilled workers have found their jobs and even their industries threatened by technological and economic restructuring. These groups have begun to challenge the logic of restructuring based on considerations of profitability, and to argue that such restructuring means wasting equipment and skills that could benefit society: the claim has been raised for the "right to socially useful work", over and above the defence of jobs. In various industries in the UK, for example (see footnote 18), groups of shop stewards and workers have sought to produce information on the potential reapplication of their work and workplace to social needs. In place of the restructuring dictated by capital, they have been seeking to develop

---

[17]Here it is even possible to cite partial representations of such visions in speculative fiction: e.g. Callenbach (1978), Le Guin (1974), Piercy (1978); on such literature, see various articles in *Science Fiction Studies*.

[18]The best known example of attempts to develop workers' plans in the UK recently is that of the Lucas Aerospace Workers: see Asquith (1979), Elliot (1978); for Vickers workers see Benyon and Wainwright (1979); for the motor industry see IWC Motors Group (1979); see also IWC (1978).

long-term plans which will gain the support both of workers in their industries and of the working class and its allies at large: these plans would cover the use of new technologies, the identification of areas of social need for which products may be manufactured, and the wider involvement of the work force and community in decision-making. Similar initiatives remain to be taken, at the time of writing, by public service workers: given the contradictions that have emerged recently between their industrial actions and more general solidarity, such initiatives are probably vital for the realization of the image of the future implied here, which is no less than the restructuring of the whole social formation around participatory democracy and social needs. The crisis of the welfare system may well provoke such initiatives in the new future.

For attempts at putting economic restructuring under different imperatives to those currently dominant to succeed, the first step would be to mobilize people around such plans, with a series of immediate goals oriented toward defending interests threatened by capital in its anticrisis manoeuvrings, while simultaneously enlarging the scope for action and strength of socialist forces. There would be a temporal sequence of some kind to these struggles. One plausible sequence would involve the development from action around reducing the work week, preventing redundancies, or seizing firms that are to close or create redundancy; to the institution of workers' control over strategic firms, means of public control over state enterprises, and neighbourhood control over local planning and services; to the linking up of such committees and other groups in struggle into a network of councils which would form the basis of "dual power" — providing a democratic alternative to the rule of capital.

Before discussing the emergent characteristics as such a development path in any more detail, it should be noted that a number of conditions will determine its course, and the degree of difficulty faced by its proponents. In some respects the inverse of those conditions identified as facilitating the realization of "corporate society": ruling-class cohesion and fragmentation of opposing movements, for example, make the coordination and defence of initiatives much more difficult. Conversely, crises of legitimacy where the state no longer masquerades as a representative of the "public will" may facilitate the search for alternatives. Such crises have in the past involved, for example, unpopular and expensive overseas adventurism, major scandals involving leading state officials, catastrophic failures of planning. Major conflicts within dominant groups are also significant, particularly if they involve a weakening of the coercive apparatus through a loss of support from the police and military. A counter-hegemonic struggle in cultural spheres and demystification of state policies can help to mobilize large numbers of people behind socialist groups and parties, and support from workers' movements in other countries can be vital in weakening the will and repressive ability of ruling groups.

Even more so than the previous three images of the future, a major social transformation such as that implied here is not something that happens overnight. A qualitative change in power relations in society may be achieved rapidly, but it can take a considerable time to develop and coordinate the institutions and practices that can secure a new social order. The original basis for practices that divide social classes and oppress social groups may be removed, but these practices do not disappear as if they never had any more substance than reflections of more fundamental realities! Take the social division of labour: a cook may make an excellent head of state, but some experience in administration might be necessary before this could be the case. A transitional period still must intervene between the overturning of existing systems of class hegemony and the construction of a classless society; the existence of non-socialist nations in the world may make this period of transition even more protracted than it might otherwise be.

In this transitional period, the main task would be to establish institutions which could enable the working class and its allies to work toward the abolition of class difference and the social division of labour. The form of these institutions, whose socialist democracy would need to be very different from liberal democracy or Eastern European institutions, can be deduced from the earlier discussion. The basic atoms here would be worker and neighbourhood councils, the type of organization created as the nucleus of class self-representation in "dual power" situations during revolutionary upsurges. These councils would be the real basis of political power: delegates from the councils would determine the actions of higher organs of the state, not vice versa. All workers and residents would be able to participate in these councils, and their delegates (not representatives) would be subject to rapid recall if their actions diverged unaccountably from council decisions.[19]

Are such councils a fantasy in an era of complex industrial societies? On the contrary, the new technology makes it an evermore concrete possibility. For one thing, the formation of a "new working class" under late capitalism, with technical skills and knowledge of design and planning, and which is tendentially proletarianized in the present crisis, provides the working class with a much larger set of skills and opportunities for organizing its

---

[19]This discussion, and subsequent paragraphs, draws on the literature concerning workers' control and socialist democracy. Previous socialist revolutions have led to state socialism rather than to socialist democracy, and this fact must be part of any non-utopian analysis. These past experiences have involved the decimation of committed activists in civil war and combatting foreign invasion, grievous economic problems resulting from underdevelopment of the productive forces and the isolation of the revolution, outside interference and the like. From analysis of the problems, some directions necessary to change social practices and prevent the formation of bureaucratic elites have been outlined in recent debates. The discussion here draws heavily upon work produced in close conjunction with attempts to effect such strategies: USFI, 1978; Ollman, 1977; Bodington, 1973; Vanek, 1975; Boyle and Harper, 1976; Mandel, 1977; Therborn, 1978.

own future than ever before. The potential reductions in the working day, too, made possible by automation, could give each individual much more opportunity for political participation than previously — as well as more freedom to change places in the technical division of labour, to learn new skills and so on. The task of learning new production skills, too, could be simplified via automation.[20]

The new information technologies could give each individual far greater access to knowledge about social affairs. Additionally, they would make direct democracy much more feasible, even for large numbers of participants. Councils could directly communicate with each other and with higher organs, and could have access to detailed information about conditions in different areas, about the possible consequences of proposed plans and so forth. Electronic mass meetings could bring together scattered groups of people with common interests; by decentralizing the communications networks, and introducing simple interactive systems, the process of discovering and dialoguing with people with shared aspirations could be facilitated. Referenda accompanied by free political debate would be possible on a wide range of issues.

This may sound like a rather narrowly political view of the use of the new technology — but in this future society, much of the current distinction between politics and economics would be archaic. Before going further into how decision-making might be carried out in such a future using microelectronics communications systems, it is first necessary to consider certain broader matters of political power that would be crucial to the democratic functioning of such a society. Some of the proposals cited above may sound uncomfortably like the "computerized democracy" with which futurologists have regaled us for years. What guarantees can there be that it would not slip towards a future of "bureaucratic centralism" under the monopoly of one limited group claiming to embody the general interest? Would not a heavy reliance on new communications technologies open up society to manipulation by technocrats?

To extend and maintain such a democracy, it would not be enough to simply assume that the revulsion of most Western workers against the police-state-like practices in contemporary "state socialist" societies would automatically prevent conspiracies and manipulation. This democratic spirit would have to take the form of practices distinct from those available in liberal capitalist society, especially when it comes to combatting technocratic ideology, as opposed to Stalinist bureaucratic repression. (Here the discussion draws heavily upon USFI, 1979, as well as other debates around socialist democracy, e.g. Poulantzas, 1977; Therborn,

---

[20]This would be very different from capitalist deskilling, as workers would now be acquiring new skills in overall planning and knowledge of the technical composition of production (Acero, 1979; Sohn-Rethel, 1976). On socialist education, see Castles and Wurstenberg (1978).

1978.) The main issue here is that people should not be inhibited from criticizing, and organising to press for change in, the current leadership and programme. Specifically, this means freedom to organize political parties (and oppositions within parties), and for autonomous movements of ethnic, national and sexual groups to organize independently so as to prevent the perpetuation of practices which have in the past oppressed them. It means the freedom to form unions and consumer groups, too. This does not, of course, amount to granting carte blanche to reactionary groups to go beyond democratic means and actively resort to violence in attempting to restore capitalist rule!

Given the existing fragmentation of socialist groups in Western societes, it is by no means unlikely that attempted monopolization of power by some self-proclaimed vanguard party could be resisted widely. Clashes between groups — even elements in the new state — seeking to impose "bureaucratic collectivism", and workers in their capacity as council members, cannot be ruled out, however. But only a pluralistic socialist democracy would enable criticism of policies to be developed and widely circulated, and policy errors thus deleted. The Stalinist interpretation of the "dictatorship of the proletariat" would find little support among the mass of people in the West.

What then of the state? In order to promote the economic development of socialist democracy, various complex decisions would need to be made. A "council of councils" could lay out broad directions here — for example, the amount of resources that workers would provide for various social activities would be determined collectively by the workers' councils themselves. But many specific details would need to be elaborated centrally by people with some expertise, at least in the early stages of the transition between social orders. One way of ensuring the consistency of their work with the goals formulated and expressed through the direct democracy of the councils, would be to submit it to the deliberation of new organs of representative democracy, which could complement the councils, as institutional guardians of political rights — but such representative organs would not be permitted to displace the ongoing system of direct democracy.

Whether or not involving the monitoring and guidance of parliamentary institutions in this way, however, a number of other features would be necessary for a radically different form of state. This state would have to actively promote its own dismantling — but given the class basis outlined, this does not involve the contradictions emerging in the "another development" idea of the withering away of the state. Whereas the delegates from councils would be subject to direct recall, it would be desirable that the workers in state agencies would not be career bureaucrats. As far as possible, state posts would rotate, positive discrimination applied towards those with experience of manufacturing work and members of oppressed groups in order to help demolish social divisions of labour. A long-term strategy for the decentralization of decision-making to the groups concerned would be established. Thus decisions about how to use the resources provided to them would be increasingly transferred to the agencies, neighbourhoods and organizations involved, who would in turn be able to directly express their needs to the council organizations.

These may not be sufficient, but they would certainly seem to be necessary measures to take in order to create higher forms of democracy.

The new technology would make possible a far greater degree of decentralization than has previously been possible in an interdependent society. Such decentralization could be a continuing obstacle to any attempt to monopolize state power. Elliot (1975) argues that the use of communications technology to enable a great number of decisions to be made at national and regional levels can give undue power to those state officials charged with assessing the impacts of different plans with setting out the different options to be chosen between in referenda, and the like. The argument follows that as many decisions as possible should be decentralized, so that sufficient attention and variety of experience could be brought to bear on the remaining "big issues". Workers and neighbourhood councils would thus make many of their own decisions (probably with greater efficiency than would be done without intimate knowledge of their needs and characteristics), coordinating with each other concerning shared problems concerning the overall allocation of resources, investment decisions and the like. As in "another development", neighbourhoods might be provided with tools and raw materials produced by large capital-intensive units to which all occasionally contribute labour. Shared and updated data-bases in computer networks that allowed any council to contact any other or group of others, could vastly improve the coordination and spatial organization of production, the monitoring of any trends towards inequalities, and communication concerning technological and cultural innovations. Household-to-household, and household-to-collective, communication systems would likewise be utilized, perhaps mainly for community or interest-groups development. But the distinctions between entertainment, politics and work might also be less meaningful here.

This discussion can be legitimately criticized as side-stepping the question of economic efficiency: would such a society be able to develop its productive forces in a superior fashion to that of capitalism? After all, a significant tradition within socialism has argued that one reason for the supercession of a mode of production is the emergence of economically more dynamic ones. But this question itself side-steps important issues: is the notion of efficiency applicable to societies of different sorts? Is economic dynamism an ahistorical criterion? With production oriented to needs, and the development of the productive forces including the development of labour, rather different criteria are implied to those typically evolved by terms like efficiency. Nevertheless, there remains a hard kernel in these questions: advanced capitalism has shown itself to be far more innovative in its technologies, for good and ill, than was anticipated by its radical critics of earlier generations, while state socialism has not been notable in general for new products or the quality of its goods.

Is socialism necessarily less adequate economically than capitalism? Even if it were so, it might be argued that this is not such a bad thing, given that wider views of social development will take into account ecological and psychological issues that the market ignores and degrades. Or it might be pointed out that the internal dynamics of socialist economies are at least free of the highly costly cycles and crises promoted by capitalism. But is socialism necessarily inferior in terms of technological change and product quality than a system based on entrepreneurship and market rewards? In the mid-1930s Oskar Lange was arguing that the market process was necessary for rational economic accounting; but in the 1960s he suggested that computer technology would allow for a centrally planned solution to the thousands of interactions otherwise left to the market (see Harrington, 1974; Lange, 1972). Indeed, he argued, the computer can make possible long-range planning of a sort for which the market is quite incapable. Drastically reduced costs of information processing and transmission given by the new microelectronics, however, may further make possible decentralized, non-market planning — for example, making use of computer networks whose users can restructure their linkages to each other in an ongoing interaction concerning needs and capabilities, benefits and costs (Garrett and Wright, 1978, speculate in this direction). The potentials of such developments remain unsounded, and require practical experiments rather than deskwork! But if there is reason for optimism here, what about the role of the entrepreneur? The crucial issue here is whether innovative activity is only spawned under competitive, individualistic systems of reward, or whether creative work can be carried out in public accountable institutions. Again, these issues demand resolution in practice: the systems of popular control envisaged in the discussion above are sufficiently different from the bureaucratic structures of state socialism that no direct parallels can be drawn from the stifling of much innovation in the Eastern European countries. Again, the real question concerns the relation of centralized and decentralized powers. So the answers to these questions must remain open, although it would seem to betoken a pessimism concerning human ingenuity and the possibilities for releasing the repressed creativity of large numbers of the population to assume that solutions to these problems will remain elusive.

What else can be said about such a future? It is obviously dangerous to speculate about the decisions people would formulate in an increasingly liberated world. People themselves would have changed through participation in the process of social transformation. But some of the dimensions of a society equipped with the new technologies, and freed from the logic of capital accumulation, may be deduced from the needs and visions that are expressed by exploited and oppressed groups, and socialist activists.

For example, several of the points earlier articulated in the programme of "another development" are compatible with such an image of the future: many of its major elements, indeed, can only be realized in such a social order. The labour process in high-technology industries would be transformed so as to take much more account of the health and psychological requirements of workers. Production would be related to social needs as formulated through socialist democracy, its logic formulated by the producers, not imposed by the capital relationship. With much reduced working time through job-sharing, automation and the abolition of socially wasteful production, a flowering of "informal" production would be likely — perhaps with extensive cultural production, making use of the new media. Factory work would no longer be regarded as menial, nor as a means of self-identification — at least in the longer term, it would be performed as part of the individual's own commitment to collective planning and identification with the social needs thus formulated. In an "informal" production, people would be contributing to the formation of a new system of needs.

While many new products would be made available by the development of the new technologies, these would decreasingly be obtained as means of demonstrating one's status or social affiliation. Perhaps means of expression and communication would be valued most of all: with the breakdown of class society, the "social animal" might be freer to re-emerge. Housework would no longer be a female preserve: women's movements would have made the socialization of many domestic tasks a priority. As private property itself became a less meaningful attribute, various communal forms of living might be instituted — although the debris of centuries of patriarchy and distrust in interpersonal relations would take a long time to sweep away. Perhaps much more effort would be put into group work and achieving psychological understanding — indeed, if Reich's (1972) arguments concerning the interconnection between psychosexual repression and political authoritarianism are correct, this would be a vital part of social transformation (see also Ollman, 1979). As environmental issues were treated more seriously, biology might become another science more valued than today.

It would be possible to elaborate on many more possible aspects of this scenario: the development of new forms of human settlement (overcoming the city–country distinction); the prospects for the development of individual relationships within a society where cultural diversity would by no means disappear; family life and children; and a host of matters concerning the forms of human development in non-alienated ways. But perhaps enough has been said already to provide some sort of answer to the question: *whose* desirable society is this?

In the transitional period, there would certainly be those who did not welcome the developing future, for reasons connected in some cases with lost status and material privileges, in others with fear of the forces that might be unleashed by liberation. As the economic bases for oppressive practices and mystifying ideologies are dissolved, so the ability of their victims to formulate and express their feelings should grow, and the most positive forms of criticism could be applied to change and extract what might be of value in such residual practices. There would surely be strains and reactions here, but no convincing case has been made that a society which would satisfy the vast majority of its members could not be achieved. People might not be happy all the time — it would probably arrest their psychological development if they were — but they would have the capacity to really feel in their daily lives, to know what the social relationships into which they entered were, and to actively constitute part of a self-aware community. The restricted human being of the twentieth century might appear like the strangest alien to the makers and livers of a non-alienated future.

Conclusions

Several scenarios have been outlined, differing widely in terms of their immediate possibility, and in terms of who would find them desirable. They are not exhaustive of scenarios for Western society — given the narrow focus of this paper as outlined in the introduction, they may be hardly adequate! Other possibilities would be deduced if it is incorrect to assume that the world-system is embarked on a period of crisis, for example. The scenario of "corporate society", for instance, might involve much less overt repression and misery were some unknown factor to restore the conditions of the post-war boom. (For a fictional exploration of the sort of world that might then result — dystopian enough in its own ways — see John Brunner's *The Shockwave Rider.*) Perhaps, too, hegemonic power in a crisis-ridden world could achieve this sort of stability by intensifying its exploitative activities in the rest of the world. But the four scenarios outlined should give some sense of the possibilities (again, *not* options) that are open. More importantly, they may point to some political issues in the present which are vital to the merging future(s). These issues are already discernible, of course, but have been thrown into relief in these images of the future.

In particular, this essay has set out to highlight issues arising around the new technology. At the very least, more public and better-informed discussion of these new microelectronics and communications systems, assessment of a wide range of social implications than are usually taken into account, and analysis of the different roles that may be performed by the new technology in alternative futures, are necessary. For example, it is important that critical attention be paid to the futurological literature on computerized democracy, and to the attempts to provide electronic systems for economic planning (as in Chile in the UP period). Such work is vital to prepare for questions which may be posed in the near future. Are new communications systems to be centralized and monopolized, or will they permit interactive, non-hierarchical networks to be formed? What sorts of overrides and controls are to be permitted — is the repressive apparatus to have priority of use (as in the system of emergency controls which will limit telephone services in the UK in conditions of widespread civil unrest), is surveillance and monitoring allowed, and if so is it secret or visible? Are the items that may be plugged into such a system to be monopolized by the state? Is there to be censorship of publicly available material — for example, would radical newspapers be circulated electronically? Are services to be provided on a commercial basis for individualized households and businesses, or collectively for organizations of all kinds?

A wide range of questions indeed, only partly prefigured in debates over the control of cable television, citizens radio and other mass media in the past. Yet the answers to these questions could significantly influence the degree to which the new technologies are shaped in the interests of repression or liberation. Perhaps the most important immediate issues for most activists at present are those concerning workplace, employment and environmental aspects of the current technological revolution — certainly similar and more concrete lists of questions could be formulated for each area. But it could well be that if we do not seriously address a wide range of questions concerning the new technologies, these will be employed in many ways to reinforce and restructure the old order. Theory, action research and cultural practice here are all vital if a vision of a desirable future is to be more than a vision.

Bibliography

Note: This bibliography, while anything but a complete guide to the relevant literature, contains references to works not directly cited in the text which were found to be helpful in the preparation of this essay.

ACERO, L. (1979) "Workers Skills as a Critical Issue for Self-reliance." In L. ACERO, S. COLE and H. RUSH (eds.) *Issues and Analysis of Long Term Development,* Paris: UNESCO.
ACKROYD, C., MARGOLIS, K., ROSEHEAD, J. and SHALLICE, T. (1977) *The Technology of Political Control,* Harmondsworth, Penguin.
AMIN, S. (1974) "Towards a New Structural Crisis of the Capitalist System?" (mimeo). Paper presented to Conference on Multinational Corporations in Africa, Dakar: UN African Institute for Economic Development and Planning.
ANNING, N. (1979) "Back Door Identity Cards." *The Leveller,* No. 31, p.13.
ASQUITH, P. (1979) "Workers' Control of Control of the Workers?" *Science for People,* No. 42, 8-12.
AVODBURY, LORD, COVERSON, R., HUMPHRIES, J. and MEEK, B. (1972) *Computers and the year 2000,* Manchester: National Computing Centre.
BAHRO, R., 1978. *The Alternative in Eastern Europe,* London: New Left Books.
BARRON, I. and CURNOW, R.C. (1979) *The Future with Information Technology,* London: Francis Pinter.
BELLINI, J. *et al.* (1977) *2002: Britain plus 25,* London: Henley Centre for Forecasting.

BENYON, H. and WAINWRIGHT, H. (1979) *In the Face of Corporate Power,* London: Pluto Press.

BODINGTON, S. (1973) *Computers and Socialism,* London: Spokesman.

BOYLE, G. and HARPER, P. (1976) *Radical Technology,* London: Wildwood House.

BRAVERMAN, H. (1974) *Labour and Monopoly Capital,* New York: Monthly Review Press.

BRIGHTON LABOUR PROCESS GROUP (1977) "Computers and Capital." *Capital and Class,* No. 2, 143-144.

BRUNNER, J. (1975) *The Shockwave Rider,* London: Sphere.

CALLENBACK, E. (1978) *Ecotopia,* London: Pluto Press.

CASTLES, S. and WUSTERNBERG, W. (1979) *The Education of the Future,* London: Pluto.

CDPPEC (1979) *The State and the Local Economy,* Newcastle-upon-Tyne: CDP/PEC (Brookside, Seaton Burn, Newcastle, NE13 6EY).

CHICHILNISKY, G. and COLE, S. (1978) *Technology, Domestic Distribution and North-South Relations* (progress report), New York, UNITAR.

COCKBURN, C. (1977) *The Local State,* London: Pluto Press.

COOLEY, M. (1976) "Contradictions of Science and Technology in the Productive Process." In H. ROSE and S. ROSE, (eds.) *The Political Economy of Science,* London: Macmillan.

CROZIER, B. (1979) *The Minimum State,* London: Macmillan.

DARWIN, J. (1979) "Bread and Circuses." In CDPPEC, *op. cit.*

EDINBURGH CSE GROUP (1978) "State Form and State Apparatus", "The Cuts and the Crisis of the State Form", "State Crises and Transport". In *CSE Conference 1978 Papers and Abstracts,* London: Conference of Socialist Economists.

ELGER, T. (1979) "Valorisation and Deskilling", a critique of Braverman. *Capital and Class,* No. 7, 58-99.

ELLIOT, D. and ELLIOT, R. (1976) *The Control of Technology,* London: Wykeham.

ELLIOT, D. A. (1975) "Decision Making and Decentral Society." Paper presented to "Socialism and the Environment" Conference, January.

ELLIOT, D. (1977) *The Lucas Aerospace Workers Campaign,* London: Fabian Society.

ENZENBERGER, H. M. (1976) "Constituents of a Theory of the Media." In *Raids and Reconstructions,* London: Pluto Press.

EVANS, T. and SHARP, (1979) "Micro-electronic Technology and the State." Paper presented at CSE Annual Conference.

FINE, B. and HARRIS, C. (1979) *Rereading Capital,* London: Macmillan.

FORRESTER, J. W. (1978) "A Great Depression Ahead?" *The Futurist,* **12,** 379-385.

FREEMAN, A. (1979) "Economic Strategy, Chile and the British Far Left." *CSE Annual Conference,* 1979: forthcoming in *International.*

FREEMAN, C. (1977) "Unemployment and the Direction of Technical Change." Paper prepared for OECD expert group meeting, SPRU, University of Sussex.

FREEMAN, C. (1978) "Creating More Jobs Than the Microprocessor Destroy" and "How Britain Should Face Up To Today's Technological Revolution." *Financial Times,* 24.5.78.

FREEMAN, C. (1978) "Technology and Development: Long Waves in Technical Change and Economic Development" (mimeo). Holst Memorial Lecture, SPRU, University of Sussex.

FREEMAN, C. and JAHODA, M. (1978) *World Futures: The Great Debate,* London: Martin Robertson.

GAMBAROTTA, H. (1978) "Integrated Approach Toward World Recession and Inflation in the Present Decade" (mimeo). Institute of Development Studies, University of Sussex, for IFIAS *Drought and Man Project.*

GARRETT, J. and WRIGHT, G. (1978). "Micro is Beautiful." *Undercurrents,* No. 27, 33-36.

GERBNER, G. (ed.) (1977) *Mass Media Policies in Changing Cultures,* New York: John Wiley.

GERSHUNY, J. (1978) *After Industrial Society?* London: Macmillan.

GERSHUNY, J. (1979) "The Informal Economy." *Futures.* February, 3-15.

GOUGH, I. (1979) *The Political Economy of the Welfare State,* London: Macmillan.

GRIFFITHS, D., IRVINE, J. and MILES, I. (1979) "Social Statistics: Political Perspectives." In J. IRVINE, I. MILES and J. EVANS (eds.) *Demystifying Social Statistics,* London: Pluto Press.

HARRINGTON, M. (1974) "Leisure as the Means of Production." In C. KOLAKOWSKI and S. HAMPSHIRE, (eds.) *The Socialist Idea,* London: Weidenfeld & Nicolson.

HARMAN, C. (1979) *New Technology and Socialism,* London: Socialist Workers.

HARMS, L. S. (1974) *Human Communication,* New York: Harper & Row.

HINES, C. (1978) *The Chips are Down,* London: Earth Resources Research.

HODSON, R. (1978) "Labour in the Monopoly, Competitive and State Sectors of Production." *Politics and Society,* **8** (3-4), 429-480.

HOLLOWAY, J. and PICCIOTTO, S. (1977) "Capital, Crises and the State." *Capital and Class,* No. 2, 76-101.

IL MANIFESTO (1979) *Power and Opposition in Post-Revolutionary Societies,* London: Ink Links.

IRVINE, J. and MILES, I. (1978) "Alternative Ways of Life in Britain." Paper prepared for S.I.D./GPID Project on "Alternative Ways of Life."

IRVINE, J., MILES, I. and EVANS, J. (1979) *Demystifying Social Statistics,* London: Pluto Press.

I.W.C. (Institute for Workers Control) (1978) *The Right to Useful Work,* London: Spokesman.

I.W.C. Motors Group (1979) *A Workers' Enquiry Into the Motor Industry,* London: CSE Books.

JOLLY, R. (1979) "Another Development for Europe in the 1980s." In *Alternative Ways of Life,* Rome: Society for International Development.

KITZMUELLER, E. (1979) *The Greening of Marx,* Brussels: Agenor (Issue No. 78).

LABORIT, H. (1977) *Decoding the Human Message,* London: Allison & Busby.

LABOUR RESEARCH (1979) "Microelectronics — The Impact Today." *Labour Research,* **68,** 78-79.

LANGE, O. (1972) "The Computer and the Market." In A. NOVE and D. M. NUT (eds.) *Socialist Economics,* Harmondsworth: Penguin.

LE GUIN, U. (1974) *The Dispossessed,* New York: Harper & Row.

LINDBERG, R. *et al.* (eds.) (1975) *Stress and Contradiction in Modern Capitalism,* Lexington, Mass: Lexington Books.

LONDON CSE GROUP (1979) "Crisis, The Labour Movement, and the Alternative Economic Strategy." *Capital and Class* **8,** 68-93.

MANDEL, E. (1973) *Late Capitalism,* London: New Left Books.

MANDEL, E. (1977) "Revolutionary Strategy in Europe." *New Left Review* **100,** 97-136.

MANDEL, E. (1978) *The Second Slump,* London: New Left Books.

MARSH, C. (1979) "Opinion Polls." In IRVINE, MILES and EVANS (*op.cit.*)

McHALE, J. (1971) *The Changing Information Environment,* London: Pavlelek.

McLEAN, J. M. and RUSH, H. (1978) *Impact Analysis by Industrial Sector-Case Studies,* SPRU, University of Sussex.

MESZAROS, I. (1971) *The Necessity of Social Control,* London: The Merlin Press.

MILES, I. (1975) *The Poverty of Prediction,* Farnborough, Saxon House, Lexington, Mass.: Lexington Books.

MILES, I. (1979) "Scenario Analysis: Identifying Ideologies and Issues." In L. ACERO, S. COLE and H. RUSH (eds.) *The Application of Analytic Techniques to Issues of Long-Term Development,* Paris: UNESCO (Working Title).

MILES, I. and IRVINE, J. (1979) "Establishing Alternative Ways of Life in Britain: and Investigations of Goals and Strategies" (mimeo). Paper presented to UNU/SID "Alternative Ways of Life" meeting, Trappeto, Sicily, March 1979.

MUMFORD, E. and SACKMAN, H. (eds.) (1975) *Human Choice and Computers,* Amsterdam: North-Holland.

NAIRN, T. (1977) *The Break-up of Britain,* London: New Left Books.

O'CONNOR, J. (1973) *The Fiscal Crisis of the State,* London: St. James.

OECD INTERFUTURES (1979) *Facing the Futures,* Paris, OECD.

OLLMAN, B. (1977) "Marx's Vision of Communism: a Reconstruction." *Critique,* **8,** 4-41.

OLLMAN, B. (1979) *Social and Sexual Revolution,* London: Pluto.

PAULDER, S. (1979) "Data Bases Get Set for Information Blast Off." *Electronic Times,* 29 March 1979, p. 12.

PERLMAN, J. E. (1978) "Grassrooting the System." In URPE (1978), *op. cit.*

PIERCY, M. (1978) *Woman on the Edge of Time,* London: The Women's Press.

POULANTZAS, N. (1977) "The State and the Transition to Socialism." *International,* Vol. 4, No. 1, 3-12.

REICH, W. (1972) *Sex-Pol: Essays 1929-1934,* New York: Vintage Books.
ROBERTSON, J. (1978) *The Sane Alternative,* London: 7 St. Ann's Villas, W11 4RU.
SOCIETY FOR INTERNATIONAL DEVELOPMENT (UK) (1979) "Development Alternatives and Priorities for National and International Reform — A British View" (mimeo). Draft for SID International Conference on Alternative Development Strategies.
SOHN-RETHEL, A. (1978) *Intellectual and Manual Labour,* London: Macmillan.
THERBORN, G. (1978) *What Does the Ruling Class do when it Rules,* London: New Left Books.
URPE, Economics Education Project (1978) *US Capitalism in Crisis,* New York: Union for Radical Political Economics, 41 Union Square West, NY 10003,
USFI, United Secretariat of the Fourth International (1977) *Socialist Democracy,* Toronto: Vanguard.
VANEK, J. (ed.) 1975) *Self-Management,* Harmondsworth: Penguin.
WILLIAMS, R. (1974) *Television: Technology and Cultural Form,* London: Fontana.
WRIGHT, E. O. (1978) *Class, Crisis and the State,* London: New Left Books.

15

On Types of Civilizations: A Comparison through Three Dimensions

OSCAR NUDLER

Fundacion Bariloche, Argentina

1. Introduction

A growing stream of reflection flows nowadays around the so-called "crisis of civilization". To be sure, the subject is not new. It could rightly be claimed that it has been with us at least since the days when the eighteenth-century idea of indefinite progress perished in the trenches of World War I and was officially buried by Oswald Spengler. The notion of a worldwide, planetary crisis of civilization is, however, of relatively recent diffusion, perhaps no earlier than the end of World War II. Some new facts and some highly probable possibilities which have since appeared on the human horizon have contributed much to bring to the forefront this notion of a total crisis. By way of illustration a few examples might suffice: the possibility of the destruction of civilization in a nuclear war, a possibility which can by no means be discarded in view of the armaments race, local wars involving the superpowers and, in general, the very fragile international order; the possibility of the destruction of vital parts of the earth's ecosystem, such as the Amazon jungle; the short-term exhaustion of oil reserves and other non-renewable resources; the growing population and increasing poverty in immense areas of the Third World; the development of new scientific instruments of political control, ranging from current, Watergate-type models of miniaturized electronic espionage devices to the Huxlean genetic engineering nightmare; and so on and so forth.

Faced with these discouraging facts and gloomy prospects, there are many who have chosen some form of nihilism or cynicism but there are others who have engaged in a search for ways out. In many cases, however, the proposed ways are essentially a repetition of formulas from the past: what is required is more love between people and respect for God's commandments, say the spokesmen of various religions; more justice in economic relations within each nation, says the classic Left; between the nations, say the advocates of the NEIO; more respect for individual rights and democratic institutions, say political liberals. My impression is that all these proposals, though responsible for greatly enlarging our historical and social vision, share the common shortcoming of not being based on a perception of the crisis in its real complexity or, more precisely, its multi-dimensionality. The present crisis is not a specifically economic or political or religious or moral or spiritual crisis. It is an overall crisis of this civiliza-tion and therefore cannot be understood, and much less confronted, from one perspective alone. The recurrent attempts to do so have, more often than not, ended in frustration and, so to speak, in "more of the same". And frustration becomes, in turn, an additional component, perhaps the most destructive, of the crisis.

It is certainly not my purpose to propose an alternative solution to the contemporary crisis. My intention is rather to compare our type of civiliza-tion with other types, taking for that end three dimensions, two of an in-dividual nature, namely, temporal consciousness and the state of the human needs system, and the third global, the society–Nature relationship. A com-parison with other types of civilization offers the possibility of removing from our thinking the straitjacket of seemingly opposing ideologies which are, in fact, equally committed to certain core beliefs of our type of civiliza-tion (for example, the idea of dominating Nature and the emphasis on unlimited material growth). To transcend some interpretative frames deeply rooted in the past of our civilization appears to be today a necessary con-dition for emerging from the crisis. Our century is still guided by the systems of the nineteenth and earlier centuries and although some new, powerful *idées-forces* have arisen, these have not yet brought about any coherent system. Moreover, the choice of several dimensions of comparison and, particularly, the type of dimensions chosen — not the economic, political or cultural dimensions usually considered — seeks to draw atten-tion to the multi-dimensionality of the concept of civilization. The *con-sciousness of time* dimension which, as Kant taught, lies at the very founda-tion of the human cognitive structure, was selected as a key indicator of the world and life conceptions built into a civilization. The *system of needs* dimension, which is at the base of the affective-motivational structure, was in turn chosen because through a knowledge of the emphasized and the repressed needs in a specific type of civilization we could reach an understanding of its embodied system of values. Finally, the *society–Nature relationship* was selected with the purpose of obtaining a sort of external and global vision of civilizations. This vision should be coherent with those obtained from the perspective of individual consciousness since, as we assume it here, in every civilization the macro and the micro dimensions are closely interlinked and constitute a kind of feedback system. The micro dimensions require the matrix of the macro dimensions to emerge and develop and the latter require the former to reproduce and change.

In this paper three types of civilization will be roughly outlined, each of them characterized by a peculiar form of temporal consciousness, a specific state of the human needs system and a definite style of society–Nature relationships. These types are somehow idealized since actual civilizations obviously require for their satisfactory description more dimensions than the ones considered here and, as regards the three dimensions selected, civilizations always stand at a certain — greater or lesser — distance from the pure states composing our types. Viewed from the society–Nature relationship vantage-point, the three types of civilization will be called, respectively, *dominated by Nature, antagonistic to Nature* and *in equilibrium with Nature*. The description of these types will be made in the third section. Previously, in Section II, some relevant parts of the needs theory accepted here will be introduced in a relatively detailed way.

Before ending this introduction, let us touch briefly on a semantical point — in fact, more than semantics is involved here. When speaking at the beginning about "the crisis of civilization", obviously the existence of a single, present-day civilization was implied. To a certain extent, this assumption could be defended, since in spite of the diversity of cultures which fortunately still subsists, a specific type of civilization, generated only some 400 years ago in a small region of the planet — Western Europe — has had such a tremendous power of expansion that today probably no nation, whether capitalist, socialist or whatever — has escaped its penetration. This type of civilization which is here called "antagonistic to Nature" and which, taking other perspectives, is known as industrial, technical, rational, etc., has continually expanded through interconnected processes of "peripheration" and building of new centres of expansion. Today a new Far West — in fact a Far East — is taking shape as a great historical horizon of expansion in the immediate future. The scenario in which this civilization plays its game is clearly the entire world so that its crisis is automatically a worldwide crisis. Nevertheless this fact should not make us forget another: together with this dominating type of civilization, and generally in conflict with it, other types exist in the present world, most of them historically older and others, still embryonic, perhaps the feeble seeds of some future civilization.

Strictly speaking, therefore, it is not appropriate to speak of a crisis of civilization but of a crisis of a specific type of civilization. But — to repeat — the problem is that this type of civilization is able, thanks to its universal scope, to drag the whole of humanity along with it in its crisis, something which has never happened with any civilization in the past.

2. The system of human needs and its states

In this section I shall sketch a model of the human-needs system.[1] This model assumes that needs are inner teleologically-oriented forces which

---

[1]For a more detailed, though earlier statement see O. Nudler, "Human Needs. A sophisticated Holistic Approach". Forthcoming in K. Lederer (ed.) *Human Needs. A Contribution to the Current Debate,* Berlin, 1979.

prompt the individual to act. It also assumes that some of the needs are, *mutatis mutandi,* characteristics that the human system shares with all living systems. At least insofar as this assumption is justified, the model may claim to have an objective foundation.

In what follows I shall describe the main additional features characterizing the present model:

1. According to the model, we can identify within the needs system a set of *fundamental needs* which constitute the core of the system:

(a) *Subsistence.* As its name shows, this need is the force which moves the individual to maintain his individuality both at a physical and at a psychical level (where we could call it the *identity* need). Following Spinoza's *Ethics,* we can put this in a nutshell by saying: "Every being tries to persevere in his own being."

(b) *Growth.* This need is the force which moves the individual to unfold his potentialities and, by so doing, to *change* his being in the direction of an ever-increasing internal differentiation and integration. Using a distinction introduced by Telma Nudler,[2] I shall distinguish between two kinds of growth: *primary* growth, which refers to the basic psychophysical growth that occurs in the first years of human life, and *maturity* growth, understood as a continuous psychic growth in multiple dimensions which may only stop with physical decline. The need for growth underlies both kinds of growth.

(c) *Transcendence.* Subsistence and growth needs, although generally requiring other individuals for their fulfilment, tend respectively to maintain and develop the individual as such. But transcendence is the force which moves the individual to go beyond his individuality and unite with others, with Nature or with collective abstract constructions, such as God, the State, etc. Subsistence and growth are needs characterizing all living systems but transcendence is more specifically human, particularly in its more purely psychic manifestations.

2. Fundamental needs are assumed as universal in the sense of being components of the human-needs system irrespectively of time and place. But the *total* system of needs is assumed to be variable in function of personal and cultural conditions. This difference between the universality of fundamental needs and the variability of needs systems arises, as well as from other sources, from the fact that fundamental needs undergo, according to the model, a series of transformations and these transformations are mediated by the other sub-systems making up the person system and, through them, by culture. In a first stage, fundamental needs are transformed into derived[3] needs. For example, the fundamental need for sub-

---

[2]T. Nudler, *Towards a Model of Human Growth,* Tokyo, 1979.

[3]As pointed out in the paper cited in note 1, the "derivation" I refer to in this case is not a logical but a psychological one.

sistence transforms itself into a set of derived needs ranging from the needs for food or shelter to the needs for security or meaning. In a second stage, if it is reached at all, derived needs turn into specific desires,[4] thus leaving the needs system as such and feeding the motivational system. I shall refer to this stage as the stage of *expression* of the needs.

3. Needs are not isolated forces acting upon the individual but they make up a dynamic system. The structure of this system is determined by the relative force of each need, which is highly variable according to personal and cultural differences. Among the different possible structures or *states* of the needs system, I shall consider the following:

(a) *Partialization.* In this state some needs tend to predominate permanently over the others, preventing them from emerging. In the most extreme cases of partialization one single need dominates the whole system. If E is the set of emphasized needs and D the set of displaced needs (the remainder of the needs), we could see the difference between a state of partialization and a non-partialized state through Fig. 1.

FIG. 1

The arrows represent the system's output or the expression of the needs. It will be noted that in the state of partialization only the needs belonging to group E express themselves while in a non-partialized state this limitation does not exist.

In many cases partialization occurs when subsistence needs reach a critical level of insatisfaction. However, it seems important to distinguish here, following a suggestion by Carlos Mallmann,[5] between exceptional or sudden and chronic states of needs insatisfaction. The former clearly put into motion the mechanism of partialization but what occurs in the second case is not so clear. When a human being is accustomed to find himself always at a low level of satisfaction of his subsistence needs and, moreover, is lucky enough to survive, it is quite possible that other needs may emerge and be satisfied. This is, as is well known, a frequent case in India and other regions of the Third World where most people are chronically hungry and at the same time endowed with strong religious feelings. Nevertheless this state of affairs tends inevitably to cause some form of partialization and displacement

---

[4]Here I give this term a wider scope than the usual one so that it covers not only desires in the usual sense but also related psychic states such as *interests, demands,* etc.

[5]Personal communication.

in the needs system such as, in this case, a one-sided emphasis on certain kinds of transcendence needs.

(b) *Blockage.* In this state an important part of the needs system is prevented from expressing itself. In the most extreme cases practically no part of the system can express itself, which creates a pathological state of generalized lack of motivation. This state can be represented simply as in Fig. 2.

FIG. 2

No arrow leaves the circle.

Partialization, as described in (a), provokes the blockage of the non-emphasized or displaced parts of the system. As can be seen in Fig. 1 (a), the group of needs *D* lacks expression, i.e. it is blocked. But blockage may be due also to other causes. One of them is the conflict between two or more needs which have a similar force. This can be illustrated as in Fig. 3.

FIG. 3

A and *B* have equal forces and therefore the system has no output.

Another cause (and also effect) of the blockage of the needs system which is worth mentioning is the systematic oversatisfaction of one part of the needs, usually that of subsistence, which prevents the accomplishment of the insatisfaction–expression–satisfaction–repose–insatisfaction cycle that keeps needs as psychic forces.

Figure 4 represents the above-mentioned cycle.

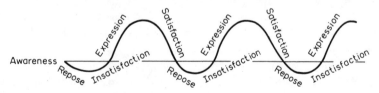

FIG. 4

Oversatisfaction maintains the needs in the right-hand descending part of the curve and prevents them from reaching the state of repose, a necessary condition for a subsequent state of insatisfaction and further continuation of the cycle. A typical illustration is provided by the over-satisfaction of the need for food in social groups which "enjoy" a high material standard of living.

(c) *Equilibrium.* In this state no needs are found permanently at a critical level of insatisfaction or oversatisfaction. All the needs have the possibility of accomplishing the insatisfaction–expression–satisfaction–repose–insatisfaction cycle to which I have just referred. We could represent this state as in Fig. 5.

FIG. 5

The equilibrium to which I refer here is a dynamic one and does not imply the absence of conflicts but only their non-destructive nature. Nor should it be understood as a constant return to the same state. On the contrary the system of human needs is certainly capable of irreversible types of change.

4. The system of human needs is a hierarchically ordered system. This means, and in this point I follow Abraham Maslow,[6] that certain needs must be satisfied before others can be expressed. The hierarchical ordering referred to here is by no means a moral or ethical one.

The hierarchy of the human needs system is not simple, or at least it does not have the simplicity which Maslow attributed to it. Thus, for example, taking the classification of fundamental needs given in point 1, it would not be adequate to postulate a simple hierarchical ordering such as subsistence, growth, transcendence. It may well happen that transcendence needs (i.e. needs derived from the transcendence need) may be satisfied without satisfying growth needs, although in that case only a particular type of transcendence needs will be those which are satisfied and only a specific type of needs of growth will be those not fully satisfied (those of maturity plus some of psychic identity). In other words, certain forms of transcendence require that the maturity growth needs be satisfied first but others do not require it. This conclusion, which I shall use later, is introduced here with the sole intention of pointing out the complex character of the hierarchical organization of the human-needs system.

5. As already stated, needs are normally expressed through desires. A simple way of representing this is as shown in Fig. 6.

---

[6]See A. Maslow, *Motivation and Personality,* 2nd edition, New York, Harper, 1970, and *Towards a Psychology of Being,* New York, Van Nost, 1968.

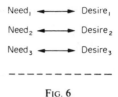

FIG. 6

Figure 6 presents, however, not only a simple but an oversimplified picture since the one-to-one relationship between needs and desires which appears therein is very far from representing what really happens in many cases. It is more likely that the opposite takes place: a need may originate several desires or a desire may be the expansion of various needs. However, for my present purpose, this oversimplified picture is enough since I only want to say that needs and desires are somehow related to each other without trying to find out the exact form of the relationship.

To go beyond the problem of univocal or multivocal representations, we find very often that there are desires which hold only very indirect and highly symbolic relationships with some need. For example, the obsessive desire to be conspicuous which some people manifest in a more or less subtle way is generally connected with a weak identity, or what is the same, with a low degree of satisfaction of identity needs. The main characteristic of desires of this kind is that their satisfaction does not really allow the satisfaction of the needs which are obscurely expressed by them and therefore they tend to become insatiable. If these needs are satisfied in some other way, however, the desires of this type tend to disappear. I shall thus divide desires into *direct* ones (expressing a need directly) and *displaced* ones (expressing only indirectly and symbolically the need in which they originate).[7]

3. The society–Nature relationship as a starting-point

I shall now introduce a typical-ideal classification of human societies based on their style of relation to Nature. The classification is the following:

1. Societies with a low degree of control over Nature or societies dominated by Nature.
2. Societies with a high degree of depredatory control over Nature or societies antagonistic to Nature.
3. Societies in an ecologically integrated relationship with Nature or societies in harmony with Nature.

---

[7]The concept of "displaced desire" introduced here is somehow reminiscent of Freud's defence mechanisms, especially sublimation. A crucial difference lies, however, in that the possibility of highly indirect and symbolic relationships between needs and desires is *not* limited here to physiologically based or "tissue" needs but extends to all needs, maturity growth and transcendence needs included.

Each of these three forms of the society–Nature relationship are peculiar, as stated in the introduction, to one type of civilization. It is obvious that forms 1 and 2 appear as undesirable ones. Nevertheless care must be taken before drawing conclusions about a whole type of civilization on the sole basis of this trait. Every type of civilization contains a form of wisdom, a wisdom obtained *between* the limits imposed by its relation with Nature. Therefore every type of civilization has something to teach the others and on this rests the "dialogue des civilizations" concept. Furthermore, the construct "society–Nature relation" is not simple. The type of relationship that a society entertains with Nature is not only a function of its degree of technological advancement but depends upon a complex interrelated set of factors. Technological advancement must be taken together with the amount and types of the demands or exigencies that a society raises in relation to Nature and these latter, in turn, are not independent of factors such as demographic pressure and prevailing value priorities. It is thus the relationship between technological advancement and exigencies towards Nature, and not technological advancement by itself, that defines a society as dominated by, antagonistic to, or in equilibrium with Nature.

Historical examples which are close to type 1 can be found, for instance, among pre-industrial European societies, this being evident especially in periods of crisis, when demographic pressure became higher, ascetic values began to be replaced and, at the same time, technological innovation was still not socially meaningful. Societies in the first stages of industrialization, such as England in the nineteenth century or the Soviet Union in the first half of the twentieth, are located half-way between types 1 and 2. The present advanced industrialized societies are, no matter their differences in political structure, good examples of type 2. Finally type 3, although examples close to it can be found especially in some so-called "primitive" societies, appears to correspond almost completely to a eutopian[8] domain, i.e. to a design of good future societies on the basis of possibilities contained in the present.

We have thus a distinction between three types of society–Nature relationships. We also have a distinction, introduced in section 2, between three types of needs states. We would require now some additional distinctions concerning our third dimension, temporal consciousness. But instead of dealing with consciousness of time separately as was done with the other two dimensions, I would rather introduce it directly into the description of the types of civilization which follows. A preliminary distinction must, however, be made. I would like to recall that "consciousness of time" can be understood in two different senses and that both senses interest me here: as reflective consciousness and as prereflective consciousness of time. Both

---

[8] I saw this term used for the first time in Jim Dator, "Neither There nor Then. A Eutopian Alternative to the Development Model of Future Society", *Human Futures,* The Rome World Special Conference on Futures Research, 1973, IPC. Business Press Limited, 1974.

forms of the consciousness of time are, as Ernest Keen has rightly pointed out, closely linked:

> ". . . the relation between reflective and prereflective modes of experiencing is circular. Reflective assessments enter into immediate experiencing, but come from immediate experiencing. I believe we can say of this relation that it is precisely dialectical."[9]

This "dialectic" between the reflective and the prereflective consciousness of time is indeed one of the problematic keys to human existence and no Utopian or futurological thinking should try to avoid confronting it.

Now the ground is prepared for a description of the three types of civilizations. Our assumption is, as stated before, that each of them is characterized, *inter alia,* by three associated features: a way of relating to Nature, a prevailing state of the human-needs system and a dominant consciousness of time. I shall now proceed to the description of the types of civilizations by taking as a starting-point the different styles of the society-Nature relationship I have just distinguished.

A. Societies with a low degree of control over Nature

These societies are in a heavily dependent relationship as regards Nature. Human life is in complete, direct function not only of certain extraordinary natural contingencies (flood, droughts, plagues, epidemics) but also of the ordinary natural rhythms and cycles. The distribution of periods of work and rest is entirely determined by them:

> "Agricultural work was longer or shorter according to the length of the days, the intensity of the sun and the frequency of rainfall. It was regulated by the seasons. Leisure time and holydays were fitted into the year to celebrate the grape-gathering and harvesting periods.[10]

Given this type of relationship between human beings and Nature, time is not considered socially as an abstract category. On the contrary, it forms part of life itself:

> "Time was thought of in terms of time in man's life, having no existence outside; the mind of the peasant was incapable of seeing beyond the implacable rhythm of nature. . . . Time, instead of being the neutral span of the real processes of life, formed an integral part of life."[11]

---

[9]E. Keen, "The Past in the Future: Consciousness and Tradition", *Journal of Humanistic Psychology,* Fall 1978, p.13.

[10]A. Jeanniere, "The Pathogenic Structures of Time in Modern Societies", *Time and the Philosophies,* UNESCO, 1977, p. 108.

[11]A. J. Gurevich, "Time as a Problem of Cultural History", *Cultures and Time,* The UNESCO Press, Paris, 1976, p. 237.

A. J. Gurevich, from whose work on time I extracted the foregoing quotation, later completes the characterization of the consciousness of time in this type of society:

"The notion of a time of unspecified quality, neutral as to content and unconnected with those who experience it and lend it emotional tone was, in general, alien to the consciousness of the men of antiquity and the Middle Ages."[12]

The foregoing does not imply, however, that in societies with low control over Nature there does not exist a reflective consciousness of temporal experience. This would obviously be false. What I am saying is that the prereflective, lived, concrete time is in these societies the *socially dominant* time. This means that the great majority of the population only knows this time and, moreover, that the educated élites who conceptualize time do so influenced by the prevailing view. Through some of these conceptualizations time appears as cyclic, as endlessly repeating itself, just as one generation of peasants keeps invariable the patterns of past generations. Through some other conceptualizations it is time itself and not just cycles of time which starts and ends. Both conceptualizations are alike in viewing human existence and time as subordinated to or included in a universal framework, whether a great cycle or non-time. In this last case, which I select as our ideal type, the myths of creation of time and the millenarist, eschatological Utopias of abolition of time provide the links between the human, temporal, corruptible side of the Universe and the divine, non-temporal, incorruptible one. There is a time and a non-time, making contact at two points. Time is endowed with a negative value and non-time with a positive value but, independently of value assignments, it is clear that the reflective consciousness of time is here able to include it in a global Weltanschauung. A diagram representing this could be as shown in Fig. 7.

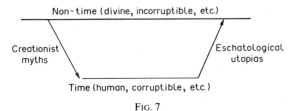

Non-time (divine, incorruptible, etc.)

Creationist myths

Eschatological utopias

Time (human, corruptible, etc.)

Fig. 7

This type of reflective consciousness of time corresponds to a prevailing state of *partialization* of the needs system. The subsistence needs, critically unsatisfied, tend to occupy the whole field and, except for the growth needs necessary for subsistence, the remainder of the growth needs cannot be expressed. The notion of personal, individual growth does not exist, or at

---

[12]A. J. Gurevich, *op. cit.*, p. 238.

least it is not socially dominant. This is quite logical since the individual, at least such as understood in the Western depredatory societies which emerged after the breakdown of medieval cosmology and anthropology, does not exist. The transcendence needs, on the other hand, can be made amply manifest although, as I pointed out previously, they involve a transcendence which as a rule does not pass through individual maturity growth. It is, so to speak, a direct transcendence, associated with a leap from the lived time to the non-time of the myth and the Utopia.

B. Societies with a high degree of depredatory control over Nature

In these societies the consciousness of time changes radically. Obviously the new conception is established long before depredatory control over Nature is achieved. It is precisely an *idée-force* which propels the change from one society to another. Time is now abstract, independent of lived cycles and rhythms. The human being becomes highly attuned to the passage of time which acquires a value in itself. Now time can be used, spent, saved, bought and sold.

Once time has been abstracted from life, the possibility appears of dividing it in a conventional manner. In this way, work time is separated unambiguously from leisure time, productivity time from time for resting, entertainment and vacations. Time has been split up into times. Correspondingly, the human being is divided up into disjointed roles. A popular text of introduction to sociology presents the following description of the social conduct of an individual as "natural":

> "How a person behaves depends to a great extent on the particular position in which he happens to be, i.e. the *status* he occupies. The tight-fisted businessman who is the very soul of generosity in his contributions to charity or the coarse blackmailer who treats his wife and children with love and tenderness, are not necessarily examples of hypocrisy or split personality; they simply behave at different moments in the manner which corresponds to the different status which they happen to be occupying."[13]

This *fragmentation* of lived, prereflective time has, of course, effects on the reflective consciousness of time. The average member of these societies has a *linear* conception of time according to which time extends indefinitely and without qualitative changes (changes in cycles, for example) into the past and the future. He usually believes in irreversible, global processes going on, especially in history. But the relationship of these processes with the time of human life is obscure and so a feeling of alienation, of being an

---

[13]E. Chinoy, *Sociological Perspective. Basic Concepts and their Application,* New York, Random House, 1975.

isolated fragment emerges. A representation of this state of the consciousness of time could be as follows:

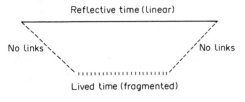

FIG. 8

The myth and the Utopia which closed the diagram of the universe in type
1 societies have been displaced now from the centre of human life and have
not been replaced. The existentialist philosophers from Kierkegaard onwards have dramatically denounced this gap in the consciousness of time.
Heidegger locates it in the very basis of what he calls "unauthentic
existence". The origin of this gap, however, does not lie, as the
existentialists claim, in a universal characteristic of the human being, or the
Dasein, but in the fragmentation and ultimately in the destruction of time
that takes place in societies which exercise a depredatory control over
Nature.

What happens to the system of human needs in this type of societies? The
satisfaction of physical subsistence needs enables other needs situated
higher in the hierarchy to emerge and be satisfied. There are, however,
forces in these societies which hinder the achievement of this possibility.
The separation of the human being from Nature, from other human beings
and his internal fragmentation expressed, as we have just seen, through the
fragmentation of the time of human life into disjointed times and the breaking of the link between that time and a universal Time, greatly adds to the
difficulty of expressing transcendence needs, which basically are needs for
unity, for overcoming the state of the individual as an isolated being. As to
the growth needs, which for the first time in history reach the possibility of
massive satisfaction, they are also affected by the fragmentation and,
moreover, by the oversatisfaction of subsistence needs. Oversatisfaction,
the same as critical insatisfaction, prevents subsistence needs from
accomplishing their cycle and thus giving place to other types of needs. The
difference between oversatisfaction and critical insatisfaction is that while
the latter allows needs to express themselves, the former does not, so instead
of a state of partialization a state of blockage is obtained. This stage
generalizes all over the entire needs system, which no longer feeds the
motivational system of the individual. In these conditions a vacuum is produced which either remains, entailing as stated above a pathological state of
lack of motivation, or else it is filled by desires which only symbolically correspond to needs, i.e. displaced desires.

C. Societies in an ecologically integrated relationship with Nature

In this type of societies the human being feels himself part of Nature although not as a passive victim of its contingencies, cycles and rhythms but as an autonomously integrated being. Along with the unity of the human being with Nature, a unification of time takes place. The fragmentation between different times which is characteristic of societies of type 2 leaves the social scene. The time for work, the time for leisure, the time to love and so on, no longer are isolated compartments for the different personalities of a single individual. The schizophrenic breaking down of personality, characteristic of depredatory societies, disappears. But this does not imply a return to the consciousness of time characteristic of the societies dominated by Nature in which the myths and Utopias of abolition of time were the escape routes from an exceedingly painful earthly time. A new consciousness of time implies an integration through reason *and* emotion between the lived time and the reflective time, between the rhythms and cycles of human life and the cycles and rhythms of Nature and the Cosmos. Some philosophers attempted to express this idea of integration of the human being with Nature and the Cosmos but perhaps no one has done it better (and this is not strange) than Chief Seattle of the North American Squawmish tribe:

> "The rocky crests — the juices of the meadows, the body heat of the pony, and man — all belong to the same family. . . . This we know: the earth does not belong to man; man belongs to the earth. This we know: all things are connected like the blood which unites one family. All things are connected. Whatever befalls the earth befalls the sons of the earth. Man did not weave the web of life; he is merely a strand in it. Whatever he does to the web, he does to himself."[14]

A diagram representing the consciousness of time in this type of societies could be simply as shown in Fig. 9.

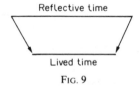

Reflective time

Lived time

Fig. 9

As regards the state of the needs system predominant in this type of societies, I think that it is the state of equilibrium in which all the needs can run again and again the insatisfaction-expression-satisfaction-repose-insatisfaction cycle. It is a living equilibrium between subsistence, growth

---

[14]Chief Seattle: "We may be brothers after all", reply to the President in Washington, 1854 — *United Nations Environment Programme — Media Pack*, 1976.

and transcendence needs, an equilibrium which tends by its own dynamics to take place at ever higher levels.

The associations which I have presented throughout this section as characterizing the different types of civilizations are summarized in Fig. 10.

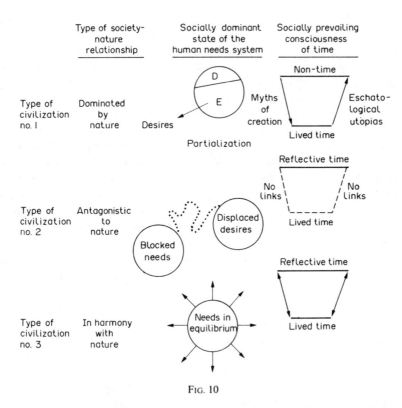

FIG. 10

4. Concluding remarks

The type of civilization which began in Western Europe, and which has expanded in a brief historical period over the whole planet, has given birth to a new type of man. This man is essentially urban, detached from Nature, insensitive to the "secret web of life", to use Chief Seattle's words. Moreover, in spite of his physical proximity to millions of fellow men, he is spiritually far from other human beings. Human relationships tend to be centred around the use of others as instruments and this dominant social style even penetrates into primary groups, making human communication a rare, difficult art. The increasing prevalence of *Gesellschaft* over *Gemeinschaft* pointed out by Ferdinand Tönnies has been so inexorable in the development of Western society that Max Weber considered it an inevitable concomitant of development processes. Finally, this type of man also tends to divide himself and to divide his activities into either-or categories. We have already mentioned the division of time and of the associated interpersonal attitudes into sharply separate compartments but this kind of separation is an entirely general feature which extends from the styles of knowledge to the whole personality. In this latter domain, internal separation has led to the substantialization of a "realm" of the unconscious, the irrational, the illogical as opposed to the conscious, the rational, the logical. Freud, impressed by the extreme forms of this opposition which he found in his patients, came to think, like Weber in the case of bureaucratic rationality, that all advance of civilization inevitably entails an advance in the process of internal separation (he believed that civilization is a product of repression).

We have thus three characteristic separations of the so-called "modern man": internal separation, separation from others and separation from Nature. The pressing question which arises is: are these separations unavoidable in any development process? Affirmative answers such as those implied by Weber's or Freud's thinking are not self-evident, even though only because this type of civilization is a relatively recent historical experiment which, given the violence with which it has been carried out, has caused severe imbalances in the society–Nature relationship, in inter-personal relationships and in the person system (the consciousness of time and the needs structure were the examples examined here in this connection). It might therefore be assumed that over a longer historical span those imbalances could be compensated. But we cannot accept either that sort of naïve historical determinism according to which the mere passage of time will bring Utopia down to earth. An active creative search for new forms of civilization is surely necessary. "Creative search" implies here that it is not historically possible, as is being attempted for example these days by the so-called "Islamic revolution" to return to an earlier type of civilization and just wipe out the influence of Western civilization. Nor is it historically possible to remain at the point where we are now, as claimed by zero-growth theorists. The unlimited-growth paradigm is certainly one of the most essential parts of the organism of this type of civilization and cannot be simply removed. The only reasonable thing which can be done is *to change the direction of growth* by redefining its goals. Maurice Strong has already made this point:

> "And it would be just as wrong to say that societies must stop growing when they reach the stage of physical maturity as it would be to say that people stop growing when they stop growing physically. The real growth of our societies in human terms can still be ahead of us. But it demands that we change our ways and adapt to a more mature kind of growth that is less physically oriented and less demanding of resources and the environment."[15]

[15]M. F. Strong, "Spaceship Earth: A Global Overview", speech at the 47th Annual Couchiching Conference on "Growth in a Conserving Society", 3 August 1978, Geneva Park, Ontario.

The historical task of the women and men who live in this type of civilization is therefore to construct a *new wisdom* regarding the relationships of the human being with Nature, with other human beings and with themselves. If this task is some day performed, it would mean that a new type of civilization would appear on this planet.

16

Democratization and Transnationals in Latin America: A Look into the Near Future

JUAN SOMAVIA
Instituto Latinoamericano Estudios Transnacionales, Mexico

THINKING about the future means to understand the past and look into the present. From a Latin American perspective this means, among other things, to deepen specially the analysis of the economic, political and cultural expansion of the transnational system in the continent. It means also to develop the intellectual and political conditions as well as those of the concrete action in order to develop the democratization of the region. Both efforts, which are inevitable, are also individable, as there are casual relations between them. It does not seem absurd today, to state that in the Latin American context, the transnational development model, ruling in a generalized way in the continent, needs for its settling, political conditions, of such a nature, that transform themselves into obstacles to the redemocratization of some countries and to the democratic perfectioning of others. In different ways, the political system is adapting itself to the complex combination of the transnational agent's interests with those which support groups and national classes looking favourably at the "transnationalization", because they reached the conclusion that this way of entering the world economy is rationally coincident with its national project of domestic domination. Hence, we cannot think of the future of Latin America without linking its aspirations to a real, participative, popular democracy, within the limits imposed by the transnational system and its local allies.

As a matter of fact, the transnational enterprises sell not only goods but also culture, or a way of life, a consumption style, different social aspirations, a sort of self-perception and a world perception, and implicitly, different parameters for the political organization of the society.

The main transnational enterprises operating in the world cover practically the whole range of human activity, from the exploitation of natural resources and the production of services and goods, to education, information and communication, through advertisement, leisure and tourism.

The typical 24 hours of a transnational consumer are marked by the systematic, permanent pressure of the transnational life model values: elitist and outside oriented. This situation looks more and more like Orwell's 1984, where the individual's manipulation, the subliminal pressure, the irresponsible socialization and the offer of a sort of transnational "El Dorado", turn into key elements for the creation of a development which is oriented towards the Third World minorities, for its own benefits and those of the transnational system of which they are part.

This model which is offered can be called mimetic. It is given as fit and necessary for the Third World, that the development model of capitalist industrialized countries should be imitated with some changes to enable it to adjust to the local characteristics. What we cannot, undoubtedly, change is its inner logic, its integrative rationality, its supportive, central ideology: the principle according to which economy and social relations develop on the basis of the market and of the so-called "laws" of its functioning. In this framework, that is to say for "law", capital is more important than work in the productive process: the private enterprise is more efficient than the public one, hence fitter to handle and orient the economy. The essential postulate is: growth first of all, and then distribution; this postulate is given as a common axiomatic self-evident feeling, where the private expense will always be more productive than the public one. All this is wrapped in the fundamental mythology that transnational capitalism frees the individual, allowing him to be the master of his destiny, stressing the concept of freedom in his consumption capacity, in a Biblical recommendation that "consumption will rescue us". It is conveniently forgotten that income is needed to consume and that one's own model, far from democratizing the income distribution towards the majorities, concentrates it among the minorities.

In this way, what we actually aim at and provoke is to concentrate capital accumulation and production capacities at the global level, in the hands of a mythical minority. So in the future this will be the source of the paternal development which will assure everybody's welfare. But in the Third World and Latin America, the people who experienced this adjustment, presented as the peak of modernization and rationality, could confirm — as a concrete experience — as I have already said, that each time, income is more and more concentrated in less hands in an increasing process presented to people as the natural development condition, where, as John Paul II said in Puebla, "We have each time richer riches and each time poorer poors". The political condition of all this is a simultaneous concentration of coercive power, embodied by the state, expressing itself in régimes, which exclude the political participation of the majorities, just as the transnational model does in the economic one. It is clear, again, that the struggle for political democracy also needs the creation of economic and social democracy.

These thoughts are important, if considered from the point of view that the leading development models in the industrialized world are the result of historical processes, the evolution and development of which took about 300 years.

What is offered to us is the final result of this process, the concrete and specific shape of this development model today. Undoubtedly the transnational proposal minimizes and overshadows the objective conditions which gave birth to the present situation of capitalist, industrialized societies.

The inevitable basic question is: if we are imitating the final model, will the historical conditions which allowed its birth be able to re-create themselves?

Analysing, from this point of view, how industrial societies have arrived where they are, the result is that their democratic perfecting of capitalist construction is lacking in the long term. But rather, we can say that the so-called "industrial democracies" were based on three essentially anti-democratic elements. Firstly, the home super-exploitation; with working days of 12 and 14 hours for both women and children: restriction of labour rights with non-existent trade unions; in the case of the US the slaveage has been a reality up to the middle of the past century, as a consequence, of course, a structure which inevitably emerged leading to an enormous income concentration in a small number of the population, then reaching a very high level of capital accumulation, which is today the basis of life-style in these countries. Secondly, it was also based on external exploitation: the colonial domination in Africa, Asia and the Middle East and the economic colonization in Latin America; all of this on the basis of interchange relations, which made the resources extraction and the natives' exploitation gratuitous. Thirdly, even if the industrial revolution leads to the past feudal democratic development conditions, it is clear that what was given was extremely formal, just as the popular participation and the economic social rights, like organization, expression and representation, were nothing but mere and solemn declarations of good will, except when they were included in constitutional texts. All that has been previously said, pointed to the fact that all the endeavours carried out in many Latin American countries to spur and develop the democratization process are restrained, not only in the repressive apparatus of authoritarian governments, but also in the pressure that domestic bourgeoisie and transnational system exert, so as not to modify the distribution logic of economic policy. It is sufficient to observe the realities presented to people through TV programmes like "Roots" and "Upstairs, Downstairs", to remind us in a synoptic way the economic and political roots of present "industrial democracies".

In this situation, the question is: is it possible to imitate the present characteristics of the transnational model without imitating the objective conditions already described which made it possible? Is it possible to use the present models of the industrialized world without re-creating in the Third World the exploitation conditions which made it historically possible? I believe the answer is negative. The Third World countries which prefer the transnational model inevitably find themselves in the conditions of re-creating the historical situations which made it possible with contemporary characteristics.

If we move this global analysis to the study of concrete situations in Latin America, we must not be surprised if the persistence of this model needs increasing authoritarian political régimes. The present ideological, political evolution has led to the general acknowledgement of workers' rights: it increased aspirations towards a real democracy and a participation to a higher level in the social organization, and each time the existence of colonies, which are able to provide surplus to reinforce the national development, is becoming less conceivable. In conclusion, it is not easy to re-create the historical conditions which marked the basis of the present transnational model.

From the above, in general terms the visible effects of the transnational development model insertion in some Third World countries and particularly in Latin America are caused by what we have described. The excluding characteristics of political régimes born under the protection of market logic renaissance, and of the neo-classic thesis covered by a "superior rationality", together with the evident lack of objective conditions which determined the kind of capitalist development in the North, hold the seed of exclusion and authoritarianism in the Third World, not as a painful stage towards a supposingly happy end, but rather as a structural and permanent outline, produced by the "logic" of the proposed model.

Hence it is perfectly understandable that the transnational model, based on its concept of freedom, on the freedom to consume and not on the freedom rising from the political and national organization of a nation, or that the efforts to maintain the national sovereignty are considered as an obstacle to transnational expansion. In this way we have seen that when Latin American societies underwent deep change processes in their economic, cultural and political structures, in order to foster the majorities' necessities and interests, they have normally met the strong and definite opposition of transnational enterprises and of the power structure they represent, together with their domestic allies. Society democratization is hardly compatible with the transnational model and the equitable distribution of income hinders the creation of the capital accumulation historical conditions.

One of the main aspects of this analysis is the contradiction between transnational offer and its concrete results in societies where transnationalization turned into a dominant phenomenon. The recommendation that transnational economic freedom is a prerequisite of political freedom and democracy is already, for many Latin American countries, a joke of bad taste. The insistence that freedom is equal to "consumption" and that true social participation is rooted in the capacity of choosing between the purchase of different substantially similar products, does not hold out against reality. In many of the places where the transnational model is rooted, this has come in close contact and will, with the régimes whose preoccupation for human rights, participation and democracy is not part, to say the least, of its priority objectives.

It seems fundamental to clarify this fallacy, to understand that the main problem is rooted not only in the necessity to "control, regulate or restrain" the transnational enterprises' activities, in view of national development and in the capacity of negotiating and applying a more or less orthodox code conduct and of international strength to the transnational enterprises' activities. The crucial problem lies in the development model and in the consumption styles a given country chooses. The only possible conduct code is to establish alternative development strategies on the basis of a real society democratization, and on a sort of social organization where participation is a generalized characteristic. In the present majority's conditions in the Third World countries, this cannot take place without deep and final structural changes — the satisfaction of material and spiritual basic needs, the respect for human dignity, the rescue of national autonomy and the true exercise of sovereignty, inevitably need a change of present minority power structures.

This points out the true option, and these are the very considerations that political operators must keep in mind when they choose a development transnational model copied from the industrialized world. It is here they must place the problem of transnational enterprises control and its impact on democracy.

This means, first, to keep in mind the majority interest as a national and consensual project, necessarily non-transnational in the sense of denying its organizational — more than antagonist — logic, geared to certain technical advancements of universal use. We need a project for "another development" which is the expression of a national self-assertion. Those who confuse this realist, necessary, nationalism, with that which they think the "cultural milieu" is overcome through a catastrophic bloodshed, are totally wrong.

Third World nationalism is very different from eurocentric chauvinism, which its own inventors' successors ridicule today. We are speaking about nationalism rising from the will not to be cancelled, from the massive will to make the communitarian conception of self true, and for this reason of a deeply democratic nationalism, really democratic, as the only possible condition for everybody's and not of a few — welfare.

This is why the exploited countries reaffirm their cultural origins, the autochthonous ways of cohabitation and of production organization become stronger, the regional peculiarities come out strongly and the spiritual strength like Islamism in the East, Buddhism in Asia and Christianity in Latin America reinforce themselves, without denying the positive Western modernity, in the search for a peaceful and democratic synthesis. The courses of actions are given and visible — the near future of Latin America will be marked by them.

Index

269